LOUISE BENNETT
AND JAMIEKAN LANGWIJ

LOUISE BENNETT
AND JAMIEKAN LANGWIJ
COMMEMORATIONS AND CRITICAL PERSPECTIVES

edited by Michele A. Johnson

AFRICA WORLD PRESS
TRENTON | LONDON | CAPE TOWN | NAIROBI | ADDIS ABABA | ASMARA | IBADAN | NEW DELHI

AFRICA WORLD PRESS
541 West Ingham Avenue | Suite B
Trenton, New Jersey 08638

Copyright © 2023

All rights reserved. No part of this publication may be reproduced, stored in a retrieval system or transmitted in any form or by any means electronic, mechanical, photocopying, recording or otherwise without the prior written permission of the publisher.

Book design: Dawid Kahts
Cover design: Ashraful Haque

The images of Louise Bennett Coverley are copyrighted, and permission to use has been granted by the executors of the LBCE, Messers Pamela Appelt (Ret. Judge, pappelt@cogeco.ca) and Fabian Coverley (fcoverley@gmail.com).

Cataloging-in-Publication Data may be obtained from the Library of Congress.

ISBNs: 9781569027905 (HB)
        9781569027912 (PB)

Table of Contents

Introduction   1

Part 1: "Pred Out Yuself Miss Lou"
1. Lillian Allen, "I Love Miss Lou."   17
2. Pamela Appelt, "Memories of Miss Lou."   23
3. Olive Senior, "Miss Lou's Teachings: The Wisdom Behind the Words."   31
4. Honor Ford-Smith, "In Her Voice, the Laughter of Freedom: Louise Bennett, the Body and Anti-Colonial Performance."   37
5. Klive Walker, "'Wherever I am—Toronto, London, Florida—I am in Jamaica': Louise Bennett's Home Away from Home."   55
6. Andrea A. Davis, "From Jamaica to Canada: Miss Lou and the Poetics of Migration."   63
7. Jennifer Walcott, "I Rejoice in Being Bilingual."   83
8. Clive Forrester, "Writing Miss Lou Right: Language, Identity, and the Official Jamaican Orthography."   85

Part 2: "…The Language of the People…The Language of Life"
1. Michele A. Johnson, "'Saying Dis, Dat, and Toder': Creating A Jamaican Language (Jamiekan Langwij) in the Eighteenth and Nineteenth Centuries."   93

2. Amah Harris, "Mother Tongue as Primary Teaching Tool—
   Jamaican Language: A Commentary." 121
3. Pamella Archer and Everton Cummings, "Patwa Discourse:
   The Perspective of Two Educators' Relationship to and
   Use of Jamaican Language." 129
4. Yewande Lewis-Fokum, Michele Kennedy, Silvia Kouwenberg,
   "School Teachers' Language Identities in Jamaica:
   The Discourses They Create and Recreate Within a
   Workshop Space." 149
5. Tka Pinnock, "Patwa a Yaad, English Abroad: Language
   and Development in Jamaica." 181
6. Annette Henry, "Patwa: Power, Politics and
   Possibilities." 193
7. Carl E. James, "'Waa Gwaan?': The Construction of Black
   Language and Identity in Toronto." 205

Author Biographies 227

Index 231

INTRODUCTION

Michele A. Johnson

In the last few months of 2019, Jamaicans at home and in the diaspora paused to reflect on, and to commemorate, the life and contributions of Louise Bennett-Coverley—Miss Lou.[1] According to the Jamaica Information Service, the communication arm of the Jamaican government, Bennett was a "poet and activist" who "remains a household name in Jamaica, a 'Living Legend' and a cultural icon" (Jamaica Information Service [JIS], Famous Jamaicans).[2] And the centenary of her birth (September 7, 1919) presented an ideal opportunity for national celebration. For its part, on September 7, 2019, the Jamaican government launched "100 days of commemorative activities in honour of the centenary of late Jamaican cultural icon Louise 'Miss Lou' Bennett-Coverley" (JIS, 2019). Organised by government agencies "including the National Library of Jamaica, the Jamaica Cultural Development Commission and the Bureau of Gender Affairs, the official celebrations began with events in each parish during September 2019 (JIS, 2019).[3] "Miss Lou," said the government "has been hailed as Jamaica's standard bearer in the popularisation of Jamaican patois and folklore on the international stage through her pioneering roles as poet, actress, comedienne, scholar, journalist, playwright, broadcaster, teacher, and lecturer" (JIS, 2019). According to the JIS:

> Through her poems in Jamaican patois, she raised the dialect of the Jamaican folk to an art level which is acceptable to and appreciated by all in Jamaica. In her poems, she was able to capture all the spontaneity of the

expression of Jamaicans' joys and sorrows, their ready and even wicked wit, their religion, and their philosophy of life (JIS, Famous Jamaicans).

While some would have insisted on the redefinition of "the dialect" as Jamaican language (Jamiekan langwij)[4] and pointed out that Jamaican Creole/Patwa is still *not* "acceptable to and appreciated by all in Jamaica" and its diasporas, the embrace of Miss Lou, cultural icon, seemed to still the disquiet around the place of Patwa in the nation and its communities overseas.

Nevertheless, there is little doubt that the sentiments presented by the JIS were indicative of a journey that Mervyn Morris may have found intriguing since his urging, in 1963, to read Miss Lou, "seriously" (Morris, 1963). As Miss Lou's creations and publications became solidified as national cultural products, (Bennett 1942, 1966, 1979, 1982/2003, 1993/2003), a scholarly tradition has emerged that has treated Bennett-Coverley's work with the gravitas it deserves. The charge has been led by Morris, who has answered his own call (1982, 2014), and two volumes of the *Journal of West Indian Literature: Critical Approaches to Louise Bennett* (April 2009, November 2009) which engage with Miss Lou's work. Contributors to volume one (April 2009) include Carol Bailey, Ifeoma Kiddoe Nwankwo, Jahan Ramazani, Janet Neigh, and Opal Palmer Adisa, all of whom celebrate Miss Lou's work in what Palmer Adisa calls a "love letter to Miss Lou" (Palmer Adisa, April 2009), a sentiment that might be echoed by Pamela Mordecai (2007).

In the second volume of the *Journal of West Indian Literature: Critical Approaches to Louise Bennett Part 2* (November 2009), contributors like Aisha T. Spencer, Katherine Verhagen Rodis, and Shalene M. Vasquez discuss Miss Lou's contributions to interrogations of gender, vernacular literature, "trickster poetics," questions of sexuality and "assertions of female agency" (Vasquez, November 2009, p. 1). In addition, Alejandra Bronfman (2017) has focused on the audio-visual media components of Miss Lou's work and, pertinent to this volume, Susan Gingell's (April 2009) examination of Miss Lou's influence on Canadian dub poets like Klyde Broox, d'bi young, amuna baraka-clarke, and Lillian Allen— a contributor to this volume—is of interest.

All of this, and more, has resulted in what Ben Ethington refers to as "a fundamental shift in the orientation of the Jamaican literary field" (2015, p. 20). Miss Lou, described by Ifeoma Kiddoe Nwankwo as "without a doubt Jamaica's definitive national poet," (Nwankwo, 2009, p. viii), and by Opal Palmer Adisa as "the preeminent purveyor of Jamaican culture, using poetry, storytelling, and the stage," as well as "the national spokesperson and advocate for nationalist sentiment after Jamaica gained its independence," is worthy of nothing less. For Palmer Adisa, as Bennett-Coverley, "a fierce advocate for all things Jamaican," has used her cultural presence "to instill pride in a people emerging from a colonial legacy that attempted to dehumanize and discredit their history" (Palmer Adisa, 2010, p. 124), her cultural productions and performances have been as significant as they have been sources of joy. It was, therefore, fitting that in Jamaica and its diasporas, the celebrations Miss Lou's hundredth birthday should be accompanied by critical and scholarly reflections. As elsewhere, this was the case in Toronto, Canada.

According to the JIS, "Although she lived in Toronto, Canada for the last decade [of her life, Bennett-Coverley] still receives the homage of the expatriate West Indian community in the north, as well as a large Canadian following" (JIS, Famous Jamaicans).[5] This was certainly the case when renown cultural studies scholar, Dr. Carolyn Cooper, presented "Disguise Up De English Language: Louise Bennett's Anansi Poetics" at the Michael Baptista Lecture at York University in 2016 and was reflected in the publication of Toronto-based children's author, Nadia Hohn, *A Likkle Miss Lou: How Jamaican Poet Louise Bennett Coverley Found Her Voice* (2019). For those who gathered, again, at York University in Toronto, on September 17, 2019, for an event "Celebrating Miss Lou," among the intersections of a "Canadian following," a "West Indian community," and Jamaicans in diaspora who came to pay "homage," this certainly seemed to be the case. However, the occasion of commemoration of Miss Lou's life and contributions and her influence and "popularisation of Jamaican patois and folklore" quickly expanded to a bracing discussion of the place, use, and politics of Patwa in Jamaica and its diasporas. This publication—which features both the presentations made at the "Celebrating Miss Lou" event at York University, contributions by some of those who were in attendance, as well as persons in Canada and Jamaica whose inputs added multiple layers to the discussion—captures both the commemoration of Miss

Lou and some of the debates around the Jamiekan langwij (Jamaican language), which she did so much to capture, celebrate, and promote.

In the first half of the volume, **"Pred Out Yuself Miss Lou"**—which is a line from Lillian Allen's poem "Heartbeat," (1993)—there are eight contributions which focus on Miss Lou's life, contributions, and influence. Lillian Allen's "I Love Miss Lou," is a fitting tribute to Miss Lou, who Allen refers to as "my Bob Dylan, My Chaucer and my Shakespeare," and speaks to Bennett-Coverley's inspiration on her own trajectory. Here, Allen offers "A Tribute to Miss Lou," a section of her seminal work, *Women Do This Every Day* (1993), in Bennett-Coverley's honour.

In her "Memories of Miss Lou," Pamela Appelt gives insight into the personal reach and many connections in Miss Lou's life, and refers to the international honours that recognize her contributions, including the designation of Louise Bennett Close in London, the Honorary Doctor of Laws from York University, and the permanent exhibition in her honour at the Louise Bennett Room, established by the Government of Ontario at Toronto's Harbour Front Centre. As co-executor (with Fabian Coverley) of Miss Lou's estate, Appelt has been instrumental in establishing the Louise Bennett Fonds in the archives of McMaster University.

In addition to the personal reflections of Allen and Appelt, the volume includes contributions by Olive Senior and Honor Ford-Smith, on the lessons that might be gleaned from an examination of Miss Lou's life, character, and cultural creations. Senior offers a poetic take on how "Once upon a time, Miss Lou donned the bandana costume of the Jamaican countrywoman, and reached deep into her pocket and pulled out words that she placed like sweeties on our tongues." In "Miss Lou's Teachings: The Wisdom Behind the Words," Senior centres Miss Lou's contributions as an educator, and the lessons she taught—about memory, history, ancestry, manners, and social harmony—and ponders if Louise Bennett should be considered a Jamaican National Hero, as she fits well the description.

In "The Laughter of Freedom: Louise Bennett, the Body and Anticolonial Performance," Ford-Smith points out that in addition to being "a serious advocate for the Jamaican language and culture over decades," Miss Lou was "the lone enduring popular voice of

Black and working-class women of the 20th century," and that she "belonged to a generation of anticolonial cultural activists who aimed to transform inherited colonial culture." According to Ford-Smith, "Bennett came to embody the iconic mother of nation—a gendered signifier of Jamaican possibility, a woman who productively negotiated the conflicting discourses of Blackness and gender to articulate a basis for national unity and progress."

In his reflections, Klive Walker discusses the life and legacy of Miss Lou, and focuses on an aspect that the JIS mentions *almost* as an aside—that "she lived in Toronto" (JIS, Famous Jamaicans). In "'Wherever I am—Toronto, London, Florida—I am in Jamaica': Louise Bennett's Home Away from Home," Walker offers an analysis of Bennett-Coverley's statement about being in Jamaica wherever she was, and argues that it simultaneously "complicated her relationship to Jamaica and to America, the UK, and Canada," and offered "different ways of understanding what Jamaica means"—beyond a specific geographical space. Rather, Walker argues that for Miss Lou (and others in the diaspora who share her sentiment), "Jamaica as a culture, as a way of being, exists in Toronto, New York, London, and elsewhere."

Similarly speaking to a diasporic sensibility, in "From Jamaica to Canada: Miss Lou and the Poetics of Migration," Andrea A. Davis focuses her discussion on Miss Lou as "an unwilling migrant," who made a "strategic choice" in moving to Canada, and who "continued to represent the spirit of a nation she may have left physically but had never left behind." Outlining Miss Lou's career and her impact on the Jamaican nation and diasporas, Davis offers a close examination of seven of what she calls Miss Lou's "migration poems . . . looking specifically at the theme of migration and cultural loss," and argues that, like Miss Lou, persons of Jamaican descent in diaspora "must increasingly grapple with . . . tensions between *here* and *there, roots* and *routes.*"

As one of those persons of Jamaican descent in diaspora to whom Davis might have referred, Jennifer Walcott makes pointed reference to Miss Lou's influence on her own writing and points out that "some ideas and emotions just cannot be expressed in Standard English." Walcott utilizes "the ballad form typical of Miss Lou," as well as her celebration of Jamaican Creole/Patwa to offer her poems "Miss Eliza" and "Sgraffito."

In his contribution to the commemoration of Miss Lou's cultural creations, and operating as a bridge between the two sections of the volume, Clive Forrester places Miss Lou's work within the linguistic world of the Jamiekan langwij (Jamaican language). In an application of the writing system developed by F.G. Cassidy and R.B. Le Page (Cassidy & Le Page, 2002), and enhanced by scholars in Di Jamiekan Langwij Yuunit (The Jamaican Language Unit) at the University of the West Indies, Forrester writes Miss Lou "right." Forrester explores some of the scholarship associated with the writing system that captures the Jamiekan langwij (Jamaican language) in a comprehensive and consistent manner, and illustrates its application in one of Bennett's popular poems, "Dutty tough" (Bennett, 1966).

The second half of the collection, " . . . **The Language of the People . . . The Language of Life**"— a line from Allen's poem "Language," (Allen, 1993)—engages with the debates about the Jamiekan langwij (Jamaican language), which became a major part of the original commemorative event from which this volume grew. Michele A. Johnson's "'Saying Dis, Dat, and Toder': Creating A Jamaican Language (Jamiekan Langwij) in the Eighteenth and Nineteenth Centuries" assesses historical records of the period, and posits that "the language system that emerged in Jamaican society during the period of slavery (Jamaican Creole/Patwa) was shared by the enslaved and their (creole) enslavers," and that "it continued to flourish through the post-slavery period, into the twenty-first century." Further, Johnson argues that "Patwa is a major cultural product in the island, and that the language operated (and operates) as a zone of convergence, conflict, and negotiation . . . combining the people in a cultural milieu, even as some among them denied and rejected that process."

In "Mother Tongue as Primary Teaching Tool—Jamaican Language: A Commentary," Amah Harris points to the politics of categorization by reminding us of Miss Lou's observation that whereas the language of the coloniser was presented as "derived from," that of the colonised was castigated as a "corruption of." Turning to questions of the use and utility of Jamaican Creole in the educational system,

Harris contends that while some argue against its use, claiming that "'standard English' was the language of commerce in the Jamaican market and the international market," her primary concern is with "the child's development as the most productive person that child could be." In rejecting Jamaican (Creole), educators and institutions reject "the child's first language," which is "the very essence of the child's being," thereby undermining the child's confidence, "a key ingredient for successful learning."

Addressing some of the concerns raised by Harris, Pamella Archer and Everton Cummings enter the conversation about the use of Jamaican Creole/Patwa in Jamaican classrooms, through "Patwa Discourse: The Perspective of Two Educators' Relationship to and Use of Jamaican Language." Using an innovative dialogical methodology, which is simultaneously "introspective and informative," Archer and Cummings reflect on their own relationships with Patwa, and their assessments of its place, use, and usefulness in Jamaican classrooms. Cummings (an educator of teachers) and Archer (a teacher-student) explore what appears to be a growing local acceptance of Jamaican Creole (JC), pushed by cultural products and media. Both reflect on their advocacy "for the use of JC in the classroom," with some limits, since English is Jamaica's official language and students' assessments are conducted in English, there is great variability in the written form of Patwa and a concern that the "transitory nature" of (the "street" parlance of) Patwa makes it difficult to ascribe meaning. For them, in addition to encouraging a comfort with Patwa, there is a benefit to having a command of English "for those who must communicate and operate within both global and Jamaican societies."

Yewande Lewis-Fokum, Michele Kennedy, and Silvia Kouwenberg, co-authors of "School Teachers' Language Identities in Jamaica: The Discourses They Create and Recreate Within a Workshop Space," come to the discussion about language in Jamaica from the perspective of linguists/teacher-educators. Cognizant of the fact that "English is the language of instruction and assessment at all levels of the educational system," but that "for a majority of children who enter that educational system, it is not the home language and does not have a significant presence in their communities," these scholars have conducted research about, and training of, teachers to become more "language-aware." The results of the Professional Development of Primary School Teachers (PDPST) project with which they are engaged point toward the directions in which educational/training institutions could move in order to acknowledge and successfully support teachers and students within "Creole-speaking environments" such as Jamaica.

In "Patwa A Yaad, English Abroad: Language and Development in Jamaica," Tka Pinnock interrogates the strategic and specific ways in which Patwa and English have been deployed within the Jamaican political economy. This exploration occurs against a background where there are references in some fora to the need for English competence in order to function within a global marketplace, and also because of a belief that "Jamaicans needed to speak English so that when they migrated, they would be able to fit into their host country and find employment." At the same time, in its promotion of "Brand Jamaica," especially in the competitive tourism market, the island's Patwa is promoted as part of an "authentic" experience that, it is hoped, will encourage millions to visit Jamaica. Between the tourism dollars based on a local culture framed by Patwa, and the remittance dollars sent by large numbers of Jamaicans (supposedly speaking English) in diaspora, this discussion brings the spectre of language as a resource to the fore.

Annette Henry's "Patwa: Power, Politics and Possibilities," discusses the potentialities inherent in Patwa, "a language of power, of self-determination, of pride, of resistance, of comfort, of inclusion, of solidarity, of struggle, and of voice." In a work that inserts questions of language in the Jamaican diaspora in Canada into the discussion, Henry argues for a "Creole-inclusive language curriculum" that "can contribute to understanding the rich cultural and political histories of the Caribbean and of Caribbean Canadians." For her, "[e]ducators need to ensure equitable access to a quality *both/and* education for students of African heritage, an education that allows students both to understand their lives, histories, and languages, and dream about their futures from their own informed, indigenous perspectives; *and* an education that affords students equitable access to 21st century knowledges with the required critical literacies to participate as confident, competent international citizens in a globalized, transnational world."

The collection concludes with Carl E. James's exploration of the developments in, and uses made of, Patwa when it is adopted and adapted by "Black youth" in Toronto, only some of whom are of Jamaican descent. In "'Waa Gwaan?': The Construction of Black Language and Identity in Toronto," James explores the complex relationship between the language and its role in the construction of Black identity in Toronto, where, as one of the participants in James's research project said, "There was this affinity for the Jamaican language by virtue of being Black." For James, as an identifiable "Black Toronto" language has developed, "its relationship to the Jamaican language" is intriguing since, as the youth said, in Toronto, "Jamaican language and culture have been synonymous with the identity of many Black Canadians," whether or not they are of Jamaican descent.

Originating from collaborations between scholars and the wider community, emerging as it did from a commemorative event, and opening as it has, further discussions about "Louise Bennett and Jamiekan langwij," this volume offers echoes and reverberations of, as well as dialogue with, a range of interested persons with a variety of perspectives. No single volume can capture the multiple, complex cultural productions of Louise Simone Bennett-Coverley. It is our hope that this commemoration and critical engagement will make a contribution to the ongoing conversations.

Endnotes

1   Louise Simone Bennett-Coverley (1919–2006) was born in Kingston, Jamaica. She attended the Ebenezer and Calabar Elementary Schools, St. Simon's College, Excelsior College, and Friends College. She was awarded a British Council Scholarship to the Royal Academy of Dramatic Art, after which she worked in Britain, including at the BBC, where she hosted *Caribbean Carnival* (1945–1946) and *West Indian Guest Night* (1950–1953). Bennett moved to New York and worked in radio, television, and on the stage (1953–1954), and married Eric Coverley (1911–2002), who was also a cultural producer. After their return to Jamaica, Bennett worked with the Jamaica Social Welfare Commission (1956–1963) and was able to travel across the island, gathering the folklore and cultural material which became the foundation of her creations. She taught drama and folklore at the Extra-Mural Department at the University of the West Indies (1959–1961). Miss Lou hosted radio programmes: *Laugh with Louise* and *Miss Lou's Views*, as well as the *Lou and Ranny Show* which she shared with her stage partner, Randolph

Samuel Williams (1912–1980)—Maas Ran. From 1970 to 1982, Miss Lou hosted the beloved television programme *Ring Ding*, which featured children's performances, Jamaican folk stories and songs. Miss Lou's contributions to the cultural life of Jamaica was recognized through a number of awards: Member of the British Empire (1960), Musgrave Silver Medal, Institute of Jamaica (1965), Norman Manley Award for Excellence (1972), the Order of Jamaica (1974), Musgrave Gold Medal, Institute of Jamaica (1978), Centenary Medal, Institute of Jamaica (1979), Hon. Doctor of Letters (University of the West Indies, 1983), Hon. Doctor of Letters (York University, 1998). Bennett-Coverley was named as Jamaica's Cultural Ambassador at Large (1998) and awarded the Order of Merit (2001). (See JIS, "Famous Jamaicans"; Louise Bennett Coverley Fonds, McMaster University; encyclopedia.com).

2   The other "Famous Jamaicans" featured on the JIS site include Ralston Milton Nettleford (1933–2010), Charles Hyatt (1931–2007), Herbert Henry McKenley (1922–2007), Randolph Samuel Williams (1912–1980), Edna Manley (1900–1987), Robert Nesta Marley (1945–1981), Usain St. Leo Bolt (1986–), all of whose accomplishments were in the fields of sports and cultural production (see JIS, "Famous Jamaicans").

3   "Miss Lou Lunch Hour Concert," at the Louise Bennett-Coverley Primary School, Gordon Town (Kingston & St. Andrew), 11 September 2019; "A Miss Lou Seh So," at the Solid Base Group of Schools, Brunswick Avenue, Spanish Town (St. Catherine), 19 September, 2019; "Lunch Hour Concert," at the Hanover Parish Church (Hanover), 20 September, 2019; "Miss Lou Concert and Bandana Competition," at the Sean Lavery Faith Hall, Savanna-la-mar (Westmoreland), 20 September, 2019; "Labrish," at the St. Ann Parish Library (St. Ann), 20 September 2019; "Miss Lou Birthday Celebration," at St. John's Methodist Church (St. James), 25 September, 2019; "Miss Lou Roots & Cultural Showbiz," at Manchester High School, Mandeville (Manchester), 26 September, 2019; "Miss Lou in Poetry and Story," at the St. Thomas Parish Library, (St. Thomas), 26 September, 2019; "Miss Lou Centennial Celebrations," at the Neville Antonio Park, Port Antonio (Portland), 26 September, 2019; "Miss Lou Tribute Concert," at the Horace Clarke High School Auditorium, Islington (St. Mary), 26 September, 2019; "Miss Lou Concert & Bandana Styling Competition," at the Denbigh High School, May Pen (Clarendon), 27 September, 2019; "Miss Lou & Maas Ran Cultural Ambassador Pageant," at Maggotty High School (St. Elizabeth), 27 September 2019; "Story Cum to Bump: A live presentation of works by Miss Lou," at the Jamaica Cultural Development Commission Parish

Office, Falmouth (Trelawny) (Jamaica Information Service, 2019).

4   This follows the reference to Di Jamiekan Langwij Yuunit (The Jamaican Language Unit) at the University of the West Indies.

5   Although the JIS inferred that Bennett-Coverley was resident in Canada in the "last decade" (of her life), according to the National Library of Jamaica, Bennett and her husband, Eric Coverley, migrated to Canada in 1987. As such, she lived in Canada for almost two decades. See https://nlj.gov.jm/project/rt-hon-dr-louise-bennett-coverley-1919-2006/.

References

Adisa, O.P. "Culture and Nationalism on the World Stage: Louise Bennett's Aunty Roachy Seh Stories." *The Global South*, vol. 4, no. 2. special issue: *The Caribbean and Globalization*, Fall 2010, pp. 124–135.

Adisa, O.P. "Love Letter to Miss Lou: Memories Intersect History." *Journal of West Indian Literature*, vol. 17, no. 2: *Critical Approaches to Louise Bennett*, April 2009, pp. 1–4.

Bailey, C. "Looking in: Louise Bennett's Pioneering Caribbean Postcolonial Discourse." *Journal of West Indian Literature*, vol. 17, no. 2: *Critical Approaches to Louise Bennett*, April 2009, pp. 20–31.

Bennett, L. *Auntie Roachy Seh*. Edited by M. Morris. Kingston: Sangster's Book Stores, 1993/2003.

Bennett, L. *Selected Poems*. Edited by M. Morris. Kingston: Sangster's Book Stores, 1982/2003.

Bennett, L. "Dutty Tough." *Jamaica Labrish: Jamaica Dialect Poems*. Edited by Rex Nettleford. Kingston: Sangster's Book Stores, 1966.

Bennett, L. *Anancy and Miss Lou*. Kingston: Sangster's Book Stores, 1979.

Bennett, L. *(Jamaica) Dialect Verses*. Kingston: Herald Ltd., 1942.

Louise Bennett, "Contemporary Black Biography." Encyclopedia.com. Retrieved August 2021, https://www.encyclopedia.com/education/news-wires-white-papers-and-books/bennett-louise.

Bronfman, A. "'This Thing is Very Much Alive': Louise Bennett on Audio-Visual Media." *Journal of West Indian Literature*, vol. 25, no. 2, November 2017, pp. 63–81.

Cassidy, F.G. and Le Page, R.B. (eds). *Dictionary of Jamaican English*, second edition. Kingston: University of the West Indies Press, 2002.

Cooper, C. "Disguise Up De English Language: Louise Bennett's Anansi Poetics." Michael Baptista Lecture, Centre for Research on Latin America and Caribbean, York University, November 3, 2016.

Etherington, B. "On Scanning Louise Bennett Seriously." *Journal of West Indian Literature*, vol. 23, no. 1–2, April/November 2015, pp. 19–34.

Gingell, S. "Coming Home through Sound: See-Hear Aesthetics in the Poetry of Louise Bennett and Canadian Dub Poets." *Journal of West Indian Literature*, vol. 17, no. 2: *Critical Approaches to Louise Bennett*, April 2009, pp. 32–48.

Hohn, N.L. *A Likkle Miss Lou: How Jamaican Poet Louise Bennett Coverley Found Her Voice*. Toronto: Owlkids, 2019.

Jamaica Information Service, "Get the Facts—The Centenary of Louise Simone Bennett-Coverley, OM, OJ, OME," September 12, 2019. Retrieved August 2021, https://jis.gov.jm/information/get-the-facts/get-the-facts-the-centenary-of-louise-simone-bennett-coverley-om-oj-mbe/.

Jamaica Information Service. "The Hon. Louise Bennett-Coverley. Famous Jamaicans," Retrieved August 2021, https://jis.gov.jm/information/famous-jamaicans/louise-bennett-coverley/.

Louise Bennett Coverley Fonds (Fonds RC0037). Archives & Research Collections, McMaster University, https://archives.mcmaster.ca/index.php/louise-bennett-coverley-fonds.

Mordecai, P. "Miss Lou—A Personal Remembrance of Louise Simone Bennett-Coverley: Poet, Folklorist, Community Worker, Lyricist, Stage and Movie Actress." *Kunapipi*, vol. 29, issue 1, 2007, pp. 8–18.

Morris, M. "On Reading Louise Bennett, Seriously." Jamaica Festival Essay Competition, 1963. Reprinted by permission of the author in *Jamaica Journal*, vol. 1, no. 1, December 1967, pp. 69–74.

Morris, M. "Louise Bennett in Print." *Caribbean Quarterly*, vol. 28, no. 1/2: *Critical Approaches to West Indian Literature*, March–June 1982, pp. 44–56.

Morris, M. *Miss Lou: Louise Bennett and Jamaican Culture*. Kingston and Miami: Ian Randle Publishers, 2014.

National Library of Jamaica, "Rt. Hon. Dr. Louise Bennett Coverley (1919-2006). https://nlj.gov.jm/project/rt-hon-dr-louise-bennett-coverley-1919-2006/

Neigh, J. "The Lickle Space of the Tramcar in Louise Bennett's Feminist Postcolonial Poetics." *Journal of West Indian Literature*, vol. 17, no. 2: *Critical Approaches to Louise Bennett*, April 2009, pp. 5–19.

Nwankwo, I.N. "(Ap)Praising Louise Bennett: Jamaica, Panama, and Beyond." *Journal of West Indian Literature*, vol. 17, no. 2: *Critical Approaches to Louise Bennett*, April 2009, pp. viii–xxv.

Nwankwo, I.N. "Preface." *Journal of West Indian Literature*, vol. 18, no. 1: *Critical Approaches to Louise Bennett, Part 2*, November 2009, pp. ix–xiii.

Ramazani, J. "The National Poet as Transnational?" *Journal of West Indian Literature*, Vol. 17, No. 2: *Critical Approaches to Louise Bennett*, April 2009, pp. 49–64.

Rodis, K.V. "Vernacular Literacy and Formal Analysis: Louise Bennett-Coverley's Jamaican English Verse." *Journal of West Indian Literature*, vol. 18, no. 1: *Critical Approaches to Louise Bennett, Part 2*, November 2009, pp. 60–72.

Spencer, A.T. "Interrogating Conceptualizations of Gender in the Shaping of a Nation, As Presented in Miss Lou's Monologues." *Journal of West Indian Literature*, vol. 18, no. 1. *Critical Approaches to Louise Bennett, Part 2*, November 2009, pp. 73–85.

The Jamaican Language Unit/Di Jamiekan Langwij Yuunit. *Writing Jamaican, the Jamaican Way/ Ou fi Rait Jamiekan*. Kingston: Arawak Publications, 2009.

Vasquez, S.M. "Slackness and a Mento Aesthetic: Louise Bennett's Trickster Poetics and Jamaican Women's Explorations of Sexuality." *Journal of West Indian Literature*, vol. 18, no. 1. *Critical Approaches to Louise Bennett, Part 2*, November 2009, pp. 1–25.

Part 1:
"Pred Out Yuself Miss Lou"

I LOVE MISS LOU

Lillian Allen

Miss Lou, the most Honourable Louise Bennett-Coverley. What an honour to have another opportunity to honour Miss Lou. I will never tire, not even to the twelfth of never. She, Miss Lou, is my Margaret Atwood, my James Baldwin, my Toni Morrison, my Bob Dylan, my Chaucer, and my Shakespeare.

Arguably, she is the most significant cultural figure to come out of Jamaica, not just for her work—the corpus of which forms a major document of Jamaica's social history and culture—but also for what she made possible for Black people and for others like Bob Marley, Lillian Allen, Linton Kwesi Johnson, Jean Binta Breeze—a whole generation of artists who trailed in the path she cleared, and looked to her, and her words, for inspiration. Her presence was a watering hole so desperately needed, as a visible and viable stance against empire.

> Ef yuh cyaan sing 'Linstead Market'
> An 'Water come a me yeye'
> Yuh wi haffi tap sing 'Auld lang syne'
> An 'Comin through de rye' (Bennett, 1993, p. 4).

In our efforts to succeed in colonial (and post-colonial) society, and ensure our children's success, we turned our backs on the spoken language of the people. It was a violence. In the introduction to my seminal poetry collection, *Women Do This Every Day* (1993), I discussed Miss Lou's impact on Jamaican culture, asserting that she is "a stunning figure of resistance, self-sufficiency, freedom, and self-determination."

While it would be easy to say she was the "voice" of the "people," she was in fact the beating heart of being Jamaican.

Miss Lou understood that "language is our skin, the blanket we live in," how language is so closely tied to culture and culture to kin, how culture is what roots you to land/place, to a past and possible futures, how culture is owned by the people, and empowers and distinguishes their identity both individually and collectively. And this is, and has always been, especially important for folks who are given access to very little ownership of anything.

As a writer and poet, I can recognize Miss Lou's inspiration to write and elevate the life of the ordinary Jamaican people. That encounter she relates of the market women in the back of a tram car—"'Pread out yuhself, one dress-oman a come"—was a moment of epiphany for the young Louise and her inspiration for her poem, "On A Tramcar."

> Pread out yuhself deh Liza, one
> Dress-oman dah look like seh
> She see de li space side-a we
> And waan foce harself een deh (Bennett, 1949, pp. 150-151; 1993, p. v).

At once, she recognized the resistance and agency in that gesture and she chose her side and dedicated her life and work to humanizing the life, aspirations, and culture of the grassroots, the silenced, the marginalized. I ask you to consider for a moment what Jamaican culture would be like if Miss Lou did not exist and persist.

However, Miss Lou is not just a Jamaican figure, but a transnational figure who traveled and worked in the UK, Europe, various Caribbean countries, and who knows where else, and often overlooked are her years and years of travel to the US Black communities, reading and performing her work, especially in the south. In fact, Miss Lou didn't need to travel anywhere to have impact because she was in the cultural and literary DNA of each and every Jamaican who spread across the globe. I love Miss Lou!

I love Miss Lou because one day, in my teens, I went to see where she was living, up a hill near Gordon Town. It was large and beautiful. She was no poor artist. I could see myself in the future. The idea of the starving poet held no relevance for me.

I love Miss Lou because she led an exemplary life. She had a persona that you would want in a friend, a neighbour, a sister, an aunt, a mother, a teacher, and in a National Hero.

Here, I would like to offer a segment of my publication, *Women Do This Every Day*, in a reproduction that honours Miss Lou.

Tribute to Miss Lou (Allen, 1993, pp. 43—46).

HEARTBEAT
Pred out yuself Miss Lou
Lawd, yu mek wi heart pound soh
yu mek we just love up wiself
an talk we talk soh

spirit words
on a riddim fire
word flame beat
pumps de heart
pulses history's heat

She writes
the heartbeat of our lives
dignity/culture/politics/history/lovingness/soul
dis dressup oman wi shinning star

HISTORY
Her story
my story
his story
our story
brukout story

THE VOICE
The voice
strug ug ugg uggling
to be heard

hear dis;
dem sey we sey she sey he sey hear sey
raw rim of soul
her mirror a poem
with room to grow

LANGUAGE
Get up
dance clap
sweat pon de ground
tambourine
sing a ring ding
sing a ring ding

If wi caant sing wi 'Linstead Market'
an 'Wata Com A Mi Yeye'
is what mek you gwine think
we coulda did feel satisfied

the language of the people
is the language of life

WINGS
She gives voice
        (and)   form
        (and)   wings to the silenced

"BEAR UP"
Candy Seller
how is business nowadays?
a *South Parade Peddle*   meddle
Problems   Problems
Hardtimes
Invasions
My Dreams
see *Jamaica Elevate*
Changes
bear up people for the *Victory Parade*
It Wut It
        It Wut It

CHO MON
when Auntie Roachie speak
cho mon
oonu know sey if a noh soh
a near soh

A TRUE
And the first and last sentence
in the book of her life reads:

Jamaican people in dem free spiritidness
in dem purity
in dem Caribbeaness
in dem Blackness
in dem cunning and industriousness
in dem 'tuppidness and imperfection
is precious

and even the ugliest among us
agents of doom and exploitation
you will hear say;
'A true mon. A true ting Miss Lou a talk, yes!'

SOUL FLICKER
Sometimes, sometimes
in the midst of oppression
a soul emerges
in the dense silence
in the conspiracy of normalcy
and officialdom

sometimes in this dimness
a flicker
a light
a path
a Miss Lou

References

Allen, L. "Tribute to Miss Lou." *Women Do This Every Day: Selected Poems of Lillian Allen*. Toronto: Women's Press, 1993, pp. 43–46.

Bennett, L. "Bans a Killin." *Aunty Roachy Seh*. Edited by Mervyn Morris. Kingston: Sangster's Book Stores, 1993.

Bennett, L. "On A Tramcar." *Miss Lulu Sez*. Kingston: Gleaner Co., 1949.

MEMORIES OF MISS LOU

Pamela Appelt

Memories of the Honourable Dr. Louise Bennett-Coverley, OM, OJ, MBE, affectionately called "Miss Lou" by her friends, colleagues, and admirers in her native Jamaica, and around the globe, leave me with an afterglow of smiles and laughter. This woman of so many talents and accomplishments, who was instrumental in preserving Jamaican culture in her beloved country and in her adopted home of Toronto, was indeed precious to me. She exuded a majestic sense of the presence of a higher power, self-confidence, and a beautiful commitment to the country of her birth and her people. Laughter, pride, joy, hopefulness, peacefulness, and a steady willingness to help were second nature to her.

My first encounter with this phenomenal woman, was in the mid-1980s, through her friend Lolita Phillips.[1] My husband and I were invited to join Dwight Whylie[2] at his home for dinner, and there was Miss Lou, who I had heard so much about. Her charm and her personality were captivating. She used the opportunity to share with the gathering her memories of Jamaica, her time in London, England, and her varied experiences. I left Dwight's home that evening extremely thankful that I had the opportunity to meet this incredible lady.

Over the next few months, we would see each other at events in the community, and we gave each other warm embraces. Miss Lou shared with me her connection with Canada going back to the 1970s when she performed to capacity crowds in the Toronto Public Library, Parkdale Branch. Later that same year, D.R.B. Grant, a well-respected Jamaican educator, did a needs assessment with respect to early childhood education in Jamaica; the report was made available to a range of organizations, institutions and persons of influence, including the Jamaican Consul General in Toronto.[3] Out of that effort emerged the organizational structure for the Project for Advancement of Childhood Education (PACE). Dr. Mavis Burke, a well-known Jamaican educator in the Ontario Ministry of Education, was selected to be the president of PACE Canada.[4] Dr. Burke asked Miss Lou to be the first patron. This gave further legitimacy to this charitable organization, as well as a sense of pride and possibility.

I was then asked to be the next patron of PACE Canada. When I shared this with my husband, his first question was, "How do you plan to support this organization?" The long and short of it is, my husband offered to host a dinner in our home, and invited guests he thought would be interested in the organization and would make a financial contribution. That fundraising effort was a huge success! Thanks to the efforts of Miss Lou, who entertained the guests, twelve schools in Jamaica were adopted that night. Today, over three hundred basic schools in Jamaica have been adopted through PACE Canada.

Over the months, I saw Miss Lou often, and she would share with pride the contributions of Jamaicans in Canada. She also shared with me her memory of her composition in 1988, "You're going home now," which won a nomination from the Academy of Canadian Cinema and Television.[5] This brought her great joy. She was especially pleased when she was the featured artiste at Westmount High School in Montreal. The invitation was extended by Thelma Johnson, the Founder of the Caribbean Pioneer Women of Canada, which sponsored the show. They were quite happy to have her because the large auditorium was packed to capacity, and it was their first fundraising event in aid of the Rev. Charles H. Este Scholarship and Bursary Fund.[6]

In 1990, I was honoured to be the judge who administered the oath of Canadian Citizenship to Miss Lou, along with many other Jamaicans. Everyone was delighted to be photographed with this remarkable lady. Miss Lou would often say, "Wherever I live, I am in Jamaica."

Many years ago, on one of my visits to England, I was walking the streets of Brixton with my brother, who lives in London, and he pointed out to me an area where many famous and world-renowned artists, such as Langston Hughes, would meet. Much to my surprise, there was Louise Bennett Close, a street that had been named in honour of this famous lady. Naturally, my brother, a photographer, was compelled to take a picture, which I took to her, and she received it with great joy.

When Miss Lou died in 2006, the Minister of Culture in the Government of Ontario made a commitment—in the presence of several hundred mourners—that Miss Lou would be remembered by the province. Soon after that pronouncement, I was invited to meet with the minister, and he asked what I would consider a fitting tribute to Miss Lou. I did not hesitate to share my thoughts with the minister and his staff. Since I was anticipating this ask, I did my research. I hastened to inform the minister that Miss Lou had received the Honorary Degree of Letters from York University for her groundbreaking contribution to literature and the performing arts, which legitimized dialect writing.[7]

Exactly six months after this meeting, the Government of Ontario named a room at Toronto's Harbour Front Centre in her memory.[8] The room houses a permanent exhibition honouring Miss Lou and her achievements. There, you'll find photographs and recordings of her storytelling and performances. Hundreds of students and teachers visit annually. Many talks and presentations are given in that room, and many cultural events are held there. Not long ago, another well-known Jamaican Canadian, Denham Jolly, had his first book launch there.[9]

In 2012, I had the pleasure as the co-executor of Miss Lou's Estate, along with Mr. Fabian Coverley, to gift McMaster University the Canadian archives of Miss Lou. The archives are used on a regular basis and have been digitized. These can be found online in the digital archive and are open to everyone.[10]

In 2012, Jamaica celebrated its fiftieth birthday. I co-chaired the committee which commemorated our independence here in Canada. We published a coffee table book, *Jamaicans in Canada—When Ackee Meets Codfish* (2012). It featured 250 individuals who have made extraordinary contributions to their adopted land. Notably, among them is Miss Lou.

In 2016, at the second annual Palaver International Literary Festival, the work and accomplishments of four outstanding individuals, including Miss Lou, were acknowledged. Miss Lou was cited for her historic achievement in getting the Jamaican people to throw off the yoke of colonialism, and to accept their own language and culture as legitimate.

Looking back, I think that Miss Lou shared these memories with me because she intended for me to play a role in maintaining her legacy. Someone once said, "We live in deeds, not years; in thoughts, not breaths; in feelings, not in figures on a dial" (Bailey, 1884). Miss Lou crossed the mysterious river to the other side in 2006, and I am honored to remember her on the anniversary of her one hundredth birthday [2019].

Thank you for carrying on her legacy of caring for others, keeping our culture alive, carrying the candle, and lighting the world. Her memories will grow more precious and will forever glow in our hearts. My sincere thanks to the Government of Jamaica, the Ministry of Culture, Gender, Entertainment and Sports for the work that you continue to do in keeping the memory of Miss Lou alive. I am indeed delighted that many individuals, organisations, and institutions, including York University, saw it fit to pay tribute to Miss Lou during her one hundredth birthday celebrations.

Endnotes

1 Lolita Phillips (1948–) was a close personal friend of Miss Lou and Eric Coverley, her husband. Born in England, to Jamaican parents, Phillips, a graduate of York University, worked in a variety of capacities in Jamaica and Canada, which is where she met Bennett. According to Phillips, Bennett and Coverley took her "under their wings." They encouraged her personal and professional development and were instrumental in her decision to return to Jamaica under the auspices of CUSO (formerly, Canadian University Service Overseas), an international development agency. When Miss Lou died, Phillips was tasked with serving as an escort for her remains and those of Eric Coverley, for burial in Jamaica. Phillips remains a close friend of the family, including Fabian Coverley, Eric Coverley's son. (Johnson, 2021).

2 Dwight Whylie (1936–2002) was a Jamaican journalist who made his mark at the Jamaica Broadcasting Corporation (JBC) and Radio Jamaica & Rediffusion (RJR), before becoming the first Black radio announcer hired by the British Broadcasting Corporation (BBC), and the General Manager of the Jamaica Broadcasting Corporation between 1973

and 1976. He joined the Canadian Broadcasting Corporation (CBC) between 1977 and 1997, and later offered his expertise to the Jamaica's Broadcasting Commission and the Caribbean Broadcasting Union (*Jamaica Gleaner*, 17 September 2002; *The Guardian*, 18 October 2002).

3   Dudley Ransford Brandyce Grant (1915–1988) was born in Santa Marta, Colombia, and taken to Jamaica at an early age by his parents. Grant served as a primary school teacher and principal in several schools, lecturer at the University of the West Indies, and as the driving force behind the Project for Early Childhood Education (PECE) and the Program for the Advancement of Childhood Education (PACE). He was labeled as the "Father of Early Childhood Education" in Jamaica (National Library of Jamaica, n.d.).

4   Mavis Burke (1928–) was born in Jamaica, and a graduate of the University of the West Indies and the University of London whose research focuses on education. After completing her doctoral studies at the University of Ottawa, she held positions in a variety of organizations, including the Ontario Social Assistance Review Board, the Ontario Women's Directorate, the Ontario Ministry of Education, and the Ontario Advisory Council on Multiculturalism and Citizenship (History, PACE Canada, n.d.; *Jamaican Proud*, 2015).

5   This nomination was for Best Original Song in the movie *Milk and Honey* (1988).

6   According to a 2015 communication by the Union United Church in Montreal, Quebec, since its inception in 1972, the Rev. Charles H. Este Scholarship and Bursary Fund had "awarded hundreds of scholarships to CEGEP [Collège d'enseignement général et professionnel] and University students annually." http://www.unionunitedchurchmtl.ca/Documents/Scholarship-Booklet-Advertisement.pdf

7   Louise Bennett-Coverley was awarded the Doctor of Letters by York University in Spring 1998. According to the Jamaica Information Service, Miss Lou was recognized for her "commanding presence in Jamaican and Caribbean literature and the performing arts, and her international reputation as a poet and folklorist" (Goulbourne-Warren, JIS 1998).

8   The provincial government made this announcement in January, 2007: https://news.ontario.ca/en/release/86205/mcguinty-government-honours-miss-lou-jamaicas-gift-to-the-world

9   Brandeis Denham Jolly, CM (1935–) was born in Jamaica, migrated to Canada in the 1960s, and has been described as a "teacher, entrepreneur,

publisher, broadcaster, philanthropist, civil rights activist, and community leader." Jolly was publisher of *Contrast* (a Black community newspaper) and founder of FLOW 93.5 (a Black radio station), both in Toronto. Jolly has published his autobiography, *In the Black: My Life* (2017), has been the recipient of wide range of honours and awards, and was made a member of Order of Canada in 2020 (Boyko, "Denham Jolly," 2020).

10   Fonds RC0037—Louise Bennett Coverley Fonds, McMaster University.

References

Bailey, P. "We live in deeds, not years; in thoughts, not breaths," 1884.

Boyko, J. "Denham Jolly," *The Canadian Encyclopedia*, 2020, Retrieved July 2021, https://www.thecanadianencyclopedia.ca/en/article/denham-jolly.

"Dudley Ransford Brandyce Grant (1915–1988)," National Library of Jamaica, Retrieved July 2021, https://nlj.gov.jm/project/dudley-ransford-brandyee-grant-1915-1988/.

Dwight Whylie, *The Guardian*, October 18, 2002, Retrieved July 2021, https://www.theguardian.com/media/2002/oct/18/broadcasting.bbc.

Goulbourne-Warren C., "Miss Lou to be Honoured by York University," Jamaica Information Service, Toronto: JAMPRESS Ltd., Great Britain, June 18, 1998, Retrieved July 2021, http://www.nlj.gov.jm/files/u8/bn_bennett_ls_0007.pdf.

Johnson, M.A. Telephone conversation with Lolita Phillips, August 7, 2021.

Louise Bennett Coverley Fonds. Fonds RC0037. Archives & Research Collections: McMaster University, Retrieved July 2021, https://archives.mcmaster.ca/index.php/louise-bennett-coverley-fonds.

"Mavis Burke, Lifetime Achievements," *Jamaican Proud*, November 29, 2015, Retrieved July 2021, https://www.youtube.com/watch?v=SzI1-aF0J3c.

"McGuinty Government Honours Miss Lou – Jamaica's Gift to the World," Ontario Newsroom, January 31, 2007, Retrieved July

2021, https://news.ontario.ca/en/release/86205/mcguinty-government-honours-miss-lou-jamaicas-gift-to-the-world.

PACE Canada, Jamaica 50 Publication Committee, *Jamaicans in Canada: When Ackee Meets Codfish*, Toronto: Jamaica 50 Celebrations Inc., 2012, Retrieved July 2021, https://www.pacecanada.org/history/.

"Veteran Broadcaster Dwight Whylie Passes On," *Jamaica Gleaner*, September 17, 2002, http://old.jamaica-gleaner.com/gleaner/20020917/lead/lead4.html.

MISS LOU'S TEACHINGS:
THE WISDOM BEHIND THE WORDS

Olive Senior

When a giant tree falls in the forest, the almighty crash echoes and resounds, followed by a deadly silence. This is meant to give Earth time to take a deep breath, mourn the loss, straighten her dress, and compose herself. For Earth knows that out of that silence, stories will start to emerge. Earth is listening and waiting for the one that begins, "Aunty Roachy seh: Listen, nuh."

Listen, nuh, we all know that once upon a time, Miss Lou donned the bandana costume of the Jamaican countrywoman and reached deep into her pocket and pulled out words that she placed like sweeties on our tongues. And we are still getting that sweet rush today. Which is why we talk so much about Miss Lou and language.

The early decision by Louise Bennett to give voice to the ordinary people of Jamaica was one that she boldly defended. In the process, Miss Lou opened the gates not only for a long list of spoken-word artists and performers, but was also a profound influence in freeing up the so-called literary heavyweights from the straightjacket of conformity.

Miss Lou did not say we must throw out or disrespect the English language. What she affirmed was that we should also claim respect for our own language, alongside our inherited English tongue. This opened a gateway for writers such as me, who were struggling to find our own voices, one that would allow us to be true to ourselves and to the culture we come from, while writing our way into a global culture.

But I will not presume to write about language and Miss Lou—there are others far more qualified than I to do that. What I would like is to ask us to move beyond the enshrinement of Miss Lou and language to see what the language of Miss Lou contained: the whole package. Yes, she gave us language, but what should we make of it? In weaving collectively the legend of Miss Lou, we need to ask ourselves: What is it we want of her? What do we yearn for? How has she managed to bring us together in a variety of places, spaces, and times, to have "listen, nuh" bring us to total alertness, in expectation of something positive and life-affirming? What are the gifts she left behind that can help us in our troubled world today?

Everything Miss Lou wrote or spoke was framed in narrative—stories and poems that made us laugh with the laughter of shared recognition. But stories are containers and transmitters of lessons, too.

Let us then consider Miss Lou as Teacher. And not just for the didactic advice given as Aunty Roachy, but also for the more subtle messages enshrined in her own persona and activities. The legacy she bequeathed to us as gifts in the form of story:

1. The gift of memory, history, and ancestry
2. The gift of manners and broughtuptcy[1]
3. The gift of social harmony

Miss Lou has said publicly, many times, that "I learned everything about history, manners, geography, love, morals, and religion from stories my grandmother told me. I grew up on stories." All culture, she affirmed, comes from stories.

To be worthy of taking ownership of Miss Lou's legacy, then, we need to ask ourselves: What stories are we passing on to our children today to counter a world of consumerism and violence? Are we simply going to continue to recite Miss Lou's poems and sayings for fun and entertainment, for the joy of having the sweetness of these words in our mouths? Or will we acknowledge that Miss Lou has left behind not just stories to make us laugh, but stories to live by? This is what I mean when I titled my talk, "Miss Lou's Teachings: The Wisdom Behind the Words."

Miss Lou continues to live in us because of what she represented in her life, as in her poems and stories: a universe with a moral centre. Our paradise might be lost now—but it is not unredeemable.

No matter how hard the time or how hot the pain, her personae always had an answer or an explanation. Even if "dutty tough," this was still a world of certainties.[2] Every act of aggression or meanness called forth a response from a Bennett persona. Bystanders were not fearful of involvement or reprisal, and spoke their minds. Evil did exist, but it came in a form that was seemingly removed or easily contained or exorcised, not stalking us into our bedrooms or schoolyards.

The tales were of Miss Lou's contemporaries, but the moral values expressed in the proverbs and sayings were from the ancestors, and her artistry created archetypal characters that will always be around—a fierce expression of the Jamaican personality as it has evolved through the ages.

Unlike politicians, preachers, teachers, and—yes—parents, Miss Lou was not talking *to* us; she was weaving us into the story. In so doing, she made the listener complicit, so we were forced to position ourselves in the drama as chorus or community. And we recognised the real possibility of becoming the objects of public condemnation or ridicule, should we ourselves transgress. Part of Miss Lou's moral universe was naming and shaming of the guilty. Guilt that did not then inhere in major crimes and violence, but in other forms of transgression. A lot of this transgression dealt with the little things, with how we relate to one another. But it is interpersonal behaviour that oils the wheels of public discourse. What we used to call manners or "broughtuptcy"; what people today call "respeck."

From her own innate sense of respect came Miss Lou's gestures of harmony that she passed on to the young in, for example, her *Ring Ding* TV shows in Jamaica: "Clap him/Clap her!" Respect for the other that can only come about from inculcating self-respect. Little things, yes . . . but it is the omission of little things—respect for others—that leads to the commission of big and terrible things: corruption, graft, greed, public kas-kas, gangs, violence, murder, and war.[3]

Miss Lou's generous spirit came from her own broughtuptcy—from the mother and grandmother who provided her with wisdom through stories, and what she called "backative."[4] Without such a talisman from her elders, she would never have been able to venture out on that heroic journey into unknown territory—territory that was then called "Dialect Verse." Her mother, a fine seamstress, is supposed to have told her that she would back her choice "if you write as well as I can sew."

All children need some kind of backative to learn to be mannersable, to earn respect, and to succeed.[5] The affirmation that comes from adults and peers willing to "clap him/clap her" for every effort, no matter how simple. Our child rearing practices in Miss Lou's homeland are not always of that school. Unfortunately, too many children are expected to succeed without backative, resulting in the terrible consequences we are seeing everywhere.

The greatest monument to Miss Lou that we can create is this: To demonstrate, by gesture and example, the value of all human life. To create stories for our youth that are woven from the fibre of the everyday, strengthened with the warp of ancestral wisdom. To find the means to allow youth to tell their own stories as a way of finding the lessons within.

We don't have to leave stories up to the professionals—writers, storytellers, or filmmakers—though, of course, they are important. Nor should we leave storytelling up to television, the Internet, or the music industry. All of us are capable of telling stories. What we need to do is build on Miss Lou's teachings and find a way of reintroducing stories about ourselves, our families, our ancestral wisdom, back into our homes and our everyday lives.

We should not see Miss Lou simply as an "icon," for that is no more than a picture—a surface representation of a revered person. Miss Lou will always be revered, but her life and work would be in vain if we do not go beyond the surface of laughter and joy, of the language she gave us—still available in her books and recordings and our memories—to find the wellspring of wisdom that lies so much deeper. Wisdom that we need now more than ever. Wisdom that can unite us.

Perhaps then, the conversation should be about Miss Lou as National Hero? Not a hero of deeds, but of words—words that are mightier than the sword. So yes, we are back to language.

I tried to find some definitions of what "National Hero" meant, and I will simply leave you to ponder this one and decide how Louise Bennett-Coverley fits the description from Wikipedia:

A hero is a person who is admired and acknowledged for their courage, outstanding achievements, and noble qualities.

A National Hero is someone who, beyond that, has made significant positive contributions to the growth and development of society, and represents all of us—that is, is seen as a representative of society as a whole.

Endnotes

1   "Broughtuptcy"—being properly brought up, or more generally having good manners.

2   "Dutty tough"—the dirt is tough or the ground is hard. Louise Bennett wrote a poem of the same name ("Dutty Tough," 1966).

3   "Kas-kas"—"dispute, contend in words" (*Dictionary of Jamaican English* 2002, p. 265).

4   "Backative"—having "backing" or "support."

5   "Mannersable"—"mannerly" or "displaying manners."

References

Bennett, L. *Jamaica Labrish: Jamaica Dialect Poems*. Edited by Rex Nettleford. Kingston: Sangster's Book Stores, 1966.

Cassidy, F.G. and R.B. Le Page, eds. *Dictionary of Jamaican English*, second edition. Barbados, Jamaica, Trinidad and Tobago: University of the West Indies Press, 2002.

THE LAUGHTER OF FREEDOM:
LOUISE BENNETT, THE BODY AND ANTICOLONIAL PERFORMANCE

Honor Ford-Smith

Louise Simone Bennett died on July 26, 2006. She was eighty-six. An outpouring of obituaries described her as one of the most influential figures in Jamaican culture: "the voice of the island's culture at home and abroad" (Moses, 2006). No other poet or performer prior to Bob Marley was more loved by Jamaicans of all classes and races than Miss Lou (as everyone called her). Though many recognise Bennett as a serious advocate for the Jamaican language and culture over decades, few are aware of the specific gendered and racialized context from which she emerged, or the remarkable breadth of her contributions.

As the lone enduring popular voice of Black and working-class Jamaican women of the twentieth century, Bennett belonged to a generation of anticolonial cultural activists who aimed to transform inherited colonial culture. She gave voice to vernacular working-class reality in performances that would shape generations of Jamaicans prior to and after independence. As she worked to create what Benedict Anderson famously called the "imagined community of nation" (Anderson, 1991), Bennett came to embody the iconic mother of nation—a gendered signifier of Jamaican possibility, a woman who productively negotiated the conflicting discourses of Blackness and gender to articulate a basis for national unity and progress. Her presence, participatory chants, invocations, and incitements to laughter, called into being an embodied and caring community. Her monologues privileged and dignified the material culture of labour and the bodies of those who worked the "dutty" or ground. Or as Sylvia Wynter would have it, the plot, or the provision ground (Boyce Davies, 2015, p. 211). Her dramatic persona was that of an African Caribbean woman who produced and marketed the food that sustained and enabled survival past and present.

Bennett came to voice in the context of the worldwide anticolonial movement—the most vibrant and varied social movement of the last century. When she was born in 1919, European colonial powers directly controlled about 80 percent of the globe. That this is no longer the case has to do with the achievements of the social movements with which her life and work intersected. Bennett's work overlapped with several generations of men who are far better known internationally than she is for their critique of the ideas and practices that underpinned colonial regime. One such writer was Aimé Césaire, the celebrated Martinican founder of Négritude, poet, playwright, and patriarch of the transformation of the French Antilles who outlived her by two years, dying in 2008. In 1933, a few years before Bennett's public debut, Césaire wrote:

> My mouth shall be the mouth of those calamities that have no mouth, my voice the freedom of those who break down in the prison of despair . . .
> And above all, my body as well as my soul, beware of assuming the sterile attitude of a spectator, for life is not a spectacle, a sea of miseries is not a proscenium, a man screaming is not a dancing bear (Césaire, 2005, p. 38).

To this Bennett might have remarked:

> Sun a shine but tings no bright;
> Doah pot a bwile, bickle no nuff;
> River flood, but water scarce, yaw;
> Rain a fall but dutty tough.
>
> Tings so bad dat nowadays when
> Yuh ask smaddy how dem do
> Dem fraid yuh tek it tell dem back,
> So dem no answer yuh.
>
> No care omuch we dah work fa
> Hard-time still eena we shut;

> We dah fight, Hard-time a beat we,
> Dem might raise we wages, but
>
> One poun gawn awn pon we pay, an
> We no feel no merriment
> For ten poun gawn awn pon we food
> An ten poun pon we rent!
>
> Saltfish gawn up, mackerel gawn up,
> Pork an beef gawn up same way,
> And when rice an butter ready
> Dem just go pon holiday! (Bennett, 1982, p. 25).

Bennett's work, unlike much of Césaire's, was marked by the use of laughter as a weapon, and with irony and mockery she broke through the bars of hunger and poverty that created those prisons of despair again and again, over a period of more than sixty years. Never a spectator separated from her audience by an imaginary fourth wall or proscenium, she insisted on smashing the barriers between spectator and participant, drawing her audience into performances through call and response, repartee, song, rhythm, laughter, and signifying gestures. As with any long career, her work took on a variety of themes, from race to food, to social pretension and respectability, but in all cases, she picked sense out of the nonsense of calamity to reveal a sea of vibrant possibility created by the people she loved.

CLR James, Trinidadian intellectual and activist, wrote *The Case for West-Indian Self Government* in 1933, and in 1936, the singer Paul Robeson played Toussaint L'Ouverture, the Haitian revolutionary, in James's play *The Black Jacobins*, in London (James, 1933). The play, like the book that followed it (James, 1938), argued that Caribbean populations had their own revolutionary approach. Tony Bogues, building on James, later called this a practice of freedom, arguing that this is different from notions of individual rights because it emerges from within the embodied traditions of the enslaved, and is made through collective action and reflection (Bogues, 2012). These approaches did not draw on or mimic the political archive of Europe, even though they borrow and reinterpret some of these while also contributing much to Western modern society.

Bennett's work voiced the intellectual and cultural difference inherent in this radical Caribbean approach. The difference between herself, and men like James, Césaire, and others was that she was a woman, and one of the only women of her generation and race to become visible and extremely popular *through* her embodiment of the persona of a working-class woman—often a peasant woman in the context of the anticolonial struggle in the Caribbean. To make her work consistently visible and appreciated in Jamaica itself, she had to find a way of negotiating a particularly treacherous terrain of images of Black women. Unlike Césaire and James, she chose to speak from the position of working class and peasant women, and to speak in their language. Many anticolonial thinkers critiqued European colonial ideas. In so doing, they engaged a tradition with which they were unable to break. They celebrated the working class, the poor, the "folk," but they often did so from a painfully conflicted distance. The great George Lamming, for example, Bennett's contemporary, writes about the particular kind of doubleness he experienced as a result of becoming middle class. He was from working-class origins, but his colonial education transformed him and made him middle class. He writes about the shame and guilt caused by this distance—describing encounters as a schoolboy with his mother in which he felt obliged to deny their relationship because of who he was with (Drayton and Andaiye, 1992, p. 26). He speaks from this place of conflicted subjectivity, and he enunciates this rupture—a rupture which made it impossible for him to simply and unproblematically write from the place of the working-class subject he sought to speak for and about.

Bennett's brilliance was that she did *not* do this, and the price she paid for it was that she was not always legible to Northern audiences, or audiences outside of the Caribbean whose ability to interpret Black bodies was always already mediated by a repertoire of stereotypes circulated in American popular cultural industries. As a result, she was, and still is, not always taken seriously as an intellectual or sophisticated artist (Morris, 1967). With her Bandana and full-body, it is easy to equate Bennett with the denigrated Black mammy, the laughing harmless servant of the Hollywood industry. But as Jamaican critic Carolyn Cooper points out: "There is nothing wrong with being a mother. A mother is a nurturer. The problem is when the Black woman looks after white people at the expense of her own children and family. This is not Miss Lou" (Ford-Smith, 2007). The full-bodied woman she portrayed was an archetypal symbol of the fertility of land and culture, and her genius lay in the fact that she was able to inhabit the domesticated stereotype of the large laughing woman in order to overturn it, and to turn the nurturing qualities toward, rather than away from, the people she wrote for and about. In doing so, she rooted herself in the ground on which she stood and from which she could speak and be heard live and direct—albeit differently—by all classes.

Other Black women writers of her time struggled to find a voice that could be recognized and heard by the working class, the literate middle classes, and the white world. Una Marson, for example, wrote about the yearning for identity and identification with Black working-class culture. She contrasted this desire with the impossibility of achieving such an identification because of the straight jacket of assimilation imposed by colonial education and by the mantle of Victorian colonial respectability which it conveyed. In her 1937 play, *Pocomania*, the Black middle-class heroine is unable to become part of the working-class band of revivalists because of her gendered class and education. This psychic division causes her enormous self-alienation, and ultimately psychological collapse because of internal division (Marson, 2016).

Bennett's success came after Marson's. Significantly, she gave her first public performance in 1938, the year of the landmark Jamaican uprising against colonial rule. Here, she was supported by two significant developments which are often forgotten in describing her trajectory. First, she was supported by the popular performance tradition which had developed a significant urban, mainly Black, audience by the 1930s. While the Caribbean had always had a yard concert tradition, in the 1920s, the Universal Negro Improvement Association (UNIA) had developed a professional version of this through its entertainment centre near Cross Roads in Kingston. It was here that Ranny Williams,[1] Miss Lou's stage partner, had come to prominence. And it was through the cultural work of the UNIA, and the training ground it provided to local entertainers, that an urban working-class audience developed for performances that treated everyday concerns and topical matters in the language of ordinary folks. While in some ways this overlapped with the literary tradition in terms of themes, the embodied codes, the music, the immediacy of improvised call-and-response, the non-verbal and the rhetorical and gestural signifying meant that performance became its own genre, one which mobilized and represented the popular.

Secondly, it is a less well-known fact that Bennett's early career was supported by women's organizations of the time which emerged within the anticolonial movement. Black feminists like Amy Bailey[2] and Madame di Mena Aitken[3] of the UNIA, had been influenced by the Garvey movement (Ford-Smith, 2004). In alliance with liberal white creoles like May Farquharson[4] and anthropologist Edith Clarke,[5] they fought for women's political rights and for women's right to enter the professions and to seek political office. In 1938, workers across the Caribbean rose up against the plantocracy and the colonial state, and the period of 1938 to 1944 was one which saw major changes. Following the formation of political parties in 1938, a reformed constitution allowing for partial self-government came into being in 1944, as the island moved toward independence. The women of the middle class supported independence from Britain, but they also supported the idea that middle-class women should become the managers of the "upliftment" of working-class women and their representatives. The political gains of the early movement of Black feminists became subsumed into the nation state and into the Jamaica Federation of Women (JFW), a broad organization of women which aimed to further "proper family life" (i.e., male-headed households) and support women's household responsibilities (French, 1988).

Bennett worked for the JFW and for Jamaica Welfare as a cultural animator, performing in rural and urban settings, advocating for programmes that developed rural food self-sufficiency, sanitation and nutrition, and social unity. At the same time, Bennett was mischievous enough to satirize the excesses of these organizations. For example, she made fun of the mass marriage campaigns of Mary Morris Knibb,[6] who she calls "Mrs. Married Knibbs" in the poem "Mass Wedding," which lampooned some of the more incongruous matches and mocked the absurdity of the fervour for respectability that, at times, suffused the JFW (Bennett, 1966). Travelling throughout Jamaica, Bennett performed for women's groups in yards and church halls, reciting and affirming proverbial wisdom, and supporting the teaching of nutrition and hygiene in rural communities. In part, as a result of this work, she garnered a scholarship to study drama at the Royal Academy of Dramatic Art in the UK, and left Jamaica.

It has been widely recognized that Bennett's work was not taken seriously by the cultural establishment of her time—that she was seen as a "mere" entertainer, a light poet who could make people laugh. She was left out of many anthologies of Jamaican verse until artist-scholars Mervyn Morris and Rex Nettleford made a strong case for her importance. Since then, much attention has been paid to her verse and its content, but less attention has been paid to her skill and contribution as a performer. It is my argument that it was through her presence in embodied performance that Bennett was able to straddle the divide between the written, the oral, and the embodied, and to perform as someone through whose body what she spoke about could materialize. It is through her persona and presence that she won popularity and never lost it. She became the South Parade Pedlar and the Candy Seller in the poems with those names, turning the curse into a sophisticated art form, levelling hilarious commentary with an inventive targeting of the vulnerabilities of hapless buyers. In her hands the sonic quality of the "tracing match" (cursing match) and the proverbial utterance became a formidable weapon, as well as a place for the laughter and the release of anxiety about social tensions and the desire for respectability. She was fond of saying, "Yuh haffi tek kin teet kibba heart bun." But, in fact, she used laughter not to cover, but to reveal heart burn (and heart ache)—satirizing and revealing social pretension, racism, and hypocrisy.

It was in her pointed gestural communication with her living audience that the immanence of her performance worked its alchemy. Her use of rhythm and song, her ironic and well-timed chuckle, her laughter, her non-verbal repartee, the way she constantly signified with a roll of the eye, a point of the lips, a motion of the hands, a sigh, a groan, all without verbalizing and with impeccable timing—these were the things that her drew her audience into a community she invoked and prefigured in the moment. Audiences finished her sentences, sang along with her, asked her questions, which she answered in the middle of a poem or story, picking up the thread and thrust of her narrative without missing a beat. She never allowed her audience to be, in Césaire's terms, spectators. She pulled them in and then built on their contribution to complete and add to a total performance.

To achieve this, Bennett had to formally study Black Jamaican peasant culture. She was a city-dweller, but she studied the countryside, sometimes moving around with the dancer and choreographer Ivy Baxter,[7] visiting communities in rural Jamaica to learn the particularities of language, proverbial philosophy, song, and dance from them. From this careful study, she developed and embodied a specific persona, usually (until the 1970s) a higgler (huckster or market-seller), and broadened her repertoire. She was not herself working class, and she spoke perfect English, but she turned local rural and urban working-class and peasant knowledge into national knowledge by carrying traditions from community to community, interpreting the deeper meanings of everyday activities for her audiences and adding meaning to them by representing, reflecting and enriching what had all too often been denigrated. She collected countless Jamaican proverbs, stories, and riddles, and studied rituals like Dinkie Mini (a wake form) and Pukkumina (a popular religion). She assembled oral knowledge, at first privileging Anancy stories that emerged from the work of those who fed the nation, and then developing her "Aunty Roachy" persona and monologues which were broadcast on the radio.

In the beginning, she physically transported her performances in her body all over Jamaica, just as the food sellers or market women she personified carried food all over the island to feed the country. Traditions like Dinkie Mini from Eastern Jamaica became part of a national cultural iconography because of the groundwork she did. Like the female farmer who bartered to exchange food, or the higgler who walked miles carrying heavy loads, Bennett performed the idea of a nation that was based on privileging the knowledge of people who had limited access to print and to the European archive. She assembled and presented a composite notion of community performatively out of her own female body, out of the tough dutty, and the wisdom of the women who were caregivers of land and society. Through her work, she proposed that nation and community had to be based on the knowledge production of the Black working class who made meaning from the land. She did this while simultaneously drawing on the colonial representations of the full-bodied Black woman to legitimize her work with the elite.

This was an ironic act of performative doubling. She used the image of the laughing Black woman to provoke opposing interpretations in her audiences. She could be read very differently depending on the social location of her audience. If cultural memory is conveyed by the oppressed in coded images that can be interpreted in different ways by oppressor and oppressed, it follows that dominant and oppressed groups can read the same symbols in very different ways. James Scott argues that subordinate groups create a covert language of resistance which eludes the powerful while protecting the identity and intention of their authors (Scott, 1990). Louise Bennett used the tactic of deploying covert signs of resistance, but she did so while appearing to collude with dominant discourses on the good-natured, laughing Black woman. In an extremely agile way, she made the ambivalence of conflicting meanings productive by inhabiting the simultaneity of the subversive and domesticated, writing and speech, pathos and mockery, respectfulness and trickery. Her tremendous popularity as a performer lay in her ability to work this ambivalence on the spot in front of an audience, calling to them and responding to what they gave back in the moment, improvising on her feet in the persona of the figure she created.

According to Ramzani, Bennett's poetry linked the double-voiced rhetorical structure of irony to the ironies of post-colonial inheritance (Ramzani, 2001). She deployed clashing irreconcilables and set up an echoing vibration between two meanings to juggle the contradictions and uncertainties which characterized the moment of national formation. Bennett's cunning linguistic juxtapositions were, and are, citational examples of perceptual split. She extended ideas of post-colonial mimicry by opening up the gap between signifier and signified, making audible the disharmony between colonial and postcolonial (Ramzani, 2001, p. 115). In my view, it is not just her linguistic juxtapositions that accomplish this, but her physical presence in persona in conjunction with her gestural and oral utterance. It is what she did with the character in the bandana whose representation in literature, welfare policy, and film constantly casts a shadow on her performance. Her utterance and gesture were constantly signifying on this image, commenting on, and undermining the objectified stereotype because what she spoke about was outside the limits of the stereotype's range. This was clear, for example, in her critiques of economic misery in "Dutty Tough," cited above.

Her strategy of soliciting double readings depended not just on the psychology of the trickster, but on the immediacy of enacting a trick. Just as domestic workers in Jamaica knew that they were not entirely defined by the work they did in middle-class homes, or by how they were treated there, they also knew that Bennett was not entirely defined by the stereotypical persona she inhabited. Their employers might dismiss Bennett's work as non-threatening folksy humour, but her trick was to deploy her monologues or poems simultaneously as a repetition of colonial discourse and as an endorsement of resistance with which the audience would find itself in collusion after the fact. "Me Bredda" is an example of how this works:

> Oonoo call me bredda fi me!
> Beg yuh tell him come yah quick!
> Tell him bring him pelt-yuh-kin cow-cod
> An bus-yuh-open stick!
>
> Me naw mek no joke wid yuh, mah!
> Quick and brisk an pay me off,
> Or ah call me bredda in yah
> Meck him beat you till yuh sof!
>
> Yuh answer me advertisement,
> Yuh come slap a me yard
> Come tell me how de pay is big
> And how de work no hard.
>
> Me never like yuh face, but when
> Me bredda tell me seh
> Dat yuh husban is a nice man
> Mi decide fi come tedeh.
>
> Me oversleep dis mornin, never
> Wake till after eight.
> Is a taxi-cab me teck come yah
> Fi hinder me from late.
>
> An now yuh start form fool bout yuh
> No want me! What is dis!

Oonoo call me bredda fi me!
It naw go so, missis.

Yuh wi haffi beg me pardon loud
Meck all de neighbours hear!
Yuh wi haffi pay me two weeks
Wages, plus me taxi fare!

So ah talking stupidness?
Oonoo call me bredda deh!
Ah-oh, yuh change yuh mine? Tank yuh.
Goodbye. Wha dat yuh seh?

Yuh woulda like fi know me bredda?
Me cyaan help yuh eena dat
Me hooda like know him meself,
For is me one me parents got! (Bennett, 1982, pp. 18–19).

Here, Bennett physically inhabits the stock figure of the domestic servant and pushes the doubleness implicit in the genre, appearing to validate stereotypes of laziness while standing up for her persona. Just as she undermines the slipperiness of performance in writing and the stability of writing in performance, the mammy is undermined by the angry, aggressive speaker, and vice versa. The speech begins as a caricature of a lazy, loud, *mouta massi*.[8] But the performance twists and turns in a series of clever reversals and absences that depend on Bennett's body. The expected weak-strong binary is reversed because of the stage presence of the large and aggressive domestic servant (Miss Lou) exerting power over the silenced, invisible employer. To working-class audiences in the 1950s, it was a delight—a feminized David and Goliath. Bennett stages subjunctively the taboo desire of many a domestic worker who had no recourse to formal justice at that time. The audience is drawn into the performance, becoming partners in her strategy of confrontation becoming the unu (*oonoo—you*, plural) who are asked to call her brother. By the end of the monologue, it is clear that the loudness and the brashness were only a strategic deception in which the audience is now implicated as witness. The trick wins the speaker exactly what she wants, and she drops the mask, explaining that the first part of the poem was an act of survival. It is the pathos of the last line—"Is me one me parents got"—that wins over witnesses.

It is a subtle statement of the desperation that motivates the character. Those who find Anancy[9] amoral can view the domestic worker as a wutliss (worthless, vulgar) woman lampooned. Others can see it as the work of a female Anancy whose majestic cunning is on display in the moment in which the poem is spoken.

There are therefore at least two interpretations of the poem, depending on one's social identification. Bennett's preferred meaning can only be discerned by reading and analysing her work as a whole, and by attending to the issues and the people she consistently embodied and for whom she advocated. But in the immediacy of performance, she was always able to produce an illusion of unity of understanding while sustaining conflicting interpretations based on one's social location. She got away with this finally because she diffused anxiety about the depth of potential class and race conflict through laughter. In performance, Bennett repeatedly offered her audiences symbols of social difference which they read and used differently depending on their social location. To become impatient with the covert disguises of Bennett's performance is to lose track of their subtle doubling and the subversive possibilities these open up.

I began by arguing that Bennett emerged from a particular anticolonial moment, and from a context in which social movements were shifting roles and assumptions. I argued that this context shaped her work. She intervened in the making of ideas of nation through her presence in performance. This presence was embodied in the persona of women of the working class who were often caregivers like Aunty Roachy,[10] food producers and distributors of food and whose language, wisdom, and labour enabled the survival and reproduction of the society. Cleverly negotiating a discursive minefield of gendered and racialized images, she embodied the role of the mother of nation or aunty of everyone in a way that no other artist of her time did. At the same time, she created a model of what an engaged postcolonial artist can be—becoming the teacher who cleverly prefigured ideas of nation, culture, and identity in public places—like the stage, the yard, the community hall. She worked through her presence to productively juggle the social divisions, race, and class antagonisms to prefigure an illusion of national unity and social progress. This prefiguring rested finally on her connection to land and labour on the land, to food, and to an empirical form of care. This was to break down in the 1980s with the destruction of already fragile ideas of self-reliance and food sovereignty, the deterritorialization of food producers and their denigration as ignorant and backward and the replacement of agriculture with the increased reliance on an economy built around tourism and mining. Rather than incentivizing food production what took place was the inauguration of neoliberal globalization. But that is another story. It is in the 1980s that Louise Bennett left Jamaica for Canada. Up till then, in her voice and body, we can hear the distant laughter of a freedom that is based on privileging the labour of the women and the men who care for the land, feed the people, name this hard work of care in their language. In her actions, this freedom is prefigured. In remembering her performances, it seems to draw nearer.

Endnotes

1   Randolph Samuel Williams (1912–1980) was born in Panama and moved with his family to Jamaica at age six. Williams attended Calabar High and Kingston Technical High Schools and made his name as a popular performer, appearing in several national pantomimes, films, and television programmes. He was also Louise Bennett's partner on radio shows and in pantomimes, achieving enormous popularity. According to the Jamaica Information Service, "his greatest accomplishment is that of the love of the people of Jamaica."

2   Amy Bailey (1895–1990) was born in Jamaica to a family of schoolteachers and attended Shortwood Teachers' College. She was co-founder and first Chairman of the Women's Liberal Club, which championed and won political rights for Jamaican women. As a newspaper columnist, she was a strong critic of racism and advocated for Black women's right to visible employment in clerical and professional positions, and an end to the exclusion of women from professional advancement. She was a relentless organizer on behalf of the Save the Children Fund, and a co-organizer of the island's first birth control league. Bailey was inspired by the tenets of the Universal Negro Improvement Association (UNIA) and was particularly concerned with the circumstances of young Black women. She founded the Housecraft Training Centre to professionalize domestic labour.

3   Maymie di Mena Aitken (1879–1953) was an African American stalwart of the Universal Negro Improvement Association (UNIA) and one of

the leaders of the Pan-African movement. De Mena Aitkin "became a legendary image" when, during one UNIA parade, "she rode a 'gray charger with a drawn sword.'" (Ford-Smith, 2004, p. 25).

4   Gladys May Farquharson (1894–1992) was born and educated in Jamaica. According to Smith College Special Collections, she was also educated in "the U.S., and Jersey Channel Islands, and she attended Cheltenham Ladies College." The daughter of Sir Arthur Farquharson, a lawyer and influential liberal planter, she assisted her father until his death. With Amy Bailey, in 1939, May Farquharson helped to advocate for political rights for women and formed the Birth Control League of Jamaica (later the Family Planning League of Jamaica). She was active in many philanthropic organizations, and as justice of the peace, she sat for years in juvenile court. (Smith College Libraries and French, J. and Ford-Smith, H., 1984).

5   Edith Clarke (1896–1979) was born in Jamaica, the daughter of Hugh Clarke, Custos of Westmoreland. She was educated at Abbey School, Malvern, UK, and University College, London (1921–1923), the London School of Economics (1926–1931). Clarke studied anthropology (1932–1933), after which she returned to Jamaica and worked in the local civil service. Among other positions, she served as director of Jamaica Welfare Ltd., was appointed as the first female member of the Jamaican Legislative Council in 1958 and worked with a wide range of social organizations (including the Child Welfare Association, 4-H Clubs, the Central Council of Voluntary Services and the Jamaica Society for the Prevention of Cruelty to Children). Clarke's publication *My Mother Who Fathered Me: A Study of the Families in Three Selected Communities of Jamaica* (Allen and Unwin, London, 1957) remains a seminal contribution.

6   Mary Morris Knibb was a Moravian social reformer, and like Amy and Ina Bailey, a member of the Women's Liberal Club, an early organization of Black feminists. She was the first woman to be elected to local government, and she won on a feminist ticket that stressed childcare as a principal policy to be addressed. She advocated for marriage because unmarried women were barred from professional advancement under colonial law. She initiated a mass marriage campaign as a misguided means to address this issue, and as a means to win respectability for working-class women. Mass weddings were later endorsed by Molly Huggins, the wife of the governor, who used her offices to broaden the reach of this performance of respectability. (Robinson, 2020).

7   Ivy Baxter (1923–1993) was a pioneer in what Sabine Sörgel refers to as "a new approach towards dance theatre as a community art form."

One of the leading figures of dance in the Caribbean, Baxter was at the forefront of "what was called the barefoot movement in the 1950s." She was "the first Jamaican dance choreographer to explore the island's diverse Africanist folk forms," and founded the Ivy Baxter Dance Group in 1950. According to Sörgel, Baxter "became part of the national independence movement reformulating an African Jamaican national identity by celebrating African cultural roots and traditions" (2018). It was this company that produced many of the dancers who became part of the National Dance Theatre Company of Jamaica.

8   According to Cassidy and LePage "mouta massi" or "mout-a-massy" (mouth+have+mercy) refers to "[o]ne who talks too much" or a "hypocrite." (Cassidy and LePage, 2002, p. 309). See also Bennett, "Mout-Amassi," (1982, pp. 50-51).

9   Cassidy and LePage identify Anancy as "The central character of numerous fables, West African in origin, and extremely popular in Jamaica and many other parts of the West Indies. Anancy, the spider, pits his cunning (usually with success) against superior strength; he also symbolizes greed and envy" (Cassidy and LePage, 2002, p.10).

10 Louise Bennett created a character—Aunty/Auntie Roachy—through whom she spoke, often beginning her statements with, "My Aunty Roachy seh . . ." (See Bennett, 1993, 2003).

References

Anderson, B.R.O.G. *Imagined Communities: Reflections on the Origin and Spread of Nationalism*, revised edition. London: Verso, 1991.

Bennett, L. "Mass Wedding." *Jamaica Labrish*. Edited by Rex Nettleford. Kingston, Jamaica: Sangster's Book Stores, 1966, pp. 29—30.

Bennett, L. "Dutty Tough." *Selected Poems*. Edited by M. Morris. Kingston, Jamaica: Sangster's Book Stores, 1982, pp. 25—26.

Bennett, L. "Me Bredda." *Selected Poems*. Edited by M. Morris. Kingston, Jamaica: Sangster's Book Stores, 1982, pp. 18—19.

Bennett, L. "Mout-Amassi." *Selected Poems*. Edited by M. Morris. Kingston, Jamaica: Sangster's Book Stores, 1982, pp. 50—51.

Bennett, L. *Auntie Roachy Seh*. Edited by M. Morris. Kingston, Jamaica: Sangster's Book Stores, 1993, 2003.

Bogues, A. "And What About the Human?: Freedom, Human Emancipation, and the Radical Imagination." *Boundary 2*, vol. 39, no. 3, 2012, pp. 29–46.

Boyce Davies, C. "Masquerade to Maskarade: Caribbean Cultural Resistance and the Rehumanizing Project." *Sylvia Wynter*. Edited by Katherine McKittrick. New York: Duke University Press, 2015, pp. 203–225.

Cassidy, F.G. and Le Page, R.B. (eds). *Dictionary of Jamaican English*, second edition. Kingston: University of the West Indies Press, 2002.

Césaire, A. "Return to My Native Land." *The Oxford Book of Caribbean Verse*. Edited by S. Brown and M. McWatt. Oxford: Oxford University Press, 2005.

Edith Clarke. Archives Hub. JISC (originally Joint Information Systems Committee). https://archiveshub.jisc.ac.uk/search/archives/02e19b7a-280d-3cad-9122-ac1a136c5eb9.

Drayton, R. and Andaiye. *Conversations, George Lamming: Essays, Addresses and Interviews 1956–1986*. London: Karia Press, 1992.

Ford-Smith, H. Unpublished Interview with Carolyn Cooper. "Colonizin' in Reverse: Louise Simone Bennett: A Commemoration." New College, University of Toronto, March 9, 2007.

Ford-Smith, H. "Unruly Virtues of the Spectacular: Performing Engendered Nationalisms in the UNIA in Jamaica." *Interventions: International Journal of Postcolonial Studies*, vol. 6, no. 1, 2004, pp. 18–44.

French, J. "Colonial Policy Towards Women After the 1938 Uprising: The Case of Jamaica." *Caribbean Quarterly*, vol. 34, no. 3/4, 1988, pp. 38–61.

French, J. and Ford-Smith, H. *Women, Work and Organisation in Jamaica: 1900–1944, Research Report*. The Hague: Institute of Social Studies, 1985.

Jamaica Information Service. Randolph Samuel Williams. *Famous Jamaicans*. Retrieved August 2021, https://jis.gov.jm/information/famous-jamaicans/randolph-samuel-williams/.

James, C.L.R. *The Case for West-Indian Self Government*. Published by Leonard and Virginia Woolf. London: Hogarth Press, 1933.

James, C.L.R. *The Black Jacobins: Toussaint L'Ouverture and the San Domingo Revolution*. London: Secker & Warburg, Ltd., 1938.

Marson, U. *Pocomania and London Calling*. Kingston: Blouse & Skirt Books, May Farquharson Papers (SSC-MS-00057), Smith College Special Collections, 2016, https://findingaids.smith.edu/repositories/2/resources/776.

Morris, M. "On Reading Louise Bennett, Seriously." *Jamaica Journal*, 1967, pp. 69–74.

Moses, K. "Louise Bennett, Jamaican Folklorist, Dies at 86." *The New York Times*, July 29, 2006, Retrieved June 2008.

National Library of Jamaica. "Amy Bailey." Retrieved August 2021, https://nlj.gov.jm/project/amy-bailey-1895-1990/.

Ramzani, J. *The Hybrid Muse: Postcolonial Poetry in English*. Chicago: University of Chicago Press, 2001.

Robinson, T. "Mass Weddings in Jamaica and the Production of Academic Folk Knowledge." *Small Axe*, vol. 24, no. 3 (63), 2020, pp. 65–80.

Scott, J. C. *Domination and the Arts of Resistance: Hidden Transcripts*. New Haven, CT: Yale University Press, 1990.

Sörgel, S. "Baxter, Ivy (1923–1993)." *The Routledge Encyclopedia of Modernism*. Taylor and Francis, 2018, Retrieved August 2021, https://www.rem.routledge.com/articles/baxter-ivy-1923-1993.

"WHEREVER I LIVE—TORONTO, LONDON, FLORIDA—I AM IN JAMAICA":
LOUISE BENNETT'S HOME AWAY FROM HOME

Klive Walker

Toronto is where Louise Bennett navigated the twilight of her existence, the city where at eighty-six years old, she took her last breath. On July 26, 2006, her profound dedication to the beauty of Jamaican folklore as a storyteller ended. Two decades before that sad moment, she decided, in the embrace of her dramatic life's third act, to depart her Jamaican homeland. She moved to Scarborough, a Toronto community with a significant Caribbean-Canadian population. But she is so closely associated with her birth country that it is easy to overlook that she was a Canadian citizen residing in a city that was her home away from home for twenty years. It is far simpler to consider her purely as an immense cultural figure of Jamaica, which she was. No question about that. It is easy to say she earned a modest mainstream profile in her new home, which she did. She was quick to point out, though, that: "Wherever I live—Toronto, London, Florida—I am in Jamaica." Or as she actually spoke it: "Any which part mi live—Toronto-o! London-o! Florida-o!—a Jamaica mi deh."

That one-sentence declaration complicated her relationship to Jamaica and to America, the UK, and Canada. It offers different ways of understanding what Jamaica means. If you possess a mentality steeped in the idea that Jamaica is only a specific place in the Caribbean region, you may interpret her comment as another way of saying she carried the spirit of her homeland with her wherever she lived. Your take on her declaration may be different if your heritage is Jamaican and you were born, grew up, or resided for a considerable amount of time in any of the significant communities of Caribbean heritage in Toronto, London, Florida, or New York. You might interpret her statement as meaning that in those communities, Jamaican music, food, literature, theatre, and art are essential to the lifeblood of those locations. In other words, Jamaica as a culture, as a way of being, exists in Toronto, New York, London, and elsewhere.

Louise Bennett was an important and early contributor to that sense of diaspora which is better understood as Caribbean rather than something restricted just to Jamaica. In 1945, a young twenty-six-year-old Louise arrived in the UK after receiving a scholarship to attend the prestigious Royal Academy of Dramatic Art (RADA). That was three years before the Empire Windrush ship docked in Tilbury, London, with its five hundred English Caribbean immigrants (Phillips and Phillips, 1999; Mathews, 2020). Her poem "Colonization in Reverse" is a snapshot of that Windrush moment when Caribbean migration to the UK began the journey to its tipping point. Its verses establish a lyrical benchmark for the significance of Caribbean communities there.

While still a student, BBC radio's *Caribbean Carnival* recognized her exceptional talent as a storyteller by hiring her. She wasn't the first Jamaican woman to work on British radio. Una Marson, a writer, playwright and poet, was that bold pioneer as on-air personality, producer, and creator (Tomlinson, 2019).[1] Nevertheless, the initiation of Louise's broadcasting career provided her with the opportunity to help shape a foundation for the presence of Caribbean culture in the UK. She was working in a medium where the refraction of her stories and poems through the prism of Jamaican folklore and language could reach a popular audience. She also involved herself in theatre, performing in dramatic plays like *Deep Are the Roots*, a production about race in America (D'Usseau and Gow, 1945).[2]

In the early 1950s, Louise decided to live in New York City, a metropolis buzzing with an outsized Caribbean presence. There, she entered a cultural and social milieu seasoned with a prominent Jamaican zeitgeist. Marcus Garvey's huge presence preceded her as did the crucial profile of writer, activist, and Harlem Renaissance catalyst Claude McKay, whose early poems were written in Jamaican language (Garvey, 1986; McKay, 1912).[3] Louise left her own indelible diasporic imprint on New York. She was a recording artist on Folkways Records,[4] committing to vinyl, mento, a sort of Jamaican calypso. She performed at the historic Village Vanguard nightclub.[5] She advanced her radio career and her native culture by participating on Alma John's landmark radio show on WWRL.[6] And she was a deep and abiding influence on Harry Belafonte and his producer Irving Burgie, an impact evident on Belafonte's 1956 million-selling album, *Calypso* (Gordon, 1994).[7]

Louise's career in the arts didn't begin in London or New York, but in Jamaica when, at nineteen, she was on a Kingston tram car where a provocative interaction with urban market women inspired her first Jamaican language poem. That was 1938. During the next seven years, she developed a vibrant career as a writer and performer working almost exclusively in the language of the people. As a storyteller performing in the oral tradition, she was celebrated and adored by the mass of ordinary citizens. As a published writer, she was rejected by the cultural elite of her homeland as less than literary, primarily because Jamaican language was seen as inferior.

When she returned to Jamaica in the late 1950s, the response to her work didn't immediately change. Despite that, she persisted for the next thirty years, negotiating the roadblocks and potholes of her career's journey until acceptance, even from the elite, became a reality. She built a career filled with groundbreaking artistic moments in poetry, short stories, comedy, theatre, broadcasting on radio and television, and as a recording artist. In doing so, she became a lightning rod for legitimizing Jamaican language, known in her day as "patois," or the "dialect." Those are the achievements gifting her an iconic presence in the nation of her birth.

Here in Toronto, we know about the popularity of Jamaican music and food. Reggae, ska, and dancehall stain the DNA of Toronto's music history. Restaurants like The Real Jerk, for example, serve not just Caribbean-Canadians, but a cross-section of the city's dense multicultural population. Louise Bennett, though, was not a reggae musician or a restaurateur. She arrived here in 1987, as an artist with a fifty-year resume, a distinguished international profile, and as someone who had to manage a reduced schedule of appearances and performances because she was then in her late sixties and assisting an ailing husband.

Even then, her accomplishments in Canada include her Best Original Song nomination for a Genie Award (at the time regarded as the Canadian Oscar) in 1988 for her composition *You're Going Home Now*, which appeared in the Canadian film *Milk and Honey*. In 1990, her performance at the International Festival of Authors (IFOA), a prominent literary event, was well-received. In 1998, York University presented the Honorary Doctor of Letters degree to her. She was featured in *Miss Lou: Then and Now*, an episode of Frances-Ann Solomon's television documentary series *Literature Alive*, highlighting Canadian literary artists of English-Caribbean heritage.

Louise's influence on the diaspora communities of London and New York in the 1950s was as a young artist at the beginning of her career. Her impact in Toronto during the 1990s was as an elder icon operating in an environment possessing an established Caribbean-Canadian presence in the arts, on the verge of a big mainstream breakthrough. There were Dionne Brand and Austin Clarke as two outstanding non-Jamaican authors of English-Caribbean heritage. Lorna Goodison, Olive Senior, Pam Mordecai, Afua Cooper, Makeda Silvera, and Lillian Allen were just some of the gifted Jamaican poets and writers rising to prominence or raising their visibility on the Canadian literary landscape then. Many, if not all, of them owe a debt to Louise's stubborn adherence to Jamaican language and her skill in using it to tell her stories. Her camaraderie and inspiration to a number of Jamaican-Canadian playwrights, poets, and storytellers, like Honor Ford-Smith, Ahdri Zhina Mandiela, Trey Anthony, d'bi.young anitafrika, and Michael St. George can't be underestimated. The sense of fellowship Louise shared with many of those artists is possibly another reason for her feeling of being at home in Toronto.

Toronto has been host to a number of events celebrating Louise's centenary (she was born on September 7, 1919). One celebration at York University had particular significance because it offered a panel discussion with Commonwealth-Writers-Prize-winning writer and poet

Olive Senior; dub poet, recording artist, and Juno Award winner Lillian Allen; and playwright, poet, and author Honor Ford-Smith, founder of the all-female theatre collective Sistren. This York University event, through the testimony of her literary sisters, paid eloquent tribute to her: Allen, through poetry; Senior, with a lyrical meditation; and Ford-Smith's erudite history. They share with her, birthplace and love for Jamaica as it exists in the Caribbean and right here in Toronto. Through their presence and their words, they kept the diasporic flame of her connection to this city blazing.

There were two other participants, including linguist Clive Forrester, who like Ford-Smith and Allen, teaches at a Canadian tertiary institution. His presentation for the panel was laser-focused on championing the idea that the language Louise used to power all the various avenues for storytelling that she travelled should be official in Jamaica. Right now, it remains an informal means of communication. Following Forrester's exciting discussion, the audience engaged in a conversation about it, to the exclusion of any further consideration of Louise's life and work, despite the previous presentations, and despite the best efforts of the moderator, the historian Michele A. Johnson. The continued struggle for the language's recognition in its homeland is crucial to Louise's legacy. It isn't, though, the entire scope of it. Louise's career as artist, as consummate storyteller, as harbinger of culture in the Caribbean diaspora, shouldn't be reduced to a slogan for Jamaican as an official language.

Another panelist, Pamela Appelt, has many accomplishments, including that she was the judge presiding when Louise acquired her Canadian citizenship. She spoke with pride about that ceremony, Louise's IFOA performance, and her memory of Louise's appearance at a similar event at the Place des Arts in Montreal.

Louise Bennett is an icon of Jamaica and the Caribbean diaspora. She was someone who embraced her Canadian home away from home. She exemplifies the truth that the spirit of Jamaica and the larger Caribbean exists deep inside the bone marrow of Toronto.

Endnotes

1   Jamaican-born Una Marson (1905–1965) is described as influential writer of literature, drama and polemic essays, a pioneer contributor

to the broadcasting industry, and an international figure whose work embodied "anti-colonialism, anti-racism, feminism, class politics and pan-Africanism in the first half of the twentieth century" (see Tomlinson, 2019).

2   D'Usseau and Gow's work (1945) follows the experiences of an African American soldier after World War II.

3   Jamaican-born Marcus Mosiah Garvey (1887-1940) was founder and president of the Universal Negro Improvement Association. Jamaican-born Festus Claudius (Claude) McKay (1889-1948), poet, novelist, central figure of the Harlem Renaissance, published his earliest works, including *Songs of Jamaica* (1912) and *Constab Ballads* (1912), in Jamaican language.

4   Folkway Records (1948-1987) "documented folk, world, and children's music"; it is now part of the Smithsonian Institution.

5   The Village Vanguard has been in operation since the mid-1930s, and has hosted poets, folklorists, musicians and other artists.

6   African American Alma John (1906-1986) was "a radio talk show producer, registered nurse, and newspaper columnist . . . In 1952, she got her first radio program on station WWRL, covering everything from religion to teen-agers."

7   In a 2006 interview with BBC Caribbean, Harry Belafonte spoke about his relationship with and admiration for Louise Bennett who he said was "very, very central to [his] interest not only in the folklore and history of Jamaica but the literary and academic players in her own verse and the way she spoke with scholars and did analysis on Jamaican life and history."

References

Alma John Papers. The New York Public Library Archives & Manuscripts. Retrieved July 2021, http://archives.nypl.org/scm-/20710.

Belafonte Interview, British Broadcasting Corporation, August 3, 2006, Retrieved July 2021, http://www.bbc.co.uk/caribbean/news/story/2006/08/060803_belafonteqanda.shtml.

D'Usseau, A. and J. Gow. *Deep Are the Roots*, 1945.

Folkway Records. Smithsonian Institution, Retrieved July 2021, https://folkways.si.edu/folkways-records/smithsonian.

Garvey, M. *The Philosophy & Opinions of Marcus Garvey*, or, *Africa for the Africans*. Compiled by Amy Jacques Garvey. New edition. Dover, Mass: Majority Press, 1986.

Gordon, M. *Live at the Village Vanguard*. New York: Hachette Books, 1994.

Marson, U. British Library, Retrieved July 2021, https://www.bl.uk/people/una-marson.

Matthews, D. *Voices of the Windrush Generation: The Real Story Told by the People Themselves*. UK: Bonnier Books Ltd., 2020.

McKay, C. *Constab Ballads*. London: Watts & Co., 1912.

McKay, C. *Songs of Jamaica*. Kingston, Jamaica: Aston W. Garner & Co. and London: Jamaica Agency, 1912.

Phillips, T. and M. Phillips. *Windrush: The Irresistible Rise of Multi-Racial Britain*. London: HarperCollins, 1999.

Tomlinson, L. *Una Marson*. Caribbean Biography Series. Kingston: University of the West Indies Press. Windrush Stories. British Library, 2019, Retrieved July 2021, https://www.bl.uk/windrush.

FROM JAMAICA TO CANADA:
MISS LOU AND THE POETICS OF MIGRATION[1]

Andrea A. Davis

The Honorable Louise Bennett Coverley—or Miss Lou, as she is still best known to Jamaicans—represents more than any other artist, including the iconic Bob Marley, the voice of the Jamaican nation. No artist, social activist, or politician has had a deeper reach into the heart of the Jamaican folk, or was more consistently committed to the project of Jamaican self-identification. With a career beginning in the late 1930s, and spanning more than fifty years, she represented before and after independence, the poetic imagination and expressive culture of a people she believed in and loved deeply. The biting social commentary often revealed in her poetry was balanced by an unwavering belief in the flexibility and creativity of the Jamaican spirit.

When Miss Lou left her island nation in the early 1980s to live first in the United States, and then permanently in Canada in 1987, she was more than sixty years old and had already contributed a life's career in the direct service of Jamaican nation building. Like many Jamaicans, she was an unwilling migrant, moved by circumstances (an ailing husband who needed advanced medical care), rather than desire. And like many of these migrants, Canada was a strategic choice, weighed in the balance and found wanting but not intolerable. Until her death on Wednesday, July 26, 2006, at the Scarborough Grace Hospital, Toronto, Canada, became the place where she lived, but for Jamaicans at home and scattered across the Caribbean diaspora, she continued to represent the spirit of a nation she may have left physically, but had never left behind.

The questions this chapter raises circulate around Bennett's location in Canada in the last two decades of her life. How do we explain her enduring cultural and national significance long after she had left Jamaica? And as a powerful cultural symbol, how did her influence translate across these distinct borders? The answers to these questions lie in part in Bennett's poetry. Miss Lou's poetry and prose monologues had long established the relationship between migration, social unease, and cultural loss. While often critical of the bourgeoning Jamaican nation, she was also forceful in the defense of her country against external political and cultural influences. The critique of migration and cultural loss that predominates in her work has to be read, however, in relation to the imperatives of migration that have marked Caribbean living since colonization. Caribbean people, for any number of reasons, do choose to migrate. Miss Lou's own decision to leave Jamaica, and her clear location as an unwilling migrant, rather than reducing her national influence, extended it by identifying her through her poetry and lived experiences with the struggles and sacrifices, not only of Jamaicans at home, but also of a growing Jamaican diaspora abroad.

Miss Lou and Life in Canada

When I first met Miss Lou in 1995, she had already been living in Canada for almost ten years. Honor Ford-Smith and I, both graduate students at the time, had decided that we were going to convince her to come to York University for a reading of her poetry. Up to that point, Miss Lou had been larger than life for me, and the meeting, the "conspiracy" to pull off the poetry reading, all seemed incredibly audacious. I was simultaneously awed by that first meeting in her "home"—an apartment in one of Toronto's suburbs—and saddened by the sense of pathos and loss the meeting evoked. She was an exile, caught in James Clifford's (1997, p. 250) "entangled tension" of diaspora claims. She and Eric Coverley had exchanged their beautiful estate in the St. Andrew hillside, for a cramped urban apartment divided by too many walls and narrow hallways, and neighbours who had no way of knowing the weightiness of her national and cultural symbolism, and who would not have cared. Maybe for this reason, I have always hated Toronto apartments—by-products of the detached anonymity of big-city living. In metropolitan cities like Toronto, Jamaican immigrants feel both hyper-visible and invisible.

We sat and listened for hours to Miss Lou recreate stories of another "home," another time that all four of us longed for desperately, at least in that moment, but knew there was no return to. She recreated stories of her childhood and adult life: of her father who wanted a son but got the surprising daughter; the market women on the bus who propelled her into writing; her early reception in Jamaica; and her love story. And even there, in that small apartment, she recited her poetry—her audience small, but rapt. I was pregnant, and as I left the apartment she stopped me, passed her hand over my stomach, and blessed the child. She had sealed our connection as displaced Jamaican women: me, a young mother-to-be. And she, the designated mother of the nation.

The college room we reserved was cozy, but too small to hold the bodies that lined the walls and spilled into the hallways and corridors to listen to Miss Lou on the winter afternoon she finally arrived on campus. A large section of the audience came from outside the university, and despite the cold, it felt as if Jamaica had, indeed, hijacked the university. The university, after all, had no special claim to Miss Lou and had rejected her, in fact, for all of her career.[2] Jamaican Creole and the untamed laughter of Jamaican immigrants recalling their entangled lives circled and enshrined the college. There was no doubt that Miss Lou belonged to the community—a Jamaican community in Toronto, in 1995, that understood and shared the pathos of her exile and came with hands open to receive some gift that could take them through another winter away from the "home" of no return. For this group, the possibilities of diaspora living, like the promise of return, were deferred and bittersweet.

Life for Jamaican immigrants in Canada is framed in large part by precisely these diaspora tensions over social citizenship, belonging, and return. Defined in economic terms, Jamaican immigrants who have settled in Canada are generally perceived as primarily escaping poverty and educational disadvantages, and as seeking a "better" life in the "more developed" country. Yet the rigorous immigration laws and point system that scrupulously select incoming immigrants ensure that "typical" immigrants of the late twentieth and early twenty-first centuries (when Caribbean migration to the United States and Canada have soared) are highly educated and skilled, and they often have to endure a reduction in standard of living, despite earning higher wages. While domestic service is a given in Jamaican middle-class households, for example, it is an expensive luxury generally reserved for the wealthiest in Canadian society. Since service jobs, like domestic labour, have historically been reserved for non-white immigrants, African and Indian Caribbean immigrants have also come to be marked permanently by this history of undervalued working-class labour. As a result, Jamaican immigrants entering societies, like Canada, find themselves not only economically, but also culturally marginalized.

As Augie Fleras (2004, p. 431) argues, the practice of Canadian diversity is actually a practice of mono-multiculturalism that privileges an Anglo-Canadian identity and culture as the universally accepted norm, and allows other minoritized cultures expression only within carefully delineated and non-threatening boundaries. Jamaican cultural performances (including language, dress, walk) are often assumed to be too extravagant, too loud, too vulgar, and not only fall short of the "ideal," normalized British-Canadian culture, but are often perceived as threatening and in need of containment. Since Canadian society tolerates differences only as long as they are contained within private or personal spaces, the tendency of Jamaican cultural expressions and attitudes to seep into the larger society is often seen as problematic, and sometimes even dangerous.

Routed to the metropolitan city of Toronto, Miss Lou's migration must be understood within this context of simultaneous gain and loss. Migration, perhaps paradoxically, humanized her. Jamaican immigrants in Canada and elsewhere, "ketching hell a farin,"[3] could make better sense of the reasons that had dictated their own movement, and could mark their own gains as well as their losses in relationship to her. She continued to bear the weight of Jamaican national identity, rooted by a nationalist rhetoric that established her(s) as its "voice," but she was now more than an icon. Jamaicans across the Caribbean diaspora accepted her routing as a personal sacrifice. She had willingly or unwillingly entered a community of everyday suffering and struggle, accepted a fall in social status and privilege, abandoned her beloved nation in body only, but not in spirit.

Jamaicans at home, struggling with their own problems, also understood, perhaps better than Miss Lou knew, the complexities of the choices she was called to make. When Miss Lou returned to Jamaica in 2003 for the first time since migrating to Canada, adoring Jamaicans lined the streets to greet her and screamed her name as her entourage passed (Mills, 2003). While she was surprised and deeply moved by this outpouring of national appreciation (Lowrie, 2003), Jamaicans had no such misgivings. Old and young, they unabashedly reaffirmed their love of the mother of their young nation as they celebrated the fortieth anniversary of Jamaica's independence.

Establishing Miss Lou's importance as a national and cultural icon in Jamaica while locating her firmly in Canada, paradoxically reminds us, however, that cultural identities are neither fixed nor "pure." In the same way that Canadian society is being called upon to adapt to and be recreated by the non-white cultures it seeks to absorb, these cultures are also themselves constantly in processes of recreation. As I have argued elsewhere, when "culture" comes to represent any kind of hegemonic nationalist discourse (whether from the center or the margin), it runs the risk of encouraging oppressive, homogenizing narratives: "For Jamaican identities abroad, where Jamaican-ness is in large part a performance of memory based on one's own or others' past lived experiences, the need for a fixed, "pure" cultural identity is . . . problematic" (Davis, 2006, p. 25). The need to project national and ethnic identities as unalterable and pure leads to an eventual marginalization and fear of any kind of difference.

Bennett's location outside of Jamaica challenges us, therefore, to rethink the role of art as a fixed performance of nation and community. As Ramazani (2009, p. 50) explains, "Bennett helps us to see that a national poet can also, paradoxically, be a transnational poet—a poet whose work vigorously crosses, and is crossed by, national boundaries." This transnationalism can be traced "through its divided social belongings, cross-national language and allusions, diasporic consciousness, and ambivalent responses to the globe-traversing forces of modernity and decolonization" (p. 50). It is precisely this tension between roots and routes that emerges perhaps unexpectedly in Bennett's poetry and prose. As a younger woman, and years before coming to Canada, Bennett had lived briefly in Europe and the United States, and traveled widely as a performer. She was always attuned to global politics, and had distinct opinions about racial injustice and imperialism. While her poetry was rooted in the Jamaican landscape, it also traveled outward, constantly testing, as it were, the wider position of the world and Jamaica's place within it.

Miss Lou and the Context of Her Poetry

Miss Lou was born on September 7, 1919, in Kingston, Jamaica, the only child for her parents, Cornelius Bennett and Kerene Robinson, and she was raised in a single-parent household after her father died when she was seven years old. According to Mervyn Morris in his introduction to *Selected Poems* (1982; 2003, pp. iii–iv), her mother's job as a dressmaker exposed Bennett early to a wide range of Jamaican folk influences and language, especially as observed through the eyes and voices of women, and she knew early that she wanted to write. She attended Calabar Elementary School at St. Simon's College and Excelsior High School, and, encouraged by her mother, she pursued her love of poetry and published her first collection, *Dialect Verses*, in 1942. A year later, her poetry began appearing every week in the *Sunday Gleaner*. As Barbara Gloudon (1986, p. 2), a senior journalist at Radio Jamaica, explains, "Nothing like these poems had been seen before," and Jamaicans were immediately captivated by her ability to recall the spirit of their daily lives in a rhythm and language they understood.

Bennett continued her education and fascination with Jamaican folklore, pursued courses in journalism and social work, and in 1945, she won a scholarship to the Royal Academy of Dramatic Art in England. Her studies in England also initiated a successful broadcasting career in London, where she worked for the BBC. After a brief return to Jamaica, and then again to England, she lived in New York for three years, where she married Eric Coverley (a promoter of Jamaican theatre) in 1954.[4] A year later, they returned to Jamaica, and she concretized her career in poetry, theatre, radio and television performance, and social commentary.

By 1986, just before she migrated to Canada, Bennett had published nine volumes of poetry and stories; recorded several albums, including

Jamaican Folk Songs (1954) and *Children's Jamaican Songs & Games* (1957); performed in at least twenty-five Jamaican national pantomimes; worked for more than twenty years in radio (*Lou and Ranny Show*, *Laugh With Louise*, *Miss Lou's Views*, and *Smile Jamaica*); spent twelve successful years in television (*Ring Ding* 1968–1980); and appeared in the film *Club Paradise* (1986). Despite this enormous repertoire of work and her unrivalled popularity among the Jamaican working classes, Bennett's work, until at least the late 1970s, drew repeated criticism from the Jamaican middle and upper classes, who were uncomfortable with her use of the Jamaican language (Morris 1982; 2003, p. xiii). In fact, her poetry, which was not respected as "real" art, received no critical attention until Morris's essay, "On Reading Louise Bennett, Seriously," appeared in 1963, a year after Jamaica's independence and twenty years into her publishing career (Cudjoe, 1990; Morris 1982, 2003).

Bennett's "discovery" in 1963 was not accidental. She provided an emerging group of scholars, poets, and writers the context within which to enter debates about the possibilities of independence, and also a model from which to craft a distinctly Jamaican and Caribbean poetics—the need for such a poetics made necessary precisely because of the reality of independence. The project of political autonomy in the Caribbean has long been interwoven with the projects of cultural and artistic autonomy. As Rex Nettleford (1990, p. 32) explains, the work of Caribbean artists has been closely tied to movements for democratic freedom: "Foremost among such artists have been the writers—literate, healthily schizophrenic, insightful, and truly among the first to explain formally the Caribbean to itself, whether in the printed poem, the novel, or short story." In referring to Bennett specifically, Nettleford, in *Jamaica Labrish* (1966; 2005, p. 2), also concedes that in "the post-independence period when many Jamaicans are asking themselves questions about who and why they are, Miss Bennett has taken on new and important dimensions."

Kamau Brathwaite (1996) extends the relationship between political and artistic autonomy by lamenting the inability of English and the iambic pentameter—the most common meter in English poetry—to reflect the lived experiences and the cultural and geographic landscape of the Caribbean. What is needed, he argues, is "a rhythm that approximates the natural experience, the environmental experience," and "more closely and intimately approaches our own experience" (269). For Brathwaite, the rhythm most capable of carrying the weight of these emotions is one influenced by "the African aspect of our New World/Caribbean heritage" (269). Not surprisingly, Brathwaite, like Morris and Nettleford, identifies Bennett as one of the first to experiment seriously with this form of linguistic creativity, and as the literary precursor of the post-independent poet.

Selwyn Cudjoe (1990, p. 26) perhaps explains Bennett's influence best when he sums up her achievements:

> Bennett's work challenged the privileged status accorded to the poetic tradition of white discourse in Caribbean letters, empowering the voices and expressions of the masses of Caribbean people. Bennett used the power of Jamaican speech to explore the complexity of the Jamaican experience, and in so doing, forced the members of the upper and middle classes to face their own linguistic and class biases. Her use of oral and scribal forms, as she forced the language to accommodate itself to express the poetic sentiments of the people, was an important breakthrough in Caribbean literature.

The rest of this chapter turns precisely to an examination of these oral and scribal forms, looking specifically at the theme of migration and cultural loss. My desire is to attempt to reveal the ways in which Miss Lou's expression of her nation's poetic sentiments might be balanced between the imperatives of Brathwaite's homebound nation language and the claims of diaspora.

Miss Lou and the Poetics of Migration

I examine seven of what I call Bennett's migration poems from *Selected Poems*, edited by Mervyn Morris (1982, 2003). I begin with her popular poem, "Colonization in Reverse," which explores the ironic effects of Jamaican migration to England. The next two poems—"Dry-Foot Bwoy" and "No Lickle Twang"—challenge the notion of shame often associated with the use of the Jamaican language, especially after migration. Since Bennett has been most influential in her use of Jamaican Creole, this discussion is necessary. "Pass fi White," "A Merica," and "Tan a Yuh Yard,"[5] are three poems that focus on Jamaican migration to the United States. I conclude with a discussion of Bennett's only truly diasporic poem, "Home Sickness." While none of Bennett's poems engage questions of migration within a specifically

Canadian context, the questions she raises in these poems are far-reaching and resonate with the experiences of Jamaican immigrants in Canada. Her poetry, I hope, might help those of us who are Jamaican immigrants in Canada re-enter conversations about what it might mean to think about the nation state differently, even as we hold on to our cultural memories. While I cannot pretend that Bennett's poetry allows us the space to completely enact such a project, it provides a valuable context from which to examine some of the challenges of South-to-North migration and transnational coalition.

"Colonization in Reverse" is a tongue-in-cheek examination of the reverse effects of Jamaican migration on English society after World War II. The long and brutal war had left England ravaged and desperately in need of economic revitalization, and skilled and working-class labour from British colonies, like Jamaica, was seen as essential to England's recovery. Estimates of total Caribbean migration to Britain between 1951 and 1961 vary, according to Bonham Richardson (1989, p. 216), from 230,000 to 280,000. While these early Caribbean immigrants saw themselves as loyal British subjects, their presence ignited deep racial paranoia, and they were exposed to increasing expressions of racism, especially in the labour market and in housing. Citing the saturation of the labour force, the Commonwealth Immigrants Act of 1962 responded to these racial prejudices by successfully cutting off Caribbean migration to Britain (p. 217).

By playing on the meaning of the word "colonization," Bennett's poem draws a parallel between the historic cultural damage of British colonialism on Caribbean peoples, and the feared cultural imposition and resettlement of Jamaican immigrants in England. The poem rewrites the project of colonization, with its assumptions of European conquest and subjugation, by bestowing agency and autonomy on the colony itself. The poem, thus, celebrates the Jamaican Anancy-like propensity to triumph over the larger and more powerful adversary. The poem's humor and irony derive, however, from the fact that the speaker understands that the colony's perceived ability to conquer and subdue the "motherlan" is indeed born entirely out of the colonizer's misplaced fear of the growing numbers of Jamaican immigrants. By invoking the fear that immigrants take away jobs from other citizens, the poem reverses the history of settlement and conquest in specifically Jamaican terms:

> Oonoo see how life is funny,
> Oonoo see de turnabout?
> Jamaica live fi box bread
> Out a English people mout.
>
> For when dem catch a Englan
> An start play dem different role
> Some will settle down to work
> An some will settle fi de dole (Bennett 1982; 2003, p. 107).

The multiple meanings of the word *settle* destabilize the immigrants' motives so that they constantly shift between earnestness and calculated deception. While the poem once again celebrates Jamaican resilience, it also reveals as either potentially naïve or morally suspect those too willing to abandon their island home for the unknown promises of the "mother country." In the end, however, English society will have to decide how to best interpret these shifting social clues because in the short term, at least, the colony has won: "What a devilment a Englan! / Dem face war an brave de worse; / But ah wonderin how dem gwine stan / Colonizin in reverse" (Bennett, 1982; 2003, p. 107).

In examining the two poems that directly address the question of language in *Selected Poems* (1982, 2003), it is clear that Bennett's critique of Jamaican middle-class aspirations, as part of a linguistic debate, is framed by an awareness of the ways in which migration alters Jamaicans' understanding of themselves as immigrants or travelers originating in the Global South. "Dry-Foot Bwoy" offers a scathing critique of a young man's abandonment of his island history once he is exposed to life in England. This abandonment is noted most powerfully in his rejection of the Jamaican language in which he was raised. It is at first unclear whether Mary's son—derogatorily referred to as *dry-foot bwoy* to register his humble origins and false pretensions—is actually living in England, or has recently returned home. While the tone of the poem and the images it invokes suggest the feeling of a communal Jamaican yard, the use of the word *come*, instead of the word *go*, implies that the encounter the poem narrates does, in fact, take place outside of the island: "Me tink him *come* a foreign lan / *Come* ketch bad foreign cole!"

(Bennett 1982; 2003, p. 1, italics mine). Read in this way, the poem becomes a commentary on a young Jamaican man's inability to navigate the challenges of English society without abdicating his cultural values.

To explain the sharp disjunction between the boy's pretentious behavior and his humble Jamaican roots, the speaker at first identifies the cultural dis-ease the boy voices through his body as a kind of physical illness brought on by the harshness of the European environment. The cold he figuratively catches symbolizes the coldness and isolation of British society, as well as his growing alienation from his own sustaining community. While the speaker empathizes with the immigrant's struggle within the harshness of the European cultural terrain, she has no sympathy for his easy abandonment of his childhood memories.

In the poem, meaningless English words displace the richness of Jamaican cultural history and erect a barrier of miscommunication between the speaker and the boy. The speaker, then, must re-educate the young man:

> Me seh, 'Yuh understand me, yaw!
> No yuh name Cudjoe Scoop?
> Always visit Nana kitchen an
> Gi laugh fi gungoo soup!
>
> 'An now all yuh can seh is "actually"?
> Bwoy, but tap!
> Wha happen to dem sweet Jamaica
> Joke yuh use fi pop?' (Bennett 1982; 2003, p. 2)

While being careful to connect the boy's laughter to Nana's (Nanny's) kitchen, the narrator undercuts the weightiness of the historical references with the lines, "Gi laugh fi gungoo soup," and "Joke yuh use fi pop" (Bennett 1982; 2003, p. 2). In this way, the speaker eloquently links a long tradition of Jamaican warriorhood to a tradition of cultural resilience.[6] The word *pop* suggests the creativity and vitality of the language, but also alludes to its secondary meaning in Jamaican speech, to fool or to trick. Yes, Jamaicans have been through difficult times, but have always found a way, like Anancy, to survive. Thus, the narrator again subtly registers a note of empathy with the boy's struggle to find himself in a foreign country, but suggests that the clues to his survival lie within the very language and cultural traditions he has abandoned. The boy's resulting anger and stubbornness—"Him get bex and walk tru de door, / Him head eena de air" (Bennett 1982; 2003, p. 2)—indicate an unfortunate willingness to comply with the colonial project of African self-erasure. He fails to realize that his pride is misplaced, and that by uncritically walking through the door of British opportunity, he runs the risk of losing more than he gains. The mocking laughter of the community of women that follows him is a final ominous reminder of the consequences of his short-sighted choices.

"No Lickle Twang" shifts the debates about language from a context of British colonialism to one of US cultural imperialism. While again relying on the social and cultural disparities between a mother and her son as its framing device, the poem reverses the central problem by shifting the narrative perspective. By making the mother the poem's speaker, and by having her voice her disappointment over her son's refusal to mimic Euro-American speech and dress, the poem signals cultural loss as a cross-generational problem that may be exacerbated by migration, but also functions beyond it.

The poem suggests that the male persona who spent six months in the United States, and has now returned home, with the money to show for his absence, but nothing else, is perhaps a temporary labourer.[7] While the young man's labour abroad seems to have been motivated by a desire to improve his economic situation rather than any desire to romanticize US society, the mother clearly privileges migration as a sign of cultural "improvement." Post-independence Jamaican society has, indeed, increasingly modeled middle-class success, less after English cultural standards, and more after the "ideal" of the American Dream. Thus, this mother believes her son's migration, no matter how temporary, should bring with it an enhancement of the family's social privilege. Since the most visible marker of a "real" improvement in class status in Jamaica is facility in British or American English, and not just economic success, she demands this facility as the ultimate sign of her son's proven cultural capital.

The mother's demand that the changes in her son's speech and behavior be distinct and rapid simultaneously alludes to and ignores the potential pain involved in such a process. The mother fails to recognize her son's self-awareness as a positive trait and sees him instead as trapped in the "ugliness" of Jamaican working-class culture. The contest between the American Dream and Jamaican cultural memory appears most powerfully in the poem's juxtaposition of the words, *Merica* and *Mocho*—one meant to mark the Global North, progress, and advancement. And the other meant to mark smallness, "backwardness," and the lingering memory of Africa in Jamaica:

> Suppose me laas me pass go introjooce
> Yuh to a stranger
> As me lamented son what lately
> Come from Merica!
>
> Dem hooda laugh after me, bwoy!
> Me couldn tell dem so!
> Dem hooda seh me lie, yuh wasa
> Spen time back a Mocho! (Bennett 1982; 2003, p. 3).

The poem finally ends on a note of dramatic irony when the mother urges her son, in one last act of familial redemption, to call his father *Poo*, instead of *Pa*. While readers immediately recognize the linguistic slip (*poo* refers to excrement or feces) and know how such a greeting will be received, the mother in her over-zealousness to impress is unaware of her own malapropism. While she uses the word *shame* repeatedly to describe her disappointment in her son's lack of linguistic prowess, in the final analysis, the shame is hers since the word she chooses for her husband, rather than a sign of respect and veneration, is one of insult.

The next group of poems—"Pass fi White," "A Merica," and "Tan a Yuh Yard"—offer more explicit critiques of Jamaican immigrants' attempts to integrate into US society. In "Pass fi White," as the title suggests, the problem is one of both cultural and physical erasure. While sensitive to the challenges non-white immigrants have historically faced in negotiating US Jim Crow laws, the poem is, nonetheless, impatient with the strategies they have sometimes employed for survival. The success of the poem revolves around the pun on the word *pass*, and the speaker's clever identification of the link between the young woman's inability to pass her exam, and her ill-advised attempts at racial camouflage. By reminding us that "Her brain part not so bright," the speaker reaffirms the immediate assessment that this is not a smart decision. The poem's repeated rhyming patterns —*write* and *white*, *bright* and *white*, *right* and *white*—progressively emphasize the link between whiteness and rightness, and whiteness as test of citizenship. A test we know the young woman will fail. The tone of anxiety in the poem heightens when her love relationship is revealed. The undercurrent of anxiety is mirrored in the bodily discomforts she experiences, both literally in the form of heart palpitations and cold sweat, and in her metaphoric self-annihilation.

While her mother recognizes the challenges of migration her daughter faces, and identifies her attempts to perform the racial "ideal" as one response to the pressures of a racialized society, she dismisses the young woman's choices as ineffectual: "She no haffi tan a foreign / Under dat deh strain an fright / For plenty copper-colour gal / Deh home yah dah play white" (Bennett 1982; 2003, p. 101). Ironically, she recognizes that her daughter's colour, combined with an education, would afford her far more cultural leverage in Jamaican society.

By inserting the father's perspective, the poem more clearly establishes the reasons for the daughter's social subterfuge, by explicitly naming the United States as racist, and critiquing its Jim Crow laws. The father powerfully unmasks the fluidity of racial identities and the shifting social constructions of "race" in a US society that pretends racial rigidity. His attempt to justify her choices as a covert form of cultural resistance is, however, quickly exposed:

> Him dah boas all bout de distric
> How him daughter is fus-class,
> How she smarter dan American
> An over deh dah pass!
>
> Some people tink she pass B.A.,
> Some tink she pass D.R.—
> Wait till dem fine out seh she ongle
> Pass de colour bar (Bennett 1982; 2003, p. 102).

Ultimately, the risks involved in trying to conform to the rules of "race" in US society leave his daughter exposed not only to the damaging effects of racial prejudice, but also to social criticism and cultural ostracization within the very community on which her rehabilitation might depend.

In "A Merica," and "Tan a Yuh Yard," Bennett examines the social frenzy around migration to the United States that reached its peak in Jamaica in the late 1970s and 1980s. Two factors combined to encourage this dramatic out-migration. The *Hart-Cellar Immigration Reform Act* of 1965 removed explicitly racist criteria from US immigration law by emphasizing skill and family reunification over place of origin, making it easier for immigrants from newly independent countries in the Caribbean to settle in the United States (Kasinitz, 1992, p. 26–27). Increasing political tensions in Jamaica and fear among the Jamaican middle classes over the growing influence of socialism and ties to Cuba's communist government were also powerful push factors driving Jamaican migration (Kaufman, 1985, p. 122). As Philip Kasinitz (1992, p. 27) confirms, by the early 1980s, approximately twenty thousand Jamaican immigrants were arriving annually in the United States. These incoming immigrants, like those coming from elsewhere in the Caribbean, represented a wide variety of class positions: "well-educated members of the urban elite seeking to protect their wealth in volatile economies, children of the middle class searching for broader opportunities, and large numbers of poor people looking for a standard of living above mere subsistence" (p. 27–28).

In "A Merica," Bennett's first linguistic intervention into the construction of the United States as an "ideal" host society occurs in the poem's title. By physically dismantling the word America, she simultaneously reproduces Jamaican speech patterns in which *a* signifies *to* and interrupts the notion of US cultural and political hegemony. By opening the poem with a proverb, she also establishes the wisdom of the speaker and contrasts historical knowledge with erroneous contemporary belief and practice: "Every seckey got him jeggeh, / Every puppy got him flea, / An yuh no smaddy ef yuh no / Got family oversea!" (Bennett 1982; 2003, p. 109).

The accumulation of voices in the poem emphasizes the sense of frenzied movement and action sustained throughout the poem and reflected in the widespread and growing urgency to migrate. By further invoking the images of a series of natural disasters, the speaker accentuates the poem's sense of out-of-control movement, as well as the near-hysterical social response of those seeking to leave: "Me ask meself warra matter, / Me ask meself wha meck: / Is tidal wave or earthquake or / Is storm dem dah expec?" (Bennett 1982; 2003, p. 109). By pointing to the disjuncture between the departing emigrants and the Jamaican landscape, the poem reveals a deep social problem in Jamaican society. Despite the cautionary question—"Ah wonder is what fault dem fine / Wid po li Jamaica / Meck everybody dah lif-up / An go a Merica?"—the poem closes with the speaker's resolve to "falla fashin" and migrate (Bennett 1982; 2003, pp. 109, 110). The poem thus suggests that while many reasons might be offered for migrating, the real reason might be that it is simply in style.

"Tan a Yuh Yard" responds directly to "A Merica" by cautioning Jamaicans to consider their options more carefully and "Lef Merica alone" (Bennett 1982; 2003, p. 110). By once again invoking a Jamaican tradition of resiliency and flexibility, the speaker suggests that with some amount of creativity, Jamaicans can survive without risking the loss of cultural and political autonomy that often results from migration. While the speaker in "A Merica" is caught up in the excitement of the perceived promises of migration, the tone in "Tan a Yuh Yard" is far more reflective and self-consciously cautionary. Here, Bennett appears to invoke an unapologetic Jamaican nationalism by indicting "First World" racism and revealing the sacrifices often encoded in the notion of American "progress": "Win yuh mine offa foreign lan – / Koo how some a de man-dem / Run back home like foreigner / Dis set bad dog pon dem!" (Bennett 1982; 2003, p. 110). By linking images of 1960s civil rights with more contemporary stories of US racism, the poem explicitly reveals the high personal and social costs involved in migration.

In the poem "Home Sickness," the only Bennett poem in which the speaker is an immigrant recording her own experiences, the persona invokes, as the title suggests, a deep desire for the past. Her homesickness is conjured up in an overwhelming desire for the cultural symbols, the food and landscape of her island home. Yet, in an unexpected turn at the end of the poem, Bennett interrupts any easy resolution of the speaker's romanticized longing for the past by powerfully reminding us of the deep ambivalence of our choices and our divided loyalties. Even as the poem's persona longs for return to a historically suspended home of her past, she realizes that return is impossible because "home" has been reconfigured by the relentless circumstances of migration: "Go back to me Jamaica, / To me fambly! To me wha? / Lawd-amassi, me figat – / All a me fambly over yah!" (Bennett 1982; 2003, p. 108). Her final assertion, "All a me fambly over yah!" registers her awareness of a sense of uncontested responsibility within the new host society. The meanings of home and family are fluid rather than static.

Conclusion

It is impossible to avoid the difficult questions Bennett's poems raise. How does one balance the explicit nationalist critique of a poem like "Tan a Yuh Yard," with Bennett's later personal decisions to migrate first to the United States and then to Canada? Is it enough to mark her as an unwilling migrant, like the speaker in "Home Sickness," forced to depart her beloved nation because of circumstances outside her control? The reality is that Bennett's position is never quite as rigid as one might initially assume. Indeed, even in "Tan a Yuh Yard," her warnings against the desire to migrate are balanced by a genuine awareness of social hardship in Jamaica. Her migration poetry, thus, shifts constantly between empathy and critique, and her nationalism is almost always balanced by a tongue-in-cheek self-mockery.

Among the bodies pressed into the university classroom in 1995 to hear Miss Lou perform, the personal stories of migration would have been too many and too complex to recount. What Jamaicans saw in Miss Lou on that cold winter afternoon was the symbol of their cumulative sacrifices and a reminder of their collective flexibility. We invoked, out of necessity, her cultural and national significance in order to delineate the contours of a shared community, however fleeting and illusory. Whether in Jamaica or in Canada, we could resist complete self-erasure by holding on, for one evening, to our island language and laughter; by making them reverberate in that room; by overtaking with our too-loud, too-vulgar, and too-colourful bodies the sacred spaces of a re-colonized Canadian university where not so long ago we would not have studied anything called postcolonial or Caribbean poetry— and even then, certainly not Miss Lou. Yes, many of us were Canadian citizens—our family and children "over yah"—but our present in that moment joined hands with a shared past to help us rejoin two nations—one here, and one a "yard."

Canadians of Jamaican descent must increasingly grapple with these tensions between *here* and *there*, *roots* and *routes*. In demanding that Canada recognize its social responsibility to all its citizens, what might it also mean to take responsibility for a country that has been home to a Jamaican diaspora now for several generations? Perhaps what Bennett's poetry best teaches us is that we respond most effectively to Canada's practices of mono-multiculturalism when we join our cultural memories across the borders of race, class, gender, language, and geography we share. It is only then that we can realize the creative power of diaspora living, and its ability to recreate, to re-imagine both the local and transnational.

Endnotes

1   This chapter first appeared in *Jamaicans in the Canadian Experience: A Multiculturalizing Presence*. Carl E. James and Andrea Davis, eds. Halifax: Fernwood Press, 2012, pp. 230—245.

2   Although Bennett's first published volume of poetry appeared in 1942, she was not included in any anthology of West Indian poetry before 1960. The first critical essay on Bennett's work was Mervyn Morris's 1963 essay, "On Reading Miss Lou, Seriously."

3   The Jamaican phrase, "ketching hell a farin," translates in English to "catching hell in foreign (countries)" or "catching hell abroad" and is an acknowledgement of the hardships inherent in migration.

4   Eric Winston Coverley died on August 7, 2002, at the age of 91, in Toronto, Canada.

5   The pervasiveness of the Jamaican language in defining Black cultures in Toronto is evident in a 2021 video message recorded in fifteen languages in which the premier of Ontario, Doug Ford, encouraged residents to stay at home during the COVID-19 pandemic. Ironically, one of these messages, "Tan a yuh yard," recorded in what the video labeled as *Patois*, is the title of one of Louise Bennett's poems. ("Doug Ford Uses Jamaican Patois to Tell People to Stay Home," Brandon Gonez Show, January 29, 2021, YouTube, 1:00, https://youtu.be/lYHs0WGcvr0.)

6   Cudjoe was the leader of the Leeward Maroons, and Nanny (suggested by the name *Nana*) was leader of the Windward Maroons. She was recognized as a Jamaican National Hero in 1975.

7   The most popular seasonal worker program in the United States that

hires temporary Jamaican labourers is the H-2A Temporary Agricultural Workers program. These workers, mostly men, are not immigrants and cannot become permanent residents or citizens. They also have little protection under US law (Hahamovitvh, 2008). Canada has a similar program known as the Seasonal Agricultural Worker Program (SAWP)

References

Bennett, L. *Auntie Roachy Seh*. Kingston: Sangster's Book Stores, 1993, 2003.

Bennett, L. *Selected Poems*. Edited by M. Morris. Kingston, Sangster's Book Stores, 1982, 2003.

Bennett, L. *(Jamaica) Dialect Verses*. Kingston: Herald Ltd., 1942.

Brathwaite, E.K. "English in the Caribbean: Notes on Nation Language and Poetry." *Using English: From Conversation to Canon*. Edited by Janet Maybin and Neil Mercer. New York: Routledge, 1996, pp. 266–271.

Clifford, J. *Routes: Travel and Translation in the Late Twentieth Century*. Cambridge: Harvard University Press, 1997.

Cudjoe, S. (ed). *Caribbean Women Writers: Essays from the First International Conference*. Wellesley: Calaloux Publications, 1990.

Davis, A. "Translating Narratives of Masculinity across Borders: A Jamaican Case Study." *Caribbean Quarterly* 52: 2/3, June–September 2006, pp. 22–38.

Fleras, A. "Racializing Culture/Culturalizing Race: Multicultural Racism in a Multicultural Canada." *Racism, Eh? A Critical Interdisciplinary Anthology of Race and Racism in Canada*. Edited by Camille A. Nelson and Charmaine A. Nelson. Concord, Ontario: Captus Press, 2004, pp. 429–443.

Gloudon, B. "The Hon. Louise Bennett, O.J.: Fifty Years of Laughter." *Jamaica Journal* 19, August–October 1986, p. 2.

Kasinitz, P. *Caribbean New York: Black Immigrants and the Politics of Race*. Ithaca, NY: Cornell University Press, 1992.

Kaufman, M. *Jamaica Under Manley: Dilemmas of Socialism and Democracy.* London: Zed Books, 1985.

Lowrie, T. "Jamaica's Beloved 'Miss Lou' Departs." *Jamaica Observer,* August 21, 2003.

Mills, C. "Noh lickle twang: JA's Cultural Icon Returns." *Jamaica Gleaner,* August 6, 2003, http://old.jamaica-gleaner.com/pages/roots/lou1.html.

Morris, M. "On Reading Louise Bennett, Seriously." *Jamaica Journal vol.* 1, no. 1, December 1967, pp. 69–74.

Morris, M. "Introduction." *Selected Poems* by Louise Bennett. Kingston: Sangster's Book Stores, 1982, 2003.

Nettleford, R. "Introduction." *Jamaica Labrish* by Louise Bennett. Kingston: Sangster's Book Stores, 1966, 2005, pp. 1–22.

Nettleford, R. "Communicating with Ourselves: The Caribbean Artist and Society." *Caribbean Affairs* vol. 3, no. 2, 1990, pp. 30–38.

Ramazani, J. "Louise Bennett: The National Poet as Transnational?" *Journal of West Indian Literature* vol. 17, no. 2, April 2009, pp. 49–64.

Richardson, B.C. "Caribbean Migrations, 1838–1985." *The Modern Caribbean.* Edited by F.W. Knight and C.A. Palmer. Chapel Hill: UNC Press, 1989, pp. 203–228.

I REJOICE IN BEING BILINGUAL

Jennifer Walcott

The poetry of Miss Lou, which I grew up hearing and reciting, made it perfectly natural for me to write in Creole. Some ideas and emotions just cannot be expressed in Standard English, and I rejoice in being bilingual.

Using the ballad form typical of Miss Lou, I offer "Miss Eliza," and in a poem inspired by her use of Creole, I present "Sgraffito."

MISS ELIZA

When Miss Eliza dead
Bans a people come fi mourn.
De whole a Lucea town come out,
Dem was lookin' so forlorn.

Dem sey ovva a t'ousan' did
Come fi sing and pray.
Some beat dem chest, an' de rest
Stan' up inna sun whole day.

Nuff police did come deh
Fi hol' de rank an' file,
An' to show how much we love she,
De parson preach in style.

Miss Eliza live up tap de hill
An' she run de family shop.

She play de organ inna church,
De lady work non stop.

She talk polite to everyone,
She give her love to Jesus.
She keep de Red Cross books an'
She tek har duty serious.

Mi nevva go de funeral,
But mi hear dat it was said
Dat everybody talk di truth
When dear Miss Eliza dead.

SGRAFFITO

Look inna de pictcha good.
Yu' see say de fadda ha'
him han' roun' de gal pickni dem?
 Dat han' nevah use fe hug.
 If yu' was to scrape off
de surface a de pictcha
yu' woulda see de knife
wha' him use fe stab de gal
dem inna dem back.
How him cut dem heart
an' lef dem hungry
fe fill dem belly
wid fadda love.
Dis ya pictcha
no show how dem tek dem
self-esteem fe stuff up
hole, nyam dirt, an' spit
blood, cut dem tongue on
sharp wud, an' cry.
 Lawd, how dem cry.
 Yu' haffi wuk fe see de
tears behin'
de laugh dem a laugh
in de lyin' photograph.

WRITING MISS LOU RIGHT:
LANGUAGE, IDENTITY, AND THE OFFICIAL JAMAICAN ORTHOGRAPHY

Clive Forrester

Whenever, in a debate, one Jamaican says to another Jamaican that they didn't write a Jamaican word "right," it is usually the case that their yardstick for correct Jamaican orthography is based on the writing style of Miss Lou. Louise Bennett's collection of work stretches across some six decades, beginning in the years leading up to Jamaica's independence in 1962, and into the new millennium. Her cultural impact in the areas of poetry, prose, stage performance, and language advocacy have established her as the veritable "Queen" of Jamaican culture, and an authority on the origin and usage of the Jamaican language. A longitudinal survey of Miss Lou's work throughout the years, especially in the case of her poetry, reveals that the orthography is not as consistent as some would think. Essentially, even as Miss Lou's style of writing Jamaican is treated by some as the gold standard for Jamaican orthography, its inconsistencies serve to embolden critics who feel a written form of the language is pointless.

The Relevance of Writing Systems

Writing has been a part of human civilizations for over five thousand years, ever since the Sumerians in ancient Mesopotamia started to use chisels to carve into stone in around 3500 BCE. While writing systems are useful, it is important to point out that many languages are born, live a long life, and eventually die without ever adopting a writing system. Writing is not synonymous with language; it is merely a visual representation of speech. A case in point is children who are learning the writing system of English for the first time who are told that English has five vowels. This, of course, is not accurate; the English writing system has five letters which, depending on your regional dialect of English, can represent up to sixteen different vowel sounds. Writing systems facilitate the preservation of cultural knowledge, the transmission of literacy, and the modernization of commerce. Yet the absence of a writing system does not strip away *languagehood*—a language is still a language without a writing system.

The writing system for Jamaican Creole was first published in 1967, with the release of the *Dictionary of Jamaican English*, compiled by Jamaican lexicographer Frederic Cassidy. The background work to compiling the dictionary started in 1955, and Cassidy made a point to survey Jamaicans from across the breadth of the island to collect as many words and meanings as possible. The lexicon spanned a wide range of Jamaican words from the archaic to modern, many of them indigenous to Jamaica, some with their West African roots still intact, but all of them authentically Jamaican. However, Cassidy was faced with a decision while compiling the dictionary: How would the words be written in such a way that they accurately capture their pronunciation and clearly show that the language is different from English, as opposed to merely a "bad" version of that language? A Jamaican writing system would have to be developed.

Developing a new writing system for a language involves two main choices—whether to use phonetic symbols or use an alphabet. The benefit of using phonetic symbols, such as those represented in the International Phonetic Alphabet (IPA), is that it would capture all the various ways speech is produced in Jamaica, since the IPA is designed to capture all the ways speech is produced in all languages. Incidentally, this is also the downside. Speaking is much more variable than writing—no two persons pronounce words exactly alike, in all contexts, all the time. Indeed, there is even variability in how the same speaker will produce a word as they move from one context to another (e.g., formal vs. jovial), and from one emotional or psychological state to another (e.g., happy to pensive to fearful, etc.). A writing system, however, needs to be consistent among all speakers of the same language, regardless of these changes. As such, the IPA would not serve as a suitable writing system, not least of all because the symbols are quite complex.

The next obvious choice then is to use an alphabet with letters instead of phonetic symbols. Again, two more choices arise—to continue using the informal writing system based on the spelling of English (the one used by Miss Lou), or to develop a new alphabet specific to Jamaican speech. The informal style of writing Jamaican speech, made popular by Miss Lou, has the benefit of familiarity. Aside from being prominent in Miss Lou's poetry, it has been adopted by other poets and authors, and is featured from time to time in cartoons published by the national newspapers. This writing system however is highly variable. There is no official document or resource each author can draw from when representing Jamaican speech, and as such, each writer simply improvises as they go along. This problem is compounded even more now in the digital age, as more persons are representing Jamaican speech in electronic formats. With no reliable benchmark, what emerges is a "chaka-chaka"[1] writing system which is susceptible to the whims of each individual writer. The final obvious solution, then, is to construct a uniquely Jamaican writing system from the ground up.

The Writing System for Jamaican Creole

The Cassidy Writing system for Jamaican Creole, first published in the *Dictionary of Jamaican English* in 1967, was updated in 2009 by the Jamaican Language Unit (JLU) at the University of the West Indies, Mona, with the release of the instructional manual "Writing Jamaican Right." This manual laid out the writing system in a user-friendly textbook inclusive of exercises, readings, and an audio CD. The main differences between the informal writing system based on English and the official Cassidy/JLU writing system can be summarized thus:

A. In the Cassidy/JLU writing system, one letter has only one sound. In the informal English writing system, one letter may have several sounds.

B. The Cassidy/JLU writing system has no silent letters—all letters are pronounced. The informal English writing system has many silent letters.
C. Some letters are not used in the Cassidy/JLU writing system, such as *c, q, x,* since these are replaced by other letters, and h does not occur unless in the form of a double consonant.

The full alphabet chart with examples is below:

The Jamaican Language Unit/Di Jamiekan Langwij Yuunit, 2009, p. 12

As seen in the diagram above, the Cassidy/JLU writing system has a separate representation for each vowel sound—twelve total—and uses duplicate letters to indicate lengthened vowels. Some consonantal sounds make use of two letters. The "hn" symbol indicates that the vowel has a nasal quality.

Though the writing system made its debut in the 1960s, it was never formally taught in public schools, and as such, generations of Jamaicans grew up without the benefit of learning the official writing system for their native language. The publication of the JLU manual in 2009 has made the writing system much more accessible, and its usage has increased due to attempts by authors to incorporate more of the writing system into their work. But by and large, there is still no national drive to popularize the writing system. It is simultaneously the best way to represent Jamaican speech and the method which is least used by the majority.

Writing Miss Lou Right

It is tempting to ask how differently things would've been if Miss Lou had used the Cassidy writing system all along. That she even decided to represent Jamaican speech in written form was already an act of subversion, so she wouldn't have been any worse off. At worst, it might have taken the reading audience slightly longer to acclimatize to this style of writing, which would not have been problematic, seeing as how Miss Lou's work is usually enjoyed orally. But eventually, what would seem strange and unusual would become natural and second nature.

To learn Miss Lou's poetry to perform at drama festivals, students in primary school would first have to be introduced to the writing system. It would only be a matter of time before the writing system would be at a stage of national saturation, all so that the beauty of Miss Lou's work could be unlocked. Indeed, we stand to lose nothing if this initiative is undertaken now, and we start to *write Miss Lou right*.

One of Miss Lou's themes in her role as language advocate was to drive home the point that the Jamaican language, Patwa, is in no way less a language than any other, least of all the English language of Jamaica's former colonizer. She urged Jamaicans to be proud of the language and the fact that it served as a powerful tool of cultural transmission. She maintained, contrary to public opinion, that Patwa was not a bad version of English, but instead a language in its own right. It is for this reason that we should promote the use of an original writing system for the language, rather than one fashioned on a bad version of the English writing system.

To this end, I close by presenting the first stanza of Miss Lou's "Dutty Tough"—first, in its original version from her *Selected Poems*. Then the same stanza, using the Cassidy/JLU writing system:

"Dutty Tough" (original with informal writing system)
Sun a shine but tings no bright;
Doah pot a bwile, bickle no nuff;
River flood but water scarce, yaw;
Rain a fall but dutty tough (Bennett, 2003, p. 25).

"Doti Tof" (modified with Cassidy/JLU writing system)
Son a shain bot tingz no brait,
Duo pat a bwail, bikl no nof,
Riva flod bot waata skiers yaa,
Rien a faal bot doti tof!

Endnote

1   "Chaka-chaka"—"disorderly, irregular" (Cassidy and LePage, 2002, p. 97).

References

Bennett, L. "Dutty Tough." *Selected Poems.* Edited by M. Morris. Kingston: Sangster's Book Stores, 2003.

Cassidy, F.G. and Le Page, R.B. *Dictionary of Jamaican English.* Kingston: University of the West Indies Press, 2002.

The Jamaican Language Unit/Di Jamiekan Langwij Yuunit. *Writing Jamaican the Jamaican Way/Ou fi Rait Jamiekan.* Kingston: Arawak Publications, 2009.

Part 2:

". . . The Language of the People . . . The Language of Life"

"SAYING DIS, DAT, AND TODER":
CREATING A JAMAICAN LANGUAGE (JAMIEKAN LANGWIJ) IN THE EIGHTEENTH AND NINETEENTH CENTURIES[1]

Michele A. Johnson

With European incursions into the Caribbean at the end of the fifteenth century, the ensuing colonial project resulted in the demographic collapse of Indigenous communities, the indentureship of poor and criminal/ized Europeans, primarily as agricultural workers,[2] and the development of commercial agricultural enterprises which featured plantation-based economies (Pietschmann, 1999; Rouse, 1992; Boucher, 1992; Beckles, 2000; Beckles, 1989; Patterson, 1967; Beckford, 1972). Featured among the shifts to plantation agriculture were enormous demographic, sociopolitical, and cultural changes wrought by the "sugar revolution,"[3] and the enslavement and transportation of millions of ethnically and culturally diverse Africans[4] across the yawning chasm of the Atlantic to colonial sites such as Jamaica. There, they were treated as units of production/reproduction and classified as property—although, as Elsa Goveia points out, they were "a special kind of property" (Goveia, 1965; 1980, p. 153). While the enslavers and those who invested in and benefitted from the brutality of the system of slavery, as well as those who wielded imperial power and their local counterparts in Jamaica invested in race-based social hierarchies (Smith, 1965; Smith 1984) and controlled the society through legalised violence and oppression, there is little doubt that the island's cultural creations, including the language by which the people communicated, were shaped by the majority of the population—enslaved Africans and their descendants.

In considering the incredibly rich cultural heritage that emerged from horrific slave societies such as Jamaica, scholars have debated about the emergence of new Atlantic cultures, African cultural retentions, and how it was that those who settled in these places, whether voluntarily or by force, "contributed to the development of a distinctive society and culture that was neither European nor African, but Creole" (Bolland, 1998, p.10; see Brathwaite, 1971; 1974; Mintz and Price, 1992; Nettleford, 1988; Alleyne, 1988; Scott, 1991; Lovejoy, 1997; Thornton, 1998; Besson, 2003). For Mervyn Alleyne, this cultural confluence—this process of creolisation—can be observed in the emergence of creole languages around the region which, he says, resulted from the long struggle between enslavers and enslaved over the medium of communication (Alleyne, 1988). As Nigel Bolland points out, Alleyne (1988) concludes that "[t]he outcome of this struggle reflects the metropolitan hegemony and becomes a further means of maintaining social inequalities" (Bolland, 1998, p. 14), as the nation-languages of the people continue/d to be devalued and defined as deficient, corrupt, and mutilated versions of European originals. For Alleyne, creolisation in Jamaica is, at heart, a political process where "Black people constantly struggled to maintain their African heritage in the teeth of slavery, colonialism, neo-colonialism, and imperialism in the guise of modernisation" (Alleyne, 1988, p. 152).[5] This contribution enters into dialogue with Alleyne's analysis and argues that the language system that emerged in Jamaican society in the eighteenth and nineteenth centuries—Jamaican Creole/Patwa—was shared by the enslaved and their (creole) enslavers, and that it continued to flourish through the post-slavery period and twentieth century, into the twenty-first century. It argues that the Jamaican language (Jamiekan langwij) is a major cultural product, and that the language operated (and operates) as a zone of convergence, conflict, and negotiation between and among the many and varied "arrivants" (Brathwaite, 2000) in the colony (and nation), combining the people in a cultural milieu, even as some among them denied and rejected that process.

In its emergence and influence, Jamaican Creole/Patwa shares a history with other creole languages that developed in the region. According to Natalie Zemon Davis:

> Caribbean creole languages are especially instructive for the historical study of communication. These creoles were created by people wrenched from their own language communities and by the children of such uprooted parents; by people eager to have a language in which to conduct their lives amidst a surrounding babel of tongues and in lands far away from those of their progenitors. They illustrate the ingenuity of human populations in difficult straits and the wide range of situations and subjects they wanted to be able to talk about in relatively short order (2009, p. 268).

As was the case in Suriname, the focus of Zemon Davis's analysis, during the period of slavery (and well beyond the formal demise of the system), while the creation of Jamaican Creole/Patwa offered recognizable structure and phrasing, poetic renderings, and pithy pronouncements, it faced deep-rooted, colonially shaped and racially driven prejudices against a language created primarily by enslaved Africans and their descendants. Not surprisingly, then, for much of the island's history, Jamaican Creole/Patwa was described as broken, improper, and vulgar. As was the case in Suriname where, according to Zemon Davis, "[l]inguists took their time to decide that colonial creoles were not just 'broken' or 'bastard' or 'aberrant' versions of genuine languages, but were new languages in their own right and worthy of study" (2009, p. 268), creole language construction in Jamaica was given short shrift. Those circumstances would change to some extent with the popular embrace of creative productions and performances by locale artistes led by Louise Bennett-Coverley and with the emergence of local/regional scholars and institutions, as well as what Zemon Davis refers to as an "explosion" of international scholarship in the last forty years, where creoles have gained the interest of linguists.[6]

In the case of Patwa/Jamaican Creole, according to linguists Barbara Lalla and Jean D'Costa, while it is very difficult to point to a moment by which an identifiable Jamaican language (Jamiekan langwij) form emerged, it is clear that by 1700, distinctive patterns of speech were noticeable, and by the late eighteenth, nineteenth, and twentieth centuries, it had become the *lingua franca* of the people resident in the island. Patwa/Jamaican Creole (JC) used many English-derived words (as well as words from other languages), but according to linguists, it was (and is) heavily influenced in structure and syntax by languages from the West African Coast (including Kru, Mandingo, and Kwa).[7]

The influence of West/Central African languages on the emerging Jamaican language system can be ascertained from some observations from the eighteenth and nineteenth centuries. Edward Long, historian, and a member of the enslaving classes, indicated the influence of the African peoples on the mode of communication when he noted that "Many of the plantation Blacks call their children by the African name for the day of the week on which they are born; and these names are of two genders, male and female."

Male.	Female.	Day.
Cudjoe,	Juba,	Monday.
Cubbenah,	Beneba,	Tuesday.
Quâco,	Cuba,	Wednesday.
Quao,	Abba,	Thursday.
Cuffee,	Phibba,	Friday.
Quamin,	Mimba,	Saturday.
Quashee,	Quasheba,	Sunday. (Long, 2002, p. 427).

That the enslaved and subjected people were able to retain enough control over their naming practices for this to have been observed as "norm" for Long is interesting. And for our purposes, it is instructive that he mentioned one naming system and one set of names for males and females. If Long is correct that this was the dominant naming system among the "Blacks" in the period, this suggests that a negotiation had taken place, or at least was under way, among the many cultural groups of enslaved Africans and their descendants, which had resulted in the appearance of consensus among them in this plantation society. Perhaps the majority had previously shared this system; perhaps it was imposed by the most numerically and/or politically and/or culturally powerful among the enslaved. But whatever means, it was widespread enough to be recorded by this observer of Jamaican life and culture in the eighteenth century.

Where the influence of "African words" on the speech observed in the island was concerned, Long provided some other intriguing information. According to him:

There are some other words, that are remarkable for the different senses in which they are used; viz.

	Original Import.	Common Import.	Dialect.
Mungo	Bread,	Negroe's name,	Mundingo.
Bumbo	Alligator,	*Pudendum muliebre,*	*Idem.*
Coffee	Goodmorrow,	{Name of a plant, the berries of which yield an agreeable morning repast to many of the Negroes,	Fûli.
Guinnay, Guinee	Devil,	Name of the slave country	Jaloff, Fûli.
Sangara	Brandy,	Sangree, or Strong Negus,	*Idem.*
Tate	The Posteriors,	Tête, the head in French,	Jaloff.
Kénne-kénne	Small-sand,	[...], Græc. *Cinis,* Lat.	Mundingo.
Buaw,	Devil,	Bullock (Negroe phrase),	*Idem.*

(Long, 2002, pp. 426–427).

Not only had these words been "imported," but they were reportedly in frequent and "common" use. If Long's attribution of the words to "Mundingo," "Fûli," and "Jaloff" *dialects* was accurate, then it might be possible to gesture towards issues of African ethnicity through the signals of language. Further, these attributions suggest a variety of sources in what would become Patwa, and an intra-African process of creolisation: the means by which the Jamaican people constructed their language system involved many layers of complex linguistic negotiations, as well as an ability to accommodate and create. For the Jamaicans in the twentieth-first century who continue to use some of the words recorded by Long—including one which operates as a swear word—this serves to confirm the resilience of the people's culture.

If one important part of the creole language which developed in Jamaica was tied directly to the languages of the enslaved Africans who constituted the majority, another contribution came from the

Europeans whose colonial project shaped the trajectory of the island's under-development. By the second half of the eighteenth century, after more than a century of English colonialism, the language of the colonisers was in evidence: there were some remnants of the Spanish colonial period (such as in place names like *Ocho Rios* and *Rio Bueno*), and some French introductions, but by and large, the island (then as now) was labeled as "English speaking." However, according to observers, this was *not* the King's English.

Whereas Long claimed that "[t]he Africans speak their respective dialects, with some mixture of broken English," among the locally born population, he noted:

> The language of the Creoles is bad English, larded with the Guiney dialect, owing to their adopting the African words, in order to make themselves understood by the imported slaves; which they find much easier than teaching these strangers to learn English. The better sort are very fond of improving their language, by catching at any hard word that the Whites happen to let fall in their hearing; and they alter and misapply it in a strange manner; but a tolerable collection of them gives an air of knowledge and importance in the eyes of their brethren, which tickles their vanity, and makes them more assiduous in stocking themselves with this unintelligible jargon (2002, pp. 426–427).[8]

What Long portrayed as an attraction to and inclusion of these "hard" words which together created an "unintelligible jargon" might otherwise be read as a love of words which scholars, such as Roger Abrahams (1983), have identified in Caribbean culture. Among the people, the words may have been attractive due to their sounds, cadence, and perceived power. They might have ascribed new and "strange" meanings to English words, but meanings might have been less important than speaking the words, creating the language and experiencing the power of creation. According to Kamau Brathwaite, "Within the folk tradition, language was (and is) a creative act in itself; the word was held to contain a secret power" (1971, p. 237). Racist observers like Long may assessed *their* inability to understand the Jamaican people as yet another confirmation of the inferiority of the population—most of whom were enslaved and non-white. However, that population was, in fact, engaged in the creation of a means of communication by which they could share their secrets, affections, humour and "livity."[9]

Given Long's cultural myopia, it should not be surprising that he labeled the language which emerged from this process of linguistic negotiation and creation as so much "gibberish."

> The Negroes seem very fond of reduplications, to express a greater or less quantity of any thing; as *walky-walky, talky-talky, washy-washy, nappy-nappy, tie-tie, lilly-lilly, fum-fum:* so *bug-a-bugs* (wood-ants); *dab-a-dab* (an olio, made with maize, herrings, and pepper); *bra-bra* (another of their dishes); *grande-grande* (augmentative size, or grandeur), and so forth. In their conversation, they confound all the moods, tenses, cases, and conjugations, without mercy: for example, *I surprize* (for I am surprized); *me glad for see you* (for, I am glad to see you); *how you do* (for, how d'ye do?); *me tank you; me ver well*, &c. (Long 2002, p. 427).

For Long, this was little more than a garbled attempt by a substandard group to speak English "properly." It certainly did not enter his consciousness that the people were not, in fact, speaking "bad English." Rather, they were fashioning a language system that bound them together. Long may well have been surprised to find that the rules of grammar and the vocabulary that he identified persisted through the nineteenth and twentieth centuries and became the subject of scholarly engagement.

Rather than applying a label of "gibberish" to Jamaican language (Jamiekan langwij), in her seminal work in the 1960s, Beryl Bailey not only identified the language system which was extant in the island, but through her analyses of phonology, morphology, word classes, sentence structure, morpheme variants, and morphophonemics, argued that there are nine main rules of grammar that distinguish Jamaican Creole from English.[10] Similarly, through an examination of phonological processes, including nasalization, vowel epenthesis, final vowel insertion, vowel coalescence, glide formation, lengthening, final consonant deletion, initial consonant deletion, "h" deletion, and "r" deletion, linguistic scholar Glenn Akers (1981) examined the grammatical structure and demonstrated the linguistic distinctiveness of Jamaican Creole/Patwa. They and other scholars, including Mervyn Alleyne (1980), Hubert Devonish (1986), Barbara Lalla, Velma Pollard and Lawrence Carrington (1988), Barbara Lalla and Jean D'Costa (1990), Mervyn Morris (1999), Pauline Christie (2001), Gordon Collier and Ulrich Fleischmann (2003), Silvia Kouwenberg (2003), Hazel Simmons-McDonald and Ian Robertson (2006) and Frederic G.

Cassidy (2007) would have rejected Long's interpretation. For them, Jamaican Creole was/is not simply a broken or bastardised version of English, but rather a communication system worthy of recognition, study, and even celebration. That it emanated largely from the creative energies of the oppressed majority and had its roots in the midst of the slave system, makes Jamaican language (Jamiekan langwij) both a testament to the power of cultural negotiation and creativity, as well as to the resilience of the human spirit.

Moving beyond the components of the language into some of its uses, nineteenth century observers like John Stewart managed to offer both a negative portrayal of the people and a grudgingly positive recognition of aspects of their cultural lives. According to him:

> The ideas of the negroes cannot be expected to extend to abstract and metaphysical subjects. Of the existence and attributes of a Deity, of a future state, and of duration and space, they have but imperfect notions . . . yet they will often express, in their own way, a wonderfully acute conception of things. These conceptions they sometimes compress into short and pithy sentences, something like the sententious proverbs of the Europeans (1808, p. 247).

These were, in fact, not merely "something like" proverbs, but would be identified, recorded, and analysed as the poignant and often philosophical lessons which emerged from the collective consciousness of the people. Even Stewart had to admit that "These sayings often convey an astonishing force and meaning; and would, if clothed in a more courtly dress, make no despicable figure even among those precepts of wisdom which are ascribed to the wisest of men" (1808, p. 247). Like many engaged in the mental contortions of explaining the "inferiority" of the enslaved, while acknowledging their unmistakable humanity and complexity, Stewart found it possible to dismiss the possibility that the enslaved could generate ideas about "abstract and metaphysical subjects," and yet to claim that they were capable of wisdom akin to that offered by "the wisest of men." It is all but certain that the people who created these "sayings" would not have agreed that they needed to be "clothed in a more courtly dress"; the "dress" of language (langwij) that they provided was quite sufficient.

Despite his critique, Stewart then proceeded to offer illustrations of the wisdom captured in Jamaican proverbs:

When they wish to imply, that a peaceable man is often wise and provident in his conduct, they say, *"Softly water run deep:"* when they would express the oblivion and disregard which follows us after death, they say, *"when man dead grass grow in him door;"* and when they would express the humility which is the usual accompaniment of poverty, they say, *"Poor man never vex."* (1808, p. 247—248).

Often descriptive, prescriptive, and witty, the proverbs not only captured the sociocultural concerns of the people and their economic circumstances, but also philosophical and moral lessons of life. The proverbs relied on easily remembered maxims and were condensed in highly illustrative metaphors, many of which were tied to the island's environment and material culture.

So pervasive were the Jamaican proverbs that in the post-slavery period, they were recorded in increasingly systematic ways. Among the 227 proverbs listed by Charles Rampini in the 1870s, people were warned that things were not always as they appeared to be: "Alligator lay egg, but him no fowl." They were cautioned against overindulgence: "Greedy choke puppy"; that familiarity did, in fact, breed contempt: "Play wi' [with] puppy, puppy lick you face"; and that people only attacked those whom they were confident they could subdue: "Duppy (ghost) know who him frighten" (Rampini, 1873, pp. 175—182). Perhaps due to Martha Beckwith's anthropological gaze, in the 1920s, she attempted to translate, explain, and identify the provenance of an alphabetized list of 972 Jamaican proverbs (Beckwith, 1970).[11] She also recognized a direct link between some Jamaican proverbs and African traditions, and argued that in the Jamaican context:

> African wit and philosophy are more justly summed up in the proverb or aphorism than in any other form of folk art, and the proverbial sayings collected from negro settlements in [. . .] the Americas or the West Indies give a truer picture of the mental life of the negro than even story or song reveals. In them he expresses his justification of the vicissitudes of life. They are his consolation for impotence, the weapon of the weak against the provocations of the strong, in argument, an apt proverb will often win conviction. As a veiled threat, it carries almost the efficacy of a curse. Proverbs enter constantly into the life of the folk; borrowed sayings undergo a process of remolding [sic] under the influence of native conditions, being interpreted to meet the emergencies of native life, and new sayings pattern upon the old. There is no other art so thoroughly assimilated to the life of the people of Jamaica . . . as this of the aphorism, and none employed so constantly in everyday experience (1970, p. 5).

That many of these proverbs had their genesis in the period of slavery and would survive for generations speaks volumes about the creativity and resilience of the Jamaican people and the creole language culture that they fashioned.

While the proverbs were noted and sometimes reluctantly acknowledged, the almost automatically critical stance of the cultural elite towards the cultural production of the (enslaved) majority soon overtook their observations. According to John Stewart:

> Although the proverbial sayings of the negroes have often much point and meaning, they, however, no sooner begin to expatiate, and enter more minutely into particulars, than they become tedious, verbose, and circumlocutive, beginning their speeches with a tiresome exordium, mingling with them much extraneous matter, and frequently traversing over and over the same ground, and cautioning the hearer to be attentive, as if fearful that some of the particulars and points on which their meaning and argument hinged, should escape his attention. So that by the time they arrive at the peroration of their harangue, the listener is heartily fatigued with it, and perceives that the whole which has been said, though it may have taken up to half an hour, could have been comprised in a dozen of words (1808, p. 248).

If Stewart was critical of their delivery, he also made reference to the "quaint" ways in which they spoke, and which came to characterise the island's speech patterns:

> Instead of short familiar names, they give sometimes whole sentences as names to their dogs and other domestic animals, as, *"Keep what you have; take care of yourself, &c."* and those who have been baptized, give a sort of pious appellation to these animals, as *"God give, God send, bless the Lord, tell God tankee."* These latter names are exactly of a piece with the epithets assumed by the puritans in Oliver Cromwell's day . . . "Be faithful;" "Fly debate;" "Stand fast on high;" "God reward;" "Faint not;" "Fight the good fight of faith" (Stewart, 1808, p. 248).

Often unable to control many outward aspects of their lives—including the naming practices which were applied to them—it is possible that the naming of an animal by the (enslaved) majority presented an opportunity for a statement. The non-religious names mentioned by Stewart seemed to operate as reminders of life lessons, while the religious names (which even Stewart recognised might be a pattern among Christian converts) could have been both their own spiritual reminders and assurances to those in the religious community who were anxious about the authenticity of their conversions. In addition, the colourful naming of animals might have represented the determination of the enslaved to confirm their humanity and individuality as well as to extract humour out of their dire circumstances.

Other nineteenth century observers, like Alexander Barclay, also made references to the "curious" turns of phrase which appeared in the Jamaican language (Jamiekan langwij). In an 1827 publication, Barclay described the surprise expressed by a group of enslaved "African negroes," who were shipbuilders, at the ability of (European) sailors for "'*finding pass*' (finding their way) in the ocean from Guinea to Buckra Country, as they call Jamaica." According to Barclay, the enslaved workers were also "struck with . . . admiration of the first 'steam engine,' or '*smoke-mill*,' as they call it, that was set to work in the neighbourhood where [he] resided, and which they came from all quarters to see." Barclay also offered what he said was an account of what the enslaved shipbuilders said, along with his translation: "The common exclamation was, 'Massa-nigger! Wharra dem 'Buckra no savi? Wharra dem no can do?' (Fellow-servant! What is it the white people do not know? What is it they cannot do?)" (Barclay, 1827, p. 239). While his translation is mostly accurate, it is important to note Barclay's alteration of the exclamation "Massa-nigger" (Master's negro) to produce "Fellow-servant." This modification serves as a reminder that commentaries on the island's language in this early period are reliant on records made by persons other than the enslaved majority and are therefore subject to the possibility of filters and biases to mis/represent, de/construct, sensationalize, and sanitize the oral culture. Even so, it is possible to identify characteristics, patterns, and cadences of the Jamaican language (Jamiekan langwij) that were recorded throughout the period which were still discernable in post-slavery society, through the twentieth century, and into the twenty-first.

Not surprisingly, for the most part, the speech recorded for enslaved persons referred to their interactions with the enslaving classes, who were among the recorders of the language (langwij). This was certainly the case for Matthew (Monk) Lewis who, in his *Journal of a West India Proprietor*, mentioned that within his Jamaican plantation home, "many a time my delicacy has been put to the blush by the ill-timed civility of some old [enslaved] woman or other, who, wandering that way, and happening to cast her eye to the left, has stopped her course to curtsy very gravely, and pay me the passing compliment of an 'Ah massa! Bless you massa! How day?'" (Lewis, 1969, p. 150). While the greetings to the "massa" could detain us, for our purposes, it is with the old woman's economy of speech ("How day?") that many speakers and scholars of Jamaican Creole/Patwa might identify.

If observers like Lewis may have recorded, with some bemusement, the speech patterns of the enslaved majority, when those patterns were observed among *other* (white, or enslaving, or free) groups, there was considerable consternation. Edward Long, for example, was dismayed by the communication patterns of Jamaican-born (creole) women in the enslaving classes who, he said, were affected by "the constant intercourse from their birth with Negroe [sic] domestics, whose drawling, dissonant gibberish they insensibly adopt, and with it no small tincture of their aukward [sic] carriage and vulgar manners; all which they do not easily get rid of, even after an English education, unless sent away extremely young" (Long, 2002, p. 278).[12] If being "sent away" (to Britain) was an ideal solution for Long, he also believed that the slide into "drawling, dissonant gibberish" could be arrested with the importation of British governesses who were expected to isolate the plantocracy's children from the influence of the language and culture of the enslaved. Failing that, he advocated the establishment of a seminary which would take the children away from the creole language and culture, and perhaps "save" them from the barbarity with which he associated both. For Long, without one or another of these interventions, the sad state of affairs was unlikely to change because of a dependence among free/d (creole) people on enslaved domestic labour, and slavery more generally, and the cultural interchange and influence that resulted from that dependence. Although the creole colonists, who were the objects of his critique, might never have left the island, that did not absolve them, in Long's mind, from the responsibility of communicating in "proper" English, one of the most important symbols of their "civilization," and a major means by which they could claim an elevated sociocultural status. Although those who should have been "sent away extremely young" in order to ensure their proper cultural indoctrination could experience anxiety, dislocation and trauma, for Long and others of his ilk, perhaps those concerns were secondary to ridding the ruling creole enslaving classes of their supposedly poor language skills, which were influenced by the Black majority.

Given the gendered association between cultural production, maintenance, and transmission (as part of the socialization process "inherent" in child-rearing), perhaps not surprisingly, Long blamed the erosion of the culture of the local plantocracy, as was evidenced through their adoption of "dissonant gibberish," on the mothers in Jamaica's enslaving classes. For him:

> [...] a mother, who has been trained in the accustomed mode among a herd of Negroe-domestics [sic], adopts the same plan, for the most part, with her own children, having no idea of the impropriety of it, because she does not discern those singularities, in speech or deportment, which are so apt to strike the ears and eyes of well-educated persons on a first introduction to them (Long, 2002, p. 278).

The situation was particularly distressing, he said, among those who had been "bred up entirely in the sequestered country parts, and had no opportunity of forming themselves either by example or tuition"; those creole women were "truly to be pitied" (Long, 2002, p.279). He continued:

> We may see ... a very fine young woman aukwardly [sic] dangling her arms with the air of a Negroe-servant [sic], lolling almost the whole day upon beds or settees, her head muffled up with two or three handkerchiefs, her dress loose, and without stays. At noon, we find her employed in gobbling pepper-pot, seated on the floor, with her sable hand-maids around her. In the afternoon, she takes her siesto as usual; while two of these damsels refresh her face with the gentle breathings of the fan; and a third provokes the drowsy powers of Morpheus by delicious scratchings on the sole of either foot (Long, 2002, p. 279).

For him, Jamaican Creole/Patwa which was spoken by the creole residents was only a part of a larger "sub-standard culture" that increasingly defined the island; the "fine young women" who were the focus of his critique, whether they knew and admitted it or not, were part of a creole culture which they shared with the enslaved "sable hand-maids" who catered to their every need.

By the turn of the nineteenth century, when Lady Maria Nugent, self-described "Governor's lady to the *blackies*" (Wright, 2002, p. 2, emphasis in original), recorded her impressions of Jamaican slave society in her journal, she referenced the "peculiarities" of the language of the island's residents. Among her descriptions of the people she met and who spent time with her within the privileged domestic space of the governor's mansion, she included "Mrs. S. [. . .] a fat, good-humoured Creole woman, saying dis, dat, and toder..." (Wright, 2002, p. 76). If Nugent meant to mock Mrs. S's pronunciation of "this, that, and the other," she also assisted in the preservation of early renditions of Jamaican Creole—although, it is important to note once again, that these were filtered through her observations and records.

As Long had intimated in the previous century, Nugent corroborated, in a journal entry for 1802, that:

> [t]he Creole language is not confined to the negroes. Many of the ladies, who have not been educated in England, speak a sort of broken English, with an indolent drawling out of the words, that is very tiresome if not disgusting. I stood next to a lady one night near a window, and, by way of saying something, remarked that the air was much cooler than usual; to which she answered, "Yes, ma—am, him rail—ly too fra—ish" (Wright, 2002, p. 98).[13]

It is possible to argue that the so-called "broken English" that the creole ladies spoke was neither "broken" nor "English," but was in fact a Jamaican Creole/Patwa and indicated some of the features that would persist in the language through the nineteenth and twentieth centuries, into the twenty-first century. The ascription of the masculine gender to just about everything (whether animate or inanimate, and in this case, the "air" which the creole lady said was 'really too fresh'), as well as its delivery, in what Nugent described as "an indolent drawling out of the words" were/are quintessential characteristics of Jamaican Creole/Patwa. That the class of persons considered elevated enough to spend time in Lady Nugent's private chambers would be speakers of the island's nation language is indicative of how pervasive and influential the speech patterns had become by 1801—1805 (the period of Nugent's sojourn in Jamaica).

While it is clear that major contributions to the creole language had been made by the enslaved Africans and their descendants who constituted the majority of persons in the island, observers seemed to be most concerned about what they believed to be the transmission of the language to the Europeans and their descendants in the society. Like Long and Nugent, John Stewart claimed in his 1808 publication that due to early exposure to "the very manners and barbarous dialect of the negroes," many of the local creole ladies were engaged in "involuntary imitation" so that they displayed "an aukward [sic] and ungraceful sort of affectation in their language and manner, which strongly indicates ignorance and untutored simplicity." Indeed, he said, "to use an expression in common use here, many of them . . . exhibit much of the *Quashiba*" (pp. 159–160, emphasis in original). If women of the enslaving classes, and their families, were to claim cultural superiority to accompany their socioeconomic, political, and personal dominance, being referred to as "Quashiba"—the generic name often given to enslaved women in Jamaican slave society—simply would not do. While Long, Nugent, Stewart and others pointed to Africans and their descendants as the source of the allegedly poor language and culture which influenced the creole plantocracy, they also inadvertently highlighted the subversive power of the oppressed, whose cadence, carriage, and mannerisms so infused the society that the elite and middling classes who participated in the creole culture could no longer discern that influence upon themselves. While commentators like Long were clearly troubled that members of Jamaica's elite society, especially its women, were influenced by "the tricks, superstitions, diversions, and profligate discourses of black servants, equally illiterate and unpolished," (Long, 2002, p. 279), they were also painfully aware that it was *their* dependence on the labour of enslaved persons that opened the portal for the latter's enormous influence on the construction of "creolity."[14]

Lest any should think that the early creation of the Jamaican language (Jamiekan langwij) occurred within or was indicative of a harmonious, multicultural society where consensus had been reached about what constituted a national cultural identity, let us remember that these negotiations among cultures took place within the context of the enslavement, hyper-exploitation, brutality, and attempts to dehumanize the majority. So, it should not be surprising that as one of the points of contact between and among the groups which were oppressed/ oppressive, the language should be one of the means by which the relationships of domination, including the moments of confrontation and the dance of negotiation, were unveiled.

In 1827, when Alexander Barclay issued his pro-slavery publication, *A practical view of the present state of slavery in the West Indies*, he outlined both the "inevitability" of the harshness of slavery (due primarily to the temperament of the enslaved) and the hypocrisy of the anti-slavery forces through an examination of the experiences of Unitarian minister, Rev. Mr. Cooper. According to Barclay, Rev. Cooper reported that while he was resident on Georgia estate in Jamaica, after initially receiving good service from his enslaved servants, he soon ran into trouble with "a boy named John Harding," who was openly rebellious and recalcitrant (Barclay, 1827, pp. 406–416).[15] Said Cooper, "Again and again I called him to account [. . .] I spoke to my neighbours upon the subject" and was advised to whip the defiant Harding; but Cooper was initially reluctant to do so. Harding's defiance increased and a similar attitude was increasingly observed among Cooper's other enslaved workers (Barclay, 1827, p. 407). According to Cooper, "Many times I saw Mrs. C. insulted, and did myself put up with language from the domestics, which I should not think of submitting to in this country [England], no, not for an hour" (Barclay, 1827, p. 408). It was at this point, when "John was so extremely outrageous," that Cooper turned the enslaved male worker over to the overseer and "John was, in consequence, sadly overpunished [sic]" (1827, p. 408). However, these violent consequences did not result in an end to Harding's insubordinate behaviour.

Of interest is Cooper's reference to language as one of the sources of abuse to which he claimed he was subjected by the enslaved "boy." While the details of those verbal encounters are lost to us, there is every reason to assume that although Harding addressed Cooper (and his wife) with words that emanated from the creole language continuum, he spoke in terms that Cooper understood quite clearly, and by which he was offended. As Zemon Davis argues for Suriname, since "owners and their spouses," as well as "the estate manager and any proprietor who managed his own estate had to be at least conversant in creole" (Zemon Davis, 2009, p. 279), "massa" Cooper and other enslavers both used and could be assailed in Jamaican Creole/Patwa.

The potential for violent verbal confrontations, as part of a larger culture of violence, was clear early in June 1831, when Mr. A.L. Palmer, a magistrate in Port Royal parish, contacted the governor of Jamaica, the Earl of Belmore, with news about a recently completed proceeding in which an enslaved mother (Catherine Whitfield) and her enslaved daughter (Ann Amelia King) were brought before him in a case against the Honourable Mr. J.R. Jackson, the Custos of Port Royal, and his wife for "improper severity" in their punishment of the two women (Hay, 1832). As the evidence connected to the case indicated, the source of the confrontation and the severe and extended punishment that the two women suffered had to do with allegations of "insolence." When Ann King got into an argument with Mrs. Jackson, the latter hit her repeatedly with a short, heavy stick, whereupon King's mother, Catherine Whitfield (called Kate) "interfered, and with some warmth declared that her daughter did not deserve such treatment." According to Palmer, as the levels of conflict escalated, "A violent altercation took place between Kate and her mistress, during which Kate used some expressions too indecent for me to repeat in this letter" (Hay, 1832, p. 4). As punishment for their violent use of language (and use of violent language), their insolence and defiance, both women were punished by being "demoted" from the house to the fields and confined in the stocks at some point in every day for more than three months. It was this latter action that was judged to be excessive by some, for the violations were "only" in language; it was this excess that caused the case to be brought to the attention of the colonial, and later, the imperial authorities.

The cases of Kate Whitfield and Ann King allow us some access, filtered and mitigated though it is, into the language world of Jamaican slave society, where verbal confrontations between enslavers and the enslaved were regular occurrences. Even Magistrate Palmer, who was concerned enough about the case to bring it to the attention of the governor, reported that Kate was "habitually insolent to her mistress," and that on occasions she resorted to "language so grossly abusive and indecent as to render correction indispensable" (Hay, 1832, p. 5). One wonders what she and her daughter could have said that would result in their being shackled daily for three months.

The concerns about language as violence and violation came out even more clearly in the record of evidence taken from the two enslaved women who were summoned by the Council of Protection (Hay, 1832, 15—23). While we will never know the extent of interpretation and edition carried out by the minute-taker, the document reported moments of confrontation between the women and their enslavers, and the women's reported testimonies reveal the power of language, especially within the context of a culture of animosity and violence that marked slave societies such as these.

According to the testimony attributed to the enslaved mother, Catherine/Kate Whitfield, after the initial beating and whipping of her daughter, she "got into a rage," to which Mrs. Jackson and *her* mother (Mrs. Strupar) responded forcefully. According to Whitfield's recorded testimony, "Then mistress said, hold your tongue you infamous wretch, hold your tongue you wretch. Old mistress (Mrs. Strupar) was in the next room. Old mistress said, Betsy, Betsy, (meaning Mrs. Jackson,) how can you jaw with that wretch" (Hay, 1832, p. 15).[16] And when Mrs. Jackson threatened to flog her again, Kate reportedly testified, "I said to mistress, there is no occasion for you to take and flog me, you wanted to suck the little blood out of me, as my [previous] flogging was not well yet" (Hay, 1832, p. 15). Although there is a possibility that the account included a translation or interpretation of what Whitfield said, the essence of the violence, exploitation, and brutality which were hallmarks of Jamaican slave society found their way into the reported testimony attributed to the enslaved woman. This and other verbal confrontations indicated that while enslavers had the institutions of authority on their side, enslaved persons could (if only momentarily) challenge the assumptions about their subjection by calling upon the power of language and invoking their humanity, creativity, and influence in ways that their enslavers would have been loath to recognize.

In addition to moments such as these, the confrontational potential of language in Jamaican slave society could also be ascertained from contemporary cultural products. In the anonymously published novel—*Marly; or The Life of a Planter in Jamaica*—the protagonist Marly went to the field of his estate one Monday morning, to find that the overseer was in the midst of punishing the entire group of enslaved workers because "several of the negroes were behind their time."

> As they came in, the overseer ordered them to be laid down, and each received either nine or ten lashes . . . none were pardoned—all received the same punishment, without distinction of sex or age. The negroes said very little, but the moment the Busha's back was turned to go away, the whole line commenced singing in a general chorus, as if they regarded him not, "I don't care a damn, oh! I don't care a damn, oh!" and this must have sounded in his ears for at least five minutes, before he could get beyond the reach of hearing (1828, p. 104).

The defiance of the fictionalized enslaved workers, who risked another round of punishment for their declarations that they didn't "care a damn," is clear. While there is little doubt that Marly and his proxy (the overseer) wielded incredible power over the labour and bodies of the enslaved, they were unable to silence the disaffection which marked occasions such as these, and which were marked by the language of resistance.

The strength and influence of the Jamaican language (Jamiekan langwij) system are easily discerned by the fact that during slavery, in post-slavery society, through the nineteenth and twentieth centuries, into the twenty-first century, Jamaican Creole/Patwa has remained one of the main cultural products of the society. Born out of the contact among West/Central African cultural and language groups and European languages (primarily English), the Jamaican Language (Jamiekan Langwij) that was created was/is functional, colourful, dynamic and was/is an important symbol of "creolity." Armed with the power of that language, Jamaicans, enslaved and free, during slavery and after its demise, continue/d to add new layers of complexity to their "nation language," to their *Jamiekan Langwij*. In a rendering of Lillian Allen's observation in "Language," one of her poems in her "Tribute to Miss Lou," the *Jamiekan* people have made it clear that 'the *langwij* of the people is the *langwij* of life.'[17]

Endnotes

1 Jamiekan Langwij—Jamaican Language (The Jamaican Language Unit/Di Jamiekan Langwij Yuunit, 2009). An early version of this chapter appeared as "'...dis, dat, and toder': Constructing a Nation/al Creole Language in Jamaica During Slavery," in "'Métissages': Conflits épistémologiques, sociaux et culturels aux Amériques et aux Caraïbes," *Cultures-Kairós: Revue d'anthropologie des pratiques coreporelles et des arts vavants,*

no. 8, janvier 2018. http://revues.mshparisnord.org/cultureskairos/index.php?id=1602.

2 The European labour force in the Caribbean included persons who had run afoul of the law/state and whose punishment was "transportation," as well vagrants and other "undesirables." While the migratory flow of indentured servants (*"engagés,"* in the French territories) and other involuntary migrants was dominated by men and the enterprise was ultimately for the benefit of élite men, there were poor, indentured European women who worked (alongside men) in tobacco fields or who were employed as domestic servants in harsh frontier conditions.

3 According to B.W. Higman, "of the many revolutions identified by historians, only one [the sugar revolution] takes its name from a particular commodity" (Higman, 2000, p. 213).

4 According to estimates from the Trans-Atlantic Slave Trade Database, between 1501—1875, those who were engaged in the transatlantic trade in enslaved Africans transported 12,521,337 persons into the Americas. Individuals, companies and governmental authorities within the British empire enslaved and forcibly transported 3,259,441 Africans into the Americas; of that number, 1,212,352 disembarked in Jamaica (http://www.slavevoyages.org/assessment/estimates).

5 The enormous African influence on Jamaican culture is, in part, linked to demography. According to B.W. Higman, there was "a steady increase in the annual average of slaves brought from Africa to Jamaica during the eighteenth century" and up to the official end of the British trade in enslaved Africans in 1807, when he estimates that "Africans comprised roughly 45 percent of the slave population of Jamaica" (1995, p. 75). As a result, argues Higman, "it appears that the slave population must have become as heavily Africanized in 1790—1807 as in any other period, with the exception of the late seventeenth century" (1995, p. 76). After 1807, however, there was a "rapid decline in the African section" (1995, pp. 75—76) and the development of a creole society and culture with overwhelming African bases.

6 Zemon Davis (2009, p. 269). According to Zemon Davis, the debates among linguists have included discussions about whether the similar forms found in the Atlantic creoles can be explained solely by "universal properties of language inborn in all of us" or whether "similarities in phonology and syntax to be explained by substrate influences—that is, influences from West African languages." There are debates about whether "creole languages created in a single generation by slave children

who are born in the Americas and who take the pidgin of their displaced parents . . . turn it into a real 'nativized' language" or, if the creoles are "created over several generations, with the influx of new speakers from Africa making a difference."

7   Linguists have relied on the records of seventeenth-, eighteenth-, and nineteenth-century observers such as Hans Sloane, J.B. Moreton and Matthew G. Lewis, among others, as well as evaluations of the processes by which the roots/routes of the languages have been traced in order to make their arguments. (See Lalla & D'Costa, 1990, pp. 23, 100; Bryan, 1998, p. 100; Dalphinis, 1985, p. 2; Alleyne, 2003, pp. 29—42).

8   First published in London: T. Lowndes, 1774.

9   "Livity" is a Rastafarian/Jamaican term that can be defined "the totality of one's being in the world" (Lewis, 1998, p. 155).

10 According to Bailey, these rules are: i) There is no subject-verb concord in Creole; the English verb must agree in number with its subject nominal; ii) The tense system in Creole is limited to the unmarked verb for general purposes, and a participle specifying "past"; English has a more fully developed tense system; iii) The Creole verb does not have a distinct passive form; iv) The English verb "be" bifurcates in Creole into an equating verb and a locating verb, with no reflex for adjectival predication; v) The Creole adjective, like the verb, predicates without use of copula; vi) The Creole nouns and pronouns have both an aggregate and an associative plural; English has the associative plural in the first and second person pronouns only; vii) In the generic phrase the Creole noun has no article; English nouns require either the singular form with definite article (the horse) or the plural form without article (horses); viii) There is no case system in either noun or pronoun in Creole, and no indication of sex in third person pronouns and ix) The inverted sentence type is basic in Creole; its use for emphasis in English is much more limited. (Bailey, 1966, p. 146).

11 Beckwith (1970, pp. 5-6) noted that versions of many of the proverbs she collected had previously been published by T. Banbury, *Jamaica Superstitions, or the Obeah Book* (Jamaica, 1894), pp. 39-43; William C. Bates, "Creole Folk-lore from Jamaica. I. Proverbs," *Journal of American Folk-lore* 9 (1895), pp. 38-42; Frank Cundall (with Izett Anderson), *Jamaica Negro Proverbs and Sayings* (Kingston: Institute of Jamaica, 1910); Harry A. Franck, "Jamaica Proverbs," *Dialect Notes* 5: 4 (1921), pp. 98-108; Cyril F. Grant, "Negro Proverbs collected in Jamaica, 1887," *Folk-lore* 28 (1917), pp. 315-317; Rampini, 1873, pp. 175-182. See Beckwith

(1969) and (Beckwith,1970).

12 For a similar description in the context of Suriname, see Zemon Davis (2009, p. 280).

13 "Yes, ma'am, it is really fresh."

14 For discussions of this phenomenon as it appeared at the end of the nineteenth and early twentieth centuries, see Moore and Johnson, 2004 and Moore and Johnson, 2011.

15 Barclay references Thomas Cooper's, "A Letter to Robert Hibbert, Jun. Esq." in reply to his pamphlet entitled "Fact Verified Upon Oath, in contradiction of the report of the Rev. Thomas Cooper, concerning the general condition of the Slaves in Jamaica, &c. &c."; "A Letter from Mrs. Cooper to R. Hibbert, Jun. Esq. and an Appendix, containing an exposure of the falsehoods and calamities of that gentleman's affidavit, 1824." (Cooper, 1824).

16 Here, to "jaw" meant to talk or argue.

17 This is a rendering of the closing lines of Allen's poem, "Language" which states ". . . the language of the people is the language of life," (1993, p.44 and this volume.)

References

Abrahams, R. D. *The Man of Words in the West Indies: Performance and the Emergence of Creole Culture*. Baltimore: Johns Hopkins University Press, 1983.

Alleyne, M. C. *Comparative Afro-American: An Historical-Comparative Study of English-Based Afro-American Dialects of the New World*. Ann Arbor: Karoma Publishers Inc., 1980.

Alleyne, M. C. *Roots of Jamaican Culture*. London: Pluto Press, 1988.

Alleyne, M. C. "The Role of Africa in the Construction of Identities in the Caribbean." *A Pepper-Pot of Cultures: Aspects of Creolization in the Caribbean*. Edited by Gordon Collier and Ulrich Fleischmann. Amsterdam, New York: Rodopi, 2003, pp. 29—42.

Anon. *Marly; or, The Life of a Planter in Jamaica: Comprehending Characteristic Sketches of the Present State of Society and Manners in the British West Indies and An impartial Review of the Leading Questions Relative to Colonial Policy*, second edition. Glasgow: Printed for Richard Griffin & Co.,

G.&J. Robinson, Liverpool—W. Hunter, Edinburgh, and Hunt and Clarke, London, 1828.

Akers, G. A. *Phonological Variation in the Jamaican Continuum*. Ann Arbor: Karoma Publishers, Inc., 1981.

Bailey, B. L. *Jamaican Creole Syntax: A Transformational Approach*. London: Cambridge University Press, 1966.

Barclay, A. *A Practical View of the Present State of Slavery in the West Indies: or, An examination of Mr. Stephen's "Slavery of the British West India Colonies," containing more particularly an account of the actual condition of the Negroes in Jamaica: with observations on the decrease of the slaves since the abolition of the slave trade, and on the probable effects of legislative emancipation: also, strictures on the Edinburgh Review, and on the pamphlets of Mr. Cooper and Mr. Bickell*, second edition. London: Smith, Elder, & Co., 1827.

Beckford, G. *Persistent Poverty: Underdevelopment in Plantation Economies of the Third World*. New York: Oxford University Press, 1972.

Beckles, H. McD. *White Servitude and Black Slavery in Barbados, 1627—1715*. Knoxville: University of Tennessee Press, 1989.

Beckles, H. McD. "A 'Riotous and Unruly Lot': Irish Indentured Servants and Freemen in the English West Indies, 1644—1713." *Caribbean Slavery in the Atlantic World: A Student Reader*. Edited by Verene Shepherd and Hilary McD. Beckles. Kingston: Ian Randle Publishers; Princeton: Markus Wiener Publishers; Oxford: James Currey Publishers, 2000, pp. 226—238.

Beckwith, M. W. *Black Roadways: A Study of Jamaica Folklore*. Chapel Hill: University of North Carolina Press; reprinted New York: Negro Universities Press, 1928; 1968.

Beckwith, M. W. *Jamaica Proverbs*. Poughkeepsie: Vassar College; reprinted New York: Negro Universities Press, 1925; 1970.

Besson, J. "Euro-Creole, Afro-Creole, Meso-Creole: Creolization and Ethnic Identity in West-Central Jamaica." *A Pepper-Pot of Cultures: Aspects of Creolization in the Caribbean*. Edited by Gordon Collier and Ulrich Fleischmann. Amsterdam; New York: Rodopi, 2003, pp. 169—188.

Bolland, O.N. "Creolisation and Creole Societies: A Cultural Nationalist View of Caribbean Social History." *Caribbean Quarterly*, Vol. 44, Nos. 1&2, March-June, 1998, pp. 1—32.

Boucher, P. *Cannibal Encounters: Europeans and the Island Caribs, 1492—1763*. Baltimore: Johns Hopkins University Press, 1992.

Brathwaite, E. *The Development of Creole Society in Jamaica, 1770—1820*. Oxford: Clarendon Press, 1971.

Brathwaite, E. *Contradictory Omens: Cultural Diversity and Integration in the Caribbean*. Mona: Savacou Publications, 1974.

Brathwaite, K. *The Arrivants: A New World Triology*. Oxford: Oxford University Press, 1973; 2000.

Bryan, B. "Some Correspondences between West African and Jamaican Creole Speakers in Learning Standard English." *Studies in Caribbean Language II: Papers from the Ninth Biennial Conference of the Society of Caribbean Linguistics, 1992*. Edited by Pauline Christie et. al. St. Augustine, Trinidad: Society for Caribbean Linguistics, 1998, pp. 100—111.

Cassidy, F. G. *Jamaica Talk: Three Hundred Years of the English Language in Jamaica*, third edition. Jamaica, Barbados, Trinidad and Tobago: University of the West Indies Press, 2007.

Christie, P. (ed.) *Due Respect: Papers on English and English-Related Creoles in the Caribbean in Honour of Professor Robert Le Page*. Jamaica: University of the West Indies Press, 2001.

Christie, P., Lalla, B., Pollard, V., and Carrington, L. (eds). *Studies in Caribbean Language II: Papers from the Ninth Biennial Conference of the Society for Caribbean Linguists*. Trinidad: School of Education, University of the West Indies, St. Augustine, 1998.

Collier G. and Fleischmann, U. (eds). *A Pepper-Pot of Cultures: Aspects of Creolization in the Caribbean*. Amsterdam; New York: Rodopi, 2003.

Cooper, T. *Facts Illustrative of the Conditions of the Negro Slaves in Jamaica, with Notes and an Appendix*. London: G. Smallfield, 1824.

Dalphinis, M. *Caribbean & African Languages: Social History, Language, Literature and Education*. London: Karia Press, 1985.

Devonish, H. *Language and Liberation: Creole Language Politics in the Caribbean.* London: Karia Press, 1986.

Goveia, E. V. *Slave Society in the British Leeward Islands at the End of the Eighteenth Century.* Westport, Conn.: Greenwood Press, 1965; 1980.

Hay, R.W. *Jamaica: Return to an Address to His Majesty, dated 25th July 1832; for, Copy of all Correspondence relative to the Punishment of Two Female Slaves belonging to Mr. Jackson, Custos of Port Royal, and the Proceedings held theron.* Colonial Department, Downing-street, 15 August 1832 (Mr. Burge), Ordered, by The House of Commons, to be Printed 16th August 1832.

Higman, B.W. *Slave Population and Economy in Jamaica, 1807—1834*, second edition. Barbados, Jamaica, Trinidad and Tobago: The Press, University of the West Indies, 1995.

Higman, B.W. "The Sugar Revolution." *Economic History Review*, vol. LIII, no. 2, 2000, pp. 213–236.

Kouwenberg, S. (ed.) *Twice as Meaningful: Reduplication in Pidgins, Creoles and Other Contact Languages.* London: Battlebridge, 2003.

Lalla, B. and D'Costa, J. *Language in Exile: Three Hundred Years of Jamaican Creole.* Tuscaloosa: University of Alabama Press, 1990.

Lewis, M. G. *Journal of a West India Proprietor Kept During a Residence in the Island of Jamaica.* New York: Negro Universities Press, 1834; 1969.

Lewis, R. "Marcus Garvey and the Early Rastafarians: Continuity and Discontinuity." *Chanting Down Babylon: The Rastafari Reader.* Edited by Nathaniel Samuel Murrell, William David Spencer and Adrian Anthony McFarlane. Kingston: Ian Randle Publishers, 1998, pp. 145—158.

Long, E. *The History of Jamaica, or General Survey of the Ancient and Modern State of that Island: With Reflections on its Situations, Settlements, Inhabitants, Climate, Products, Commerce, Laws and Government*, vol. 3. London: T. Lowndes 1774; Kingston: Ian Randle Publishers, 2002; Montreal: McGill-Queen's University Press, 2003.

Lovejoy, P. E. "Identifying Enslaved Africans: Methodological and Conceptual Considerations in Studying the African Diaspora." *The "Nigerian" Hinterland and the African Diaspora: Proceedings of the*

UNESCO/SSHRCC Summer Institute. York University, Toronto, Canada, 1997.

Mintz, S. W. "The Caribbean as a Socio-Cultural Reality." *Peoples and Cultures of the Caribbean.* Edited by Michael M. Horowitz. Garden City, NY: Natural History Press, 1971, pp. 17—46.

Mintz, S. W. and Price, R. *The Birth of African-American Culture: An Anthropological Perspective.* Boston: Beacon Press, 1976; 1992.

Moore, B. L. and Johnson, M.A. *Neither Led nor Driven: Contesting British Cultural Imperialism in Jamaica, 1865–1920.* Kingston: University of the West Indies Press, 2004.

Moore, B. L. and Johnson, M.A. *"They do as they please": The Jamaican Struggle for Cultural Freedom after Morant Bay.* Kingston: University of the West Indies Press, 2011.

Morris, M. *Is English We Speaking and Other Essays.* Kingston: Ian Randle Publishers, 1999.

Nettleford, R. *Mirror, Mirror: Identity, Race and Protest in Jamaica.* Kingston: Collins and Sangster, 1970.

Nettleford, R. "Implications for Caribbean Development." *Caribbean Festival Arts.* Edited by J. Nunley and J. Bettleheim. Seattle: University of Washington Press, 1988.

Patterson, O. *The Sociology of Slavery: An Analysis of the Origins, Development and Structure of Negro Slave Society in Jamaica.* London: MacGibbon & Kee, 1967.

Patterson, O. "Context and Choice in Ethnic Allegiance: A Theoretical Framework and Caribbean Case Study." *Ethnicity Theory and Experience.* Edited by N. Glazer and D. P. Moynihan. Cambridge, Mass.: Harvard University Press, 1975.

Pietschmann, H. "Spanish Expansion in America, 1492 to c.1580." *New Societies: The Caribbean in the Long Sixteenth Century: UNESCO General History of the Caribbean,* volume II. Edited by P. C. Emmer. Paris: UNESCO Publishing; London, Oxford: Macmillan Caribbean, 1999, pp. 79—113.

Price, R. "The Miracle of Creolization: A Retrospective." *New West Indian Guide/Niewu West-Indische Gids*, vol. 75, No. 1 and 2, 2001, pp. 35—64.

Rampini, C. *Letters from Jamaica*. Edinburgh: Edmonston & Douglas, 1873.

Rouse, I. *The Tainos: Rise and Decline of the People who Greeted Columbus*. New Haven: Yale University Press, 1992.

Scott, D. "That Event, This Memory: Notes on the Anthropology of African Diasporas in the New World." *Diaspora*, vol. 1, no. 3, 1991, pp. 261—284.

Simmons-McDonald, H. and Robertson, I. (eds.) *Exploring the Boundaries of Caribbean Creole Languages*. Jamaica, Barbados, Trinidad and Tobago: University of the West Indies Press, 2006.

Smith, M.G. *The Plural Society in the British West Indies*. Berkeley: University of California Press, 1965.

Smith, M.G. *Culture, Race and Class in the Commonwealth Caribbean*. Mona: University of the West Indies, 1984.

Stewart, J. *An Account of Jamaica and Its Inhabitants by a Gentleman Long Resident in the West Indies*. London: Printed for Longman, Hurst, Rees, and Orme by G. Woodfall, Paternoster-Row, 1808.

The Jamaican Language Unit/Di Jamiekan Langwij Yuunit. *Writing Jamaican the Jamaican Way/Ou fi Rait Jamiekan*. Kingston: Arawak Publications, 2009.

Thornton, J. *Africa and Africans in the Making of the Atlantic World, 1400—1800*. Cambridge: Cambridge University Press, 1998.

Wright, P. (ed.). *Lady Nugent's Journal of Her Residence in Jamaica from 1801 to 1805*. Barbados, Jamaica, Trinidad and Tobago: University of the West Indies Press, 2002.

Zemon Davis, N. "Creole Languages and Their Uses: The Example of Colonial Suriname. *Historical Research*, vol. 82, no. 216, May 2009, pp. 268—284.

MOTHER TONGUE AS PRIMARY TEACHING TOOL
THE CASE OF JAMAICAN LANGUAGE: A COMMENTARY

Amah Harris

Jamaican is a Language. It is not a patois, i.e., a corruption of English. It is derived from many languages, with English and West African Languages as its base. Miss Lou often questioned the fact that when we (Caribbean people/Black people) originate something, it is said to be a "corruption of"—as in, English and the Jamaican language—but when they do it—referring to the colonizers—it is "derived from." For example, English is said to be derived from Germanic languages, including French and Latin, to name a few. The language came about because of the origins of English people, mixed with the languages of those who conquered them. This does not denigrate English; it simply establishes how so many languages the world over, are given birth. That holds true for the Jamaican Language (Harris, 2010).

Why is this topic even figuring here? It came about as the centre of a discussion on Language and Learning. The Jean Augustine Chair in Education, Community and Diaspora at York University, under the chairmanship of Dr. Carl James, hosted a "Celebration of Miss Lou: The Life and Legacy of The Honourable Louise Bennett-Coverley." The session took the form of a film, presentations by panelists, and dialogue with a participatory audience.

During her lifetime, Miss Lou stated emphatically her decision that Jamaican is a language and not a patois or a dialect. All her performances were delivered in the Jamaican Language. As far back as the 1960s and 1970s, there were energized debates at the University of the West Indies on the topic of Jamaican as a language. Miss Lou and some of the professors were on the *yes* side and there were other professors on the *no* side.

Miss Lou, as she is affectionately known to Jamaicans, Caribbeans, and people across the world who have had the privilege to experience her performances, lectures, and dialogues, was referred to as a Cultural Revolutionary and Cultural National Hero by Professor Aggrey Brown, then Director of the Caribbean Institute of Media and Communication (CARIMAC).[1] These are accolades and titles accepted and used by a large cross section of the general population, professors, artists and those who have had the experience of Miss Lou; these are terminologies for Miss Lou that I use myself. To speak in the Jamaican Language is revolutionary. It is defying the status quo. Right up to then and to some extent even now, not only in Jamaica but through the Caribbean, to speak in a language derived largely by the African component of the population and not use the colonizer's language as your accepted means of communication is taking a stand for a new definition of self; a definition 'by the people for the people.' It was a 'liberating of the mind from mental slavery' to borrow a statement from Bob Marley (Robert Nesta Marley OM). It was and is a political statement against the status quo. Using the colonizer's language as the primary language has been used as one of the determining factors to decide one's socio-economic status/social class, one's value in society, so for Miss Lou to take the stand that she did, especially in the era that she did, certainly placed her in the category of revolutionary and hero.

Why is that relevant here? Well, after the panelists had presented their papers, the floor was open for questions, comments, and discussion. The use of the Jamaican language as the primary vehicle of children's education took over the floor. Some members of the audience hotly disputed the use of Jamaican—being referred to as patois—as the primary tool for education in those areas of Jamaica where Jamaican, not English, is the mother tongue—the primary language in the household. What I understood from that argument, was that "standard English" was the language of commerce in the Jamaican market and the international market, therefore, not to use that language as the primary vehicle of education was to undermine the chances for the children in the Jamaican market and the world market.

That thought process, for me, did not zero in on the main groundings of the learning process, the child's development as the most productive person that child could be. The child is the centre of the learning process. That is indeed who is important. The focus should be, therefore, on what is the most effective tool to reach into the child's 'psyche' and arouse that interest and excitement in learning, to open up the child to 'absorb' learning. How does a teacher find a path to bringing a child to identify with the learning process? In *Mind in Society* (1978), Vygotsky argues that people are socio-cultural beings. These socio-cultural beings have their learning processes beginning in the womb and from birth, are socialized first by the home community, then the surrounding community, before entering the more structured learning arena that is the formalized school. Children begin their learning of concepts, thinking processes, self definition from the source—the home. In fact, many social scientists go as far as to say that first learning comes from the mother. To quote myself:

> [One] social scientist I wish to introduce into this socio-cultural exchange is Grumet (1988) who is a proponent of emergent education. In her work, "Conception, Contradiction, and Curriculum," she brought me to the point of registering this fact which I will share. Emergent education is vital in both the school and community setting. If it is not brought to the fore as a key element in developing pedagogy, the commitment to and depth of the learning process is weakened. It is weakened as an agent for developing a population who sees itself as transformers of society. That point resonated with me, especially as (I am) addressing the search for pedagogy that is effective in serving the diverse educational needs of diverse Peoples (Harris, 2010).

Grumet (1988) brings us into the vision of her theorizing by taking us from the process of conception through to birth and development, illustrating with clarity through day-to-day illustrations the interplay between subject and object in every action and thought process of human development. As a different approach to initiation into socio-cultural practice, therefore, Grumet guides us directly to the reproductive process which calls us into being. She walks us through the social interaction of mother and father, egg and sperm, out of which we are born into the world, and immediately move into that "external" biological and social interaction with caregivers.

Grumet's term, body knowledge, leads the way, like a torch shedding light, on how human beings make meaning of their own bodies and their environment through object resources; it is an Emergent Learning Process. This social scientist emphasizes the fact that from birth, we learn body knowledge, i.e., make meaning of our very bodies and our environment, through the "object" resource of our mothers. She posits that in the first few months, it is mainly the mother[2] who figures significantly in the child's life. If the culture or health so dictates, she breast-feeds the child. In a different situation, or culture, it is the caregiver other than the mother who bottle feeds the child, or in some cases, breast-feeds the child. It is through that personal interaction that the child learns the behaviour expected to call for feeding, have his clothes changed, and all his basic needs attended to. As we move into the next stage of development, the father begins to figure significantly as the added "object" resource with whom to interact and from whom to learn. Broad spectrums of caregivers in other areas of our lives play an important role as object resources in the process of our development. This progression of development is, indeed, bodies interacting with other bodies within specific contexts.

Grumet uses Stephen Strasser's concept of the dialogic phenomenology to explain that we only come to know ourselves through that "other" person. As Grumet aptly puts it:

> For Strasser, what is fundamental is the interpersonal basis for human experience, and so the primary question is no longer how one comes to constitute a world but how a world evolves for us. The very possibility of my thought of consciousness rests upon the presence of a "you" for whom "I" exist. My thought is a moment suspended between two primordial presences, the "you" who thinks me, and "you" whom I think (1988, p. 7).

So there is really no realization of the "I" without the "you." In fact, it is like getting one's initial sight of the world through the eyes of that significant other person. We learn the symbolic order, which defines for us the order of the world, through the eyes of the "you" responsible for us as caregivers. Concepts which we take for granted, like mother, father, sister, baby, along with the entire code of behaviour that accompanies those symbols, are socio-culturally taught to us. This occurs initially by caregivers and family culture, then the community culture, school culture,[3] and finally the society at large. Indeed, it is on the heels of these interpersonal—socio-cultural—interactions that the intrapersonal process takes place. That process of interpersonal followed by intrapersonal leads to the thinking process, i.e., our higher psychological functioning. Another human, therefore, is said not only to be responsible for one's first thought, but integral to one's first thought (Grumet, 1988, pp. 1—8). Within the context of recognizing the subject-object relationships, however, Grumet, along with the other social scientists referenced, are explicit through their choice of scenarios that subjects act with agency. They do not simply suck up learning without any sort of ability or capacity to act on discourses or take personal responsibility in sociocultural interactions (Harris, 2010, pp. 10—12).

My stand is with Vygotsky and Grumet. The child does receive early learning from the home, then community, then school. The child's first language, therefore, is the one most identified with. It is the mother tongue, the primary language. It is the one the child feels most comfortable with rather than stressed using. The primary language is, after all, the very essence of the child's being. Language is not merely a set of words. It is emotions, history, rhythms, melody couched in one's life experiences, the experiences of ancestors, the vision of how one interprets the world—a vision of SELF passed on through those with whom one first comes in contact, with whom one identifies prior to going to the formal school.

Research by UNESCO, Jim Cummins, Ellen Bialystok, Rezvan Noormohammadi (and the list goes on), has proven that learning in one's mother tongue brings the most rewarding results. The child brings her initial processes of thinking, working through concepts, solving problems with her into the more formal space of the classroom. If these are rejected, deemed unacceptable, wrong—because that is how it will appear when her language is rejected—what happens to her psychological stability?! Am I saying, "Don't teach the child English or the colonizer's language for that specific country?" No. The child should be taught that language as a second language in which she can be fluent, while her mother tongue is valued as the primary teaching vehicle. If the processes which she brings with her from home are nurtured, respected, valued, it opens up the child to learning. She can identify with the learning process. She has a foundation of stability to use as a springboard into "learning success."

"Oh! It's English, not Jamaican, Mamma!" What, then? Isn't an environment for learning supposed to be a welcoming space rather than a stressful place? Isn't it supposed to build up the child's confidence, a key ingredient for successful learning? Isn't it supposed to be an environment where a child is free to think "freely" and express herself in an atmosphere of acceptance?!

However, when a child first goes to school, which is supposed to be a welcoming, friendly, safe space for learning, and the teacher begins to speak in a language foreign to her, foreign to those who have nurtured her from birth, how does that make her feel?! Welcomed?! When a child is told that the language which is "her" is actually her not speaking "properly,"—in fact, that it is not a language at all, but a patois i.e., less than, wrong, unacceptable in the world out there, a CORRUPTION OF—has the teacher not just devalued the child in the child's eyes? Devalued the child's definition of self?! Has her culture not been measured as less than, not as good as?! And which language is the child to speak as the "right" language? Is it not the language originated by the people who don't look like her, but by those people she sees on social media or TV? What does that tell her about herself? What does that do to the child's definition of self? Does that mean that to be successful she needs to be more like them? Does that not denigrate the parents, the grandparents, relatives, community, the culture that the child has used to define the self? What does that do to the child's psychology? Doesn't that leave her with a psychological dislocation?!

Endnotes

1 Professor Aggrey Brown served as director of the Caribbean Institute of Media and Communication (CARIMAC) between 1979 and 2002 and also as Dean of the Faculty of Humanities and Education at the University of the West Indies (Mona, Jamaica). See Hopeton Dunn, "Tribute to the late Professor Aggrey Brown," *Critical Arts: South-North Cultural and Media Studies*, Vol. 26, No. 1, 2012: 1-2. CARIMAC was established in 1974 "out of research by the United Nations Economic, Scientific and Cultural Organization (UNESCO) and a subsequent

partnership between the University of the West Indies and the Friedrich Ebert Stiftung Foundation." https://www.carimac.com/about-us/

2   In more and more cases in today's world, a father has become the initial caregiver of the child.

3   In many cultures where schools are not available, the society plays an earlier role in the child's development.

References

Ball, J. *Mother Tongue Instruction in Early Childhood Education: A Selected Bibliography.* Paris: UNESCO, 2010.

Bialystok, E. *Communication Strategies: A Psychological Analysis of Second-Language Use.* Oxford, UK; Cambridge, Mass.: B. Blackwell, 1990.

Bialystok, E. *Bilingualism in Development: Language, Literacy, and Cognition.* Cambridge, U.K.; New York: Cambridge University Press, 2001.

Brown, A. *Color, Class and Politics in Jamaica.* New Brunswick, New Jersey: Transaction Books, 1979.

Cummins, J. *Language, Power and Pedagogy: Bilingual Children in the Crossfire.* Clevedon, Buffalo: Multilingual Matters, 2000.

Cummins, J. *Bilingualism and Special Education: Issues in Assessment and Pedagogy* Clevedon, Buffalo: Multilingual Matters, 1984.

Cummins, J. *Empowering Minority Students.* Sacramento: California Association for Bilingual Education, 1989.

Dunn, H. "Tribute to the Late Professor Aggrey Brown." *Critical Arts: South-North Cultural and Media Studies,* vol. 26, no. 1, 2012, pp. 1—2.

Grumet, M. R. "Conception, Contradiction and Curriculum." *Bitter Milk: Women and Teaching.* Amherst: University of Massachusetts Press, 1988, pp. 3—30.

Harris, A.B.T. "Drama as Pedagogy: Addressing Diverse Needs in Shared Learning Spaces." M.Ed., Unpublished manuscript, York University, Ontario, Canada, 2010.

Noormohammadi, R. "Mother Tongue, a Necessary Step to Intellectual Development." *Journal of Pan-Pacific Association of Applied Linguistics,* vol. 12, 2008, pp. 25—36.

UNESCO. "The Use of Vernacular Languages in Education." *Monographs on Foundations of Education*, no. 8. Paris: UNESCO, 1953.

UNESCO Bangkok. *Advocacy Brief on Mother Tongue-based Teaching and Education for Girls*. Bangkok: UNESCO, 2005.

UNESCO. *Educational Equity for Children from Diverse Backgrounds: Mother Tongue-based Bilingual or Multilingual Education in the Early Years: Literature Review*. Paris: UNESCO, 2010.

Vygotsky, L. S. *Mind in Society: The Development of Higher Psychological Processes*. Edited by Michael Cole, Vera John-Steiner, Sylvia Scribner, Ellen Souberman. Chicago: Harvard University Press, 1978.

PATWA DISCOURSE:
THE PERSPECTIVE OF TWO EDUCATORS' RELATIONSHIP TO AND USE OF JAMAICAN LANGUAGE

Pamella Archer and Everton Cummings

Introduction

Everton: I gladly accepted the invitation to write a reflective paper that would focus on my relationship to Jamaican language. In this paper, I could write about what I had observed, experienced, and critically thought about as a Black Canadian teacher who had taught Jamaican students in both Jamaica and Canada for the past thirty-one years. This being a reflective paper, I assumed that I would not have to slavishly follow the conventions of scholarly writing. And for this reason, I decided to exercise a certain casual creativity and include the experiences and ideas of others who were also thinking about Jamaican discourse and its place in education.

In thinking about how to include the voice of others, the idea of reflective dialogue came to mind. This is when I remembered a book I had read called *Breaking Bread: Insurgent Black Intellectual Life* (hooks and West, 1991), a publication which featured bell hooks and Cornel West addressing issues of race and class in a dialogical manner. This approach was not only introspective and informative, but a unique and creative form of scholarly writing. This book was the inspiration for taking a similar approach and inviting another voice to reflect on the topic of Jamaican language and schooling.

In search of another voice, I considered my graduate students from the School of Education at the University of the West Indies (UWI) and the lively class discussions we engaged in about teaching, learning, and Jamaican schooling. During several classes, we discussed the advantages and disadvantages of including certain aspects of Jamaican culture in the school curriculum. The issue regarding the use of Patwa in schools was the moot topic on several occasions. It was at this point that Pamella, a Masters' student in the Teacher Development programme, and an active participant in these class discussions, came to mind. I remember that Pam was very introspective about the topic of Jamaican culture, and she was equally as critical, comprehensive, and coherent about it in her writing. Her writing also possessed a relaxed and reflective tone, and it was easy to hear the "writer's voice" in her work. While imagining this paper, it was her narrative that I believed would provide an interesting and informative perspective in comparison to my mine. Her experience as a student, teacher, and citizen qualified her as the right candidate to speak on the topic of indigenous language and Jamaican schooling. Together, our thoughts dialogically intertwined would present how each of us related with the Jamaican language, revealing what we agreed and disagreed with in respect to the role of Patwa in the Jamaican classroom and society.

I was grateful when Pam accepted my invitation to share her views in writing. There was a sense of excitement knowing that reflections on the relationship with the Jamaican language would come from two different lived experiences. On one hand, the perspective of a Canadian-born male teacher of Jamaican parentage, and on the other a Jamaican-born female teacher. In the following sections, we talk about the relationship we have had with Patwa in our lives, and the role we have seen it play in our profession.

PATWA INNA WI LIFE

So yuh a de man, me hear bout!
Ah yuh dem seh dah teck
Whole heap a English oat seh dat
Yuh gwine kill dialec!

Meck me get it straight, Mas Charlie,
For me no quite understand —

> Yuh gwine kill all English dialec
> Or jus Jamaica one? (Bennett, 1982, p. 4).

Everton: Pam, before we start talking about Jamaican language, tell me a little bit about yourself.

Pam: I am a born Jamaican, a graduate of the primary, secondary, and tertiary school systems, and Social Science teacher for twenty-six years at a rural high school. I received my teacher training at Mico University College, Mico Teachers' College at the time, specializing in Geography and Social Studies. I completed my undergraduate and postgraduate studies at UWI in International Relations and Teacher Education respectively. I have always had a passion for the performing arts, especially speech and drama. I also enjoy writing which has been fueled by my love for reading. What about yourself?

Everton: I was born in Canada, the son Jamaican parents who had migrated to Toronto in the late 50s. I completed all of my primary and secondary schooling, and most of my higher education in Canada. I started teaching in Jamaica when I was offered a position at a local traditional high school. I also completed my teacher certification at the UWI before returning to Canada to teach for ten years in the elementary (junior high) system. My undergraduate qualifications are in Geography and Physical Health Education, and these have been my teaching subjects for most of my career. My post-graduate areas of interest are in race, class, curriculum, teaching and learning, with a special emphasis on teacher education and development. Interestingly, throughout my life, whether as a student or a teacher, in Canada or Jamaica, I have always been intricately connected to my Jamaican heritage. My parents believed that this close relationship started from the year and a half that I spent in the country, as a baby living with Grandma.

Pam: Doc, having listened to you in class, you do seem to have a special attachment to Jamaica.

Everton: Pam, you know, from since I can remember, I have been in love with the Jamaican part of my cultural identity. Audley and Carmen Cummings's culture, both born and proud Jamaicans. I've loved the music, food, dance, fashion, history, theatre, extended family, lifestyle, place, and the people (both noble and notorious). My parents encouraged my exposure to and interaction with the place they affectionately called "home." Their home was my home, although I was not physically "from there." I think my parents had good reason to keep my siblings and me in touch with Jamdown from childhood days.[1] It gave us a sense of belonging to a place where there was family, people, and things that we enjoyed and could identify with. Yes, Canada was also home, but I believe they knew that not all that is Canadian is something we could identify with. This grounding had a significant impact on who I am today—it has determined how and where I live, what I like to do, and with whom I have formed my social and professional relationships. It has factored greatly in terms of my identity and comfort with who I am. You seem to be a proud Jamaican. Are you?

Pam: I am extremely proud to be Jamaican, and equally fascinated with my culture. You seem to have been especially intrigued with the dialect, the Patwa. Why?

Everton: I've always been fascinated and in awe of Jamaican language aka creole, Patwa, "real ting" Jamaica talk.[2] I loved its expressiveness, economy with words, popular phrases, unique syntax, and clarity of meaning, particularly among fellow "Yardies."[3] I loved the drama, facial and body expressions, wit, and accent that accompanied the words that were used to communicate the thoughts, feelings, answers, questions, jokes, riddles, proverbs, and beliefs to a bredren/sistren[4] or an attentive audience. I really wished I could speak it better. When Jamaicans speak their language, there is a certain ease, poetry, fluency, intelligence, an "I get it," comfort, joy, and pride among those who were delivering the message and those receiving. What a joy it was to watch and listen to you and your classmates communicate in Patwa before and after class about schoolwork or other current events, or the enjoyment and ease with which you switched between SJE [Standard Jamaican English] and JC [Jamaican Creole] while roleplaying those pre-observation interviews. I think nervousness may have been the bigger enemy for some.

Pam: Doctor C, that's an interesting perspective, and it is not unusual to find non-Jamaicans who are in awe of the language . . . always trying to imitate the accent or adopting some of the common phrases. However, for some of us who were born and raised in Jamaica, the use of Jamaican Creole (JC) as the native tongue is not appreciated. Through the eyes of the average Jamaican, anything "foreign" [generally, a more developed nation] has always been seen as ideal. However, this perception is slowly changing with the advent of technology, since the rise of the Information Age. For a long time, any person, place, or thing "from foreign" was seen in a more favourable light, and the use of the English language was no different. The person who uses Standard Jamaican English (SJE) is usually given more prominence, deemed intelligent, and is generally seen as "better off" in terms of social class (Wassink, 1999, as cited in Frank, 2010). The Jamaican who converses using creole is . . . often criticized for "speaking badly," is deemed unintelligent, and is usually associated with the poor and underclass in the society (Evans, 2006).

Everton: Oh, this may explain why my parents did not speak much Patwa. Dad would "bruk out" every so often, and with "mother dear" Creole was basically non-existent. They were of the late-colonial, pre-independence, professional, "uptown people," who were socialized to accept the superiority, correctness, and value of the colonizer's English, aka the "good good" English, the language of kings and queens, and the ticket to upward mobility and success. I am referring to the Jamaican upper class who, in order to maintain a privileged status and identity with the more prestigious European culture, would have made sure to have a better command of SJE than those with lower income (Frank, 2010).

Pam: That's right. Your parents would have embraced the "good good" official English language, but at the same time not totally abandon their Jamaican talk—well, your daddy, anyway. This may be explained knowing that the native tongue Jamaican Creole (JC), though discredited in some circles, is extensively used in all spheres of Jamaican life. From the House of Parliament, where it is used as political satire, to the street corner, where it plays out as good-natured banter among the ordinary man. The use of JC varies as it relates to where, what, why, how, and to whom it is being directed. Such is the nature of this eclectic parlance.

Everton: So it would appear that the JC is okay if tempered and in its place. Restricted to certain times and places because it cannot achieve for someone what I suspect many Jamaicans would want—success, "move up inna life!" My upbringing in Canadian society, and eventual career path into education, ensured that I was well-acquainted and well-versed in Standard English (SE). I've noticed, especially in Jamaican society, or at a Jamaican gathering in Toronto, appreciation and acceptance of SE in certain circles. The praise I received for my strong command of it served to establish me as distinguished, sophisticated, and intelligent. Among many Jamaicans, I suspect they see me as someone who "come affa good table."[5] Surprisingly, I don't think I am even that well-versed in the SE. Regardless, I still love my Jamaican Patwa and the pleasure it brings when delivered at its best and in its most authentic form, by friends and family, and in music, theatre, and literature. I love to hear it, understand it (95% of the time), and speak it sometimes. I speak in Patwa to myself a lot! I am proud of it! The influence it has had on popular culture—"irie," "yeah mon," "real ting," "a dis yu a dis mi."[6] Oh, how I love to listen to Miss Lou "chat bout" *Colonization in Reverse*, or Shawt Mon boastfully describe in vivid detail the three goals he scored against the "Ey-talian" soccer (football) team.

Pam: So Doc, what brought you to this point—the point where you are interested in talking about Jamaican language?

Everton: Pam, I remember sitting at Carl James's dining table, casually discussing one of our favorite topics—education in Jamaica. Prof and I talked about all sorts of educational issues, from student achievement to reform. One Sunday, we were discussing teaching and learning, and how Jamaica, like much of the world, was directing its teachers to use more student-centered educational strategies as the preferred alternative to teacher-centered approaches. Our chat raised some interesting questions and ideas, which eventually evolved into co-authored article for the *Caribbean Journal in Education* (UWI). In the paper, we focused on the practicality of constructivist pedagogy within the Jamaican school system and argued that implementing and sustaining constructivist modes of teaching and learning in Jamaican schools could be a challenge given the persistence of teacher-centered pedagogy, the hesitation to use indigenous language (Patwa/Jamaican Creole), standardized testing, and overcrowded and under-resourced classrooms (Cummings and James, 2014). In the article, we focused on how the resistance to using indigenous language (Patwa) in Jamaican classrooms contradicted the principles of constructivist teaching and limited the opportunities for the language to support successful student learning and achievement (Cummings and James, 2014).

Recently, Carl invited me to write another article for this book which would focus on the Jamaican language, particularly Patwa. He suggested that the paper could be an elaboration of the indigenous language issue we had raised in the *Caribbean Journal of Education* (CJE) article but should also include my reflections regarding how I have experienced and related to the use of the Jamaican language in my life and teaching. It was easy to accept Carl's offer because studying the role that culture plays in teaching and learning is, in my opinion, intriguing and significant. I also liked the idea. I had many thoughts on the issue, and I looked forward to sharing these within the context of the publication.

Pam: But Doctor C., I noticed your slight use of Patwa earlier. Did you speak it at home in Canada, among your siblings? How did you come to appreciate it when one parent used it sparingly, and the other hardly at all?

Everton: Well, despite my middle-class upbringing and consistent use of SE, my parents never scolded or reprimanded my siblings or me for our frequent and unabashed expressions of Jamaican-ness, particularly the use of Patwa. However, although I have my affection for Patwa and the freedom to express it if I want, it has been the main aspect of Jamaican culture that I wish I had a better command of, and ability to use in social and educational spaces where the indigenous language could offer a clear and convincing explanation of what happened, was happening, or would happen. "Please don't do that," just doesn't seem to send the same message as "yu nu fi dweet!" What further contributed to my quandary was the fact that I looked, dressed, ate like a Jamaican, and understood Jamaican society and culture. However, when I spoke, it was a clear indication of not being from here, and likely from the upper echelons of Jamaican society where the language of the masses was not always spoken. I am sure this left many wondering, "Who im be?" and "Who a di speakie spokie mon?"[7] So Pam, what about you? How have you negotiated the use of your extremely popular, yet unofficial language? Was it accepted and used in your home? What about school?

Pam: Well, for me, growing up in a lower middle-class household, Patwa was spoken at home and in other informal settings. However, as children, we were expected to use SJE in more formal settings such as school and church, mainly when addressing someone in authority. Within my household, my mother was more relaxed with regards to our use of Patwa. My father, however, was adamant that certain Patwa terms should not be used. For example, we had to say, "Come ere" instead of, "Come yah."[8] (Note that we could drop the "h" sound). For "daddy dearest," although he did not speak SJE, certain JC terms were perceived as vulgar, and as such were forbidden in the Archer household. As a high school student in the 1980s, the use of JC in the school setting was frowned upon. We would not dare converse with our teachers using JC, as this was seen as unintelligent. As a result, our use of Patwa while at school was relegated to our chit-chat sessions as students outside of class time. I recall an occasion when a group of female students was sharing a joke among themselves. As the air erupted with their boisterous laughter, they were instantly admonished by the principal. "Laugh in English, girls!" was his vehement warning—a comment which triggered giggles from those of us within earshot of the exchange as we blankly stared at each other, musing, "How do you laugh in English?" As an impressionable fifteen-year-old then, my interpretation was that subdued laughter is associated with the English language, and anything contrary was unacceptable—in essence, the girls were laughing in Patwa. I believe this is what Frank (2010) is referring to when he states that "educational practice has affected the perception of JC negatively. During school classes, the use of Jamaican Creole is prohibited and often corrected when it emerges. Hence, students start to perceive JC as inferior to SJE" (p. 2).

Everton: That's funny. Imagine that—even laughter should be delivered in the vernacular of the colonizer. Pam, why doesn't JC get more respect? If it is used in all spheres of life—from the man on the street to the politician in parliament—why is it not widely accepted as an official language?

Pam: Doc, there are many rationalizations as to why Patwa is not an official language in Jamaica, despite numerous calls for its status to be upgraded. It may be as a result of the way the language is structured, in addition to our disdain for anything not aligned to "foreign," as I alluded earlier. Of note is the fact that JC is more commonly spoken than it is written. This is presumably because it has no conventional spelling, and the syntax associated with JC is informally learnt rather than taught. Although all Jamaicans understand Patwa, it is more commonly used among persons of the lower social class. With the use of the "Queen's English" being largely associated with high culture and prominence, JC is looked on as the language of the underclass, in many regards. Remember, SJE is an indication of high status and is prestigious in official domains, whereas JC is perceived as a degraded version of English, and representative of the lower class (Wassink, 1999, as cited in Frank, 2010).

Everton: Do you think this disdain for Patwa might be changing? Or has it changed?

Pam: To some extent, it has changed. For one, I have noticed that persons who use both Jamaican Creole and Standard Jamaican English fluently are given equal prominence and "respect" (Frank, 2010). For instance, Jamaican media personalities such as Mutabaruka[9] and Miss Kitty[10] are favoured by many Jamaicans usually because of their extensive use of JC in their on-air broadcasts. Their ability to fuse both English and Patwa with ease makes their programme content fun and relatable to the average Jamaican. In this way, they are able to reach the common man, as they are seen as knowledgeable, and at the same time, as ordinary Jamaicans. Consequently, their perspectives are often respected and taken as "gospel," and their authority on certain matters, more often than not, goes unquestioned.

Jamaican Creole is also used in spheres of Jamaican life where the use of Standard Jamaican English would have been the norm. Oftentimes, this is done to garner public interest or to appeal to the average Jamaican. A case in point is with the recent COVID-19 health crisis, where the catchphrase "Tan a yu yaad" became the mantra to urge Jamaicans to stay at home in order to limit the spread of the coronavirus. The phrase quickly became "viral" as various sectors of the society adopted its use. Government and health officials used it to appeal to the citizenry, while the average man used it as part of everyday banter (sometimes in jest). In such an instance, the impactful and dynamic use of the JC cannot go unnoticed. Given that the catchphrase was expressed in Patwa—"Tan a yu yaad"—as opposed to "Please stay at home," the message resonated well with the Jamaican populace mainly because it was communicated in the language of the people.

Everton: Yes, I too have noticed greater use and acceptance of Patwa. The Bigga soft drink commercials pre-2010, News Talks "News in a di Jamaica Language," Carolyn Cooper's column in the *Daily Gleaner*, and the King James Version of the *Bible* in Patwa are indicators for me that "Patwa a get nuff respec'!"[11] Not to mention the ongoing debate regarding the use of JC in schools and teaching and learning.

WHA' BOUT PATWA INNA SCHOOL?

Everton: Pam, we are both educators, so it is only natural that we talk about the role that JC can play in our classrooms. Let's talk about JC as a positive or negative factor where teaching and learning are concerned. It would seem that almost yearly, there are writers who post their views in one of the local papers on the topic of the use of JC in schools (Tucker, 2012; Moyston, 2018; Cooper, 2019; Roberts, 2019). What are your thoughts?

Pam: Well, Doc, I am taking somewhat of a middle ground. My stance is based mainly on my experience with the use of Patwa in the classroom, both as a student and as a teacher. I remember as a student, my favourite literature texts were those with a Jamaican or West Indian storyline (Shakespeare was my anathema). Sadly, West Indian novels were not commonly used as texts at that time. The texts were usually British, and there was a definite shortage of Jamaican printed literature, which I believe caused a form of cultural alienation (Frank, 2010). Notwithstanding, English Literature was one of my favourite subjects. For the most part, the literature texts which had settings and storylines outside of the Caribbean were largely unappealing, and this held true for my classmates as well. As a student, the best literature classes were those in which the novel or poem included JC.

To this day I still reminisce on the enthusiasm I felt when we read *Escape to Last Man's Peak* by Jean D'Costa (1975), as a literature text in my second year of high school. The story chronicles the journey of a group of Jamaican orphans travelling on foot from Spanish Town to Trelawny after the Matron at their orphanage died from pneumonia. I remember thinking, *Finally! A Jamaican story*. Even more thrilling was the fact that the characters were just about the same age as I was— some even had names I could relate to (I'll never forget Wuss Wuss)— and the pride I felt when places I knew were mentioned in the story. I constantly volunteered to read aloud from the text, partly because I was among the few in my class with the ability to read JC fluently. As students, we enjoyed those particular literature classes especially because of the use of Patwa.

Literature classes also entailed analysis of poems, and like Jamaican stories, poems with the Jamaican vernacular were our favourites to be recited and analysed. We always enjoyed reviewing and reciting poems written by Louise Bennett-Coverley (Miss Lou), as they were written in the Jamaican language which resonated with who we were and affirmed our cultural identity. Besides the comedic undertone of Miss Lou's poems, as children we anticipated dressing the part and portraying the actions and gestures of the characters depicted. But best of all, we would be expressing ourselves in the language we were most comfortable with—Patwa—and that spoke volumes.

Everton: That's very interesting. As you know, I was schooled in Canada, and although I attended schools with a significant representation of Jamaican students, there was never any need or reason to speak in the Jamaican language. This was reserved for hanging out in the lunchroom, parties, and sporting events. Interestingly, regardless of whether you were Canadian-born, or from another Caribbean island, or the continent of Africa, among the crew, Jamaican Patwa—or should I say, "broken" Jamaican Patwa—was the language spoken. But I can share my thoughts about the use of the language in the Jamaican classroom, from the perspective of a teacher.

Throughout my years as a teacher, practising predominantly in Jamaican schools, or Canadian schools with a high percentage of Jamaican students, I have seen the benefits of the use of Jamaican Creole. I have witnessed the participation, engagement, understanding, pride, and confidence it garners and inspires when it is used strategically and authentically. I believe that the positive effects far outweigh the negative when students are permitted to use JC in the classroom. I believe speaking in Patwa has motivated my students, reduced their anxiety about committing mistakes, and assisted them with the comprehension of content, issues, and concepts (Frank, 2010). I believe it was Miss Lou who said "there are many things which are best said in the language of the common man" (Bennett and Morris, 1982, p. xiii). Notwithstanding, the confidence of students will develop if they can communicate proficiently in the Queen's English. To speak SJE well is an achievement and a great esteem booster. However, we should not overlook the use of Patwa as a means to enhancing enjoyment, understanding, esteem building, and bilingualism in the Jamaican classroom.

Interestingly, to this day, I believe my imperfection with speaking the Jamaican Creole fluently and authentically has inhibited me from achieving some incredibly good teaching. For example, as a teacher who endorses drama and roleplay as engaging and effective strategies for teaching and learning, I wished I could take on the persona of Mas Joe to explain the importance of subsistence farming, or Leighton the farmworker to describe the push and pull factors that influence migration. Fortunately, I compensated for this limitation by enthusiastically accepting and encouraging the use of JC by my students whenever they were required to describe or explain their knowledge and understanding. I do believe that can also contribute to student academic achievement if students are encouraged to use JC and to develop a positive attitude towards its use in their schooling (Evans, 2006; Ramsay, 2007). Even in their written assignments, where appropriate and necessary, I would embrace their expressions of the Jamaican dialect. In my opinion, it is authentic student-centered learning when the student is encouraged to communicate in the manner that will best describe or explain the answer, idea, or experience they need to articulate in order to reflect meaning (Frank, 2010)

Pam: I totally agree. As a teacher, I too have always advocated for the use of JC in the classroom (within limits, of course). In much the same way as Ramsay (2007) advocates the use of texts which use both SJE and JC to promote communicative competence in English in Jamaican students, I too believe that teachers and students stand more to gain if discretionary use of the native tongue is incorporated in the learning process. I also believe that JC can, and should, be used to advance the teaching and learning process in Jamaican schools, as it can help students to better understand and grasp content. It has been shown that some Jamaican students do experience difficulty understanding SJE, and as a result, reject or resist it as the main language of communication (McCourtie, 1998 as cited in Frank, 2010). I, too, have had numerous experiences as a teacher where, in my attempt to explain a concept using SJE, some students may have difficulty understanding my explanation. However, as soon as I explain the concept using JC, or use a scenario they can relate to, their response is almost always, "Ohhh! Mi understand now, miss." Consequently, as a teacher, I use JC as part of my teaching strategy to clarify concepts, to give relatable examples, to add variety, and to make my lessons fun. Storytelling is a huge part of Jamaica's culture, and as most Jamaicans are aware, sharing one's experience in Patwa makes it much more appealing to the listener. I have also found that some students participate more willingly in class activities when given the opportunity to express themselves in their native tongue. Students are most enthused when they are required to engage in activities that give them the option of using JC in dramatizations, poetry, and songs. Additionally, some students are better able to verbally express their knowledge or understanding of a concept using JC as opposed to writing or speaking using SJE (Evans, 2006). Just imagine, permitting students who have insecurities with the use of SE/SJE, to have their knowledge and understanding assessed using JC (McCourtie, 1998 as cited in Frank, 2010).

Yet another dimension to the use of JC in school and learning is utilizing the idiomatic, and at times, witty lyrical content of songs and poems written in Patwa to develop students' skills in analysis and interpretation. This can make reading pleasurable, interesting, understandable, and culturally relevant (Frank, 2010). On this basis, reggae music, which appeals to many Jamaican youths, is the ideal way to garner interest in English Language and Literature (especially for boys, who are usually less interested in these subjects). Interpreting the lyrical content of popular songs will undoubtedly pique the interest of students, and at the same time, provide the requisite content for topics in English Language lessons, such as Figures of Speech. JC constitutes "an immense range of ironic, satiric, parodic, pathetic, and melodramatic language in which metaphor and word games [can] flourish" (D'Costa, 1992, as cited in Frank, 2010). The lyrics of "Smile Jamaica" sung by Chronixx, and "Blood Money" sung by Protoje, readily come to mind.

> . . . She [Jamaica] have a rich history
> A beautiful woman with the sweetest gifts
> Beautiful sunrise and an evening kiss
> Have nice sunset on the evening seas
> But she tell me seh she tyad
> Tyad a di exploits and di liars . . . (Chronixx, 2013).

> . . . Inna Jamaica say yu status a yu salary
> Man deh road a carry one whole heap a felony
> But dem have a family a boost up i economy so . . .
> Police cancel operation,
> 'Cause no real badman nah go station,
> Now if you check di situation,
> A blood money run the nation . . . (Protoje, 2017).

Everton: I hear you saying use the JC, but "within limits, of course." What type of limits are you referring to?

Pam: While I agree that JC should be used in the learning process, by no means am I touting for its invariable use in the classroom, as such a move would seem specious based on number of variables relating to education in general, and Jamaica's education system in particular. Firstly, English is the official language of communication in Jamaica, and in preparing global citizens, it is only practical that students be fluent in the most universally acceptable language. Secondly, students' assessments, both internally and externally, are written in Standard English. Correspondingly, their responses are expected to be in Standard English. Thirdly, the linguistic nuances associated with JC may create difficulties with its use in the written form, as there are variations in pronunciations and spelling for particular words. This lack of coherence could create confusion. JC would need to be standardized if it is to be used as a language of instruction (Frank, 2010).

Everton: So you don't agree with Jamaican creole being included in the school curriculum?

Pam: The way I see it, JC is implicit to our socialization as natives. Therefore, including the language as a subject to be taught at the primary and secondary levels would certainly be tantamount to "taking sand to the beach." It would be logical, however, to study the semantics and phonology of JC at the tertiary level. This would be of value to the education system as understanding the JC lexicon can provide greater insight into the history of the language, and serve as a catalyst for teaching subject matter, especially English Language. Hence, student-teachers could be trained to effectively use JC as a teaching technique in their respective subject areas. Studying JC at the tertiary level would also elicit a greater level of appreciation for the native language as a significant part of the island's culture.

We also need to consider the transitory nature of the language, especially in the use of "street" parlance. Wherein, some Patwa terms or phrases may reign for a limited period, as they are soon replaced by new ones. For example, "How yu a eyes mi suh?" meaning, "Why are you looking at me?" was popularly used in the 1990s. Today, the same question may be posed as "Why pree?" Such is the dynamics of the Jamaican vernacular. Additionally, the prevalent use of "street" parlance may create difficulties for students who may not be very articulate in the use of Standard English, yet are required to express themselves using SJE. Too much reliance on JC can interfere with a student's ability to speak when answering questions or writing assignments and examinations (Ramsay, 2008). I am often peeved at my students who, over the years, use the "street" term "bigga heads" to describe government officials or persons in authority. This highlights the need to create a balance in students' ability to express themselves using JC and Standard English. Therefore, inasmuch as I endorse (within reasonable limits) the use of JC in schools, care must be taken in how it is utilized in the teaching and learning process.

Everton: Good points, Pam, and I fully agree with some that you have made. I fully endorse the use of JC in classroom, but I also understand and believe that a strong command of SE is a benefit and necessary for those who must communicate and operate within both global and Jamaican societies. Like Glenn Tucker, a guest columnist in the *Daily Gleaner* (August 29, 2012), I too recognize that JC is a mere speck of all the languages spoken worldwide, and therefore not essential to doing business in the wider world. As noted by renowned Jamaican trade unionist Danny Roberts, in the *Daily Gleaner* (December 22, 2019), a total reliance on Patwa will certainly limit the Jamaican businessman, tradesman, academic or sports figure from being able ". . . to exceed beyond the shores of Jamaica's inner city . . ." Not even the musician of today can rely solely on "I an I" language. Jamaicans, to function effectively within global society, should be able to speak SE/SJE as best as possible since it is the predominant language for global communication (societies train their citizens to speak it). Speaking another predominant language or two (Spanish, French, Mandarin) would also serve as an advantage.

However, we should not dismiss the value of the "likkle" language of the Jamaican people, and the purpose it can especially serve for preschoolers, "schoolers," to express what they have learned and understand.[12] Schooling, and specifically learning, to be competent in SE should not be about exorcising the demons of Jamaican Patwa from the young citizen. There must be value in the language that most of the people speak. And as teachers, educators, we have a responsibility to include it in our classrooms and curriculum to enhance learning. Education policymakers should seriously consider the important role education can play in promoting JC as an acceptable form of communication for teaching and learning (Frank, 2010). I cannot support the idea of the high school or college graduate, or even the average citizen, speaking only JC. For me, the comfort is knowing that the Jamaican citizen is proud, versatile, intelligent, and bilingually competent enough to use the SE, SJE, JC, and any other language as means to highly effective and authentic/meaningful communication.

LAAS WORDS

Everton: Pam, it is reasonable to expect the debate regarding the value and role of Creole in the Jamaican society to continue. The topic will likely remain on the list of popular moot points such as same sex marriage, pro choice, the death penalty, and the Queen as Head of State. Having had our conversation, I believe it is safe to say that the Jamaican society—and by extension, its schools—are increasingly recognizing the normalness, importance, and pedagogical credence of the Creole language. At the same time, we also seem to agree that JC should not be without some limits, because there is also great value in being competent at communicating in SJE. We believe a strong case can be made for Jamaicans to be proficient in SJE, JC, and one other major language—therefore, developing a true bi/multilingual citizen.

Pam: Yes, Doc. And where better than our teacher education programmes to situate the pedagogy that will prepare the future teacher on how to enhance student learning and achievement through the effective inclusion of JC in his/her teaching. In Jamaica today, if you listen to what is said, and how it is said on the television, radio, chatroom, and classroom, it is not unreasonable to conclude that Patwa is assuming its rightful place and is gaining its "respec due." After all, there are things best said in the language of the people.

> Wen yuh done kill 'wit' an 'humour',
> Wen yuh kill 'variety',
> Yuh wi haffi fine a way fi kill
> Originality!
>
> An mine how yuh dah read dem English
> Book deh pon yuh shelf,
> For ef yuh drop a 'h' yuh mighta
> Haffi kill yuhself! (Bennett, 1982, 5).

Endnotes

1   "Jamdown" is a popular name for Jamaica.

2   "Real ting"—the real thing, authentic.

3   The term "Yardies" refers to Jamaicans, especially in diaspora and particularly in the United Kingdom, who are associated—and who associate themselves—with the conception of Jamaica as "Yard," that is, home.

4   "Bredren/sistren" refers to brethren/sistren or brother/sister, but the terms have wider application than labels given to relatives; they often refer to a friend or a person with whom one shares (significant aspects of) life.

5   "Come affa good table"—coming from a good home ("good table"), well brought up.

6   "Irie"—positive/good/wholesome; "yeah mon"—"yes man," a popular affirmation; "real ting"—the real thing; "a dis yu a dis mi"—"you are disrespecting me."

7   "Who im be?"—"Who is he?"; "Who a di speakie spokie mon?"—"Who is the man who is speaking in that fancy/affected way?"

8   "Come ere"/"Come yah"—"Come here."

9   Mutabaruka (Allan Hope) is a Rastafarian dub poet, author, actor and talk-show host in Jamaica. His creative works include contributions to fourteen albums—as well as the major hit "Every Time A Hear Di Soun"—four books of poetry, three films and two popular radio shows, *The Cutting Edge* and *Steppin' Razor* on Irie FM (see https://www.iriefm.net/?s=mutabaruka). In recognition of his cultural contributions, in 2016, Mutabaruka was awarded the Order of Distinction, Commander Class, by the Government of Jamaica.

10 Khadine "Miss Kitty" Hylton is a talk-show host on Nationwide FM in Jamaica. Referring to herself as "the Fluffy Diva," Miss Kitty—who is also a lawyer—is known for her direct commentary on a wide range of topics and current events on her show *Miss Kitty Live* (see https://nationwideradiojm.com/personalities/miss-kitty-live/; https://jamaica-gleaner.com/article/entertainment/20201217/it-was-always-part-my-purpose-miss-kitty-realises-childhood-dream).

11 "Patwa a get nuff respec'!"—"Patwa is getting a lot of respect!"

12 "Likkle"—little; "schoolers" is is popular term for school children.

References

Bennett, L. "Bans a Killin." *Selected Poems: Louise Bennett*. Edited by M. Morris. Jamaica: Sangster's Book Stores, 1982, 4—5.

Cooper, C. "Two Languages Are Better Than One," *Jamaica Gleaner*, October 2019.

Cummings, E.A.D. and James, C.E. "Constructivist Approaches to Education in Jamaica: Challenges, Limitations, and Possibilities." *Caribbean Journal of Education*, vol. 36, nos. 1 and 2, 2014, pp. 40–66.

Chronixx (Jamar Rolando McNaughton), "Smile Jamaica," 2013.

Evans, H. "Changing the Education Programme in Teacher Education." *Institute of Education Publication Series*. Edited by R. D. Down, vol. 2, 2006, pp. 23–43.

Frank, M. "Introducing Jamaican Creole into the Jamaican Educational Curriculum." *English Languages: History, Diaspora, Culture*, vol. 1, no. 1, 2010.

hooks, b. and West, C. *Breaking Bread: Insurgent Black intellectual life*. Boston: South End Press, 1991.

Moyston, L.E.A. "Language: The Great Neglect of School and Curriculum." *Jamaica Observer*, October 2018.

Protoje (Oje Ken Ollivierre), "Blood Money." *A Matter of Time*, 2017, 2018.

Ramsay, P. "The Use of Jamaican Literature in the Jamaican English Language Class: A Rationale and a Model." *Caribbean Journal of Education*, vol. 29, no. 2, 2008, pp. 241-289.

Roberts, D. "Patois: Figet It!" *Jamaica Observer*, December 22, 2019

Tucker, G. "Stop This Teach Patois Nonsense!" *Jamaica Gleaner*, August 29, 2012.

SCHOOL TEACHERS' LANGUAGE IDENTITIES IN JAMAICA:
THE DISCOURSES THEY CREATE AND RECREATE WITHIN WORKSHOP SPACE[1]

Yewande Lewis-Fokum, Michele Kennedy, Silvia Kouwenberg

Introduction

In 2015, two linguists and an educator met to discuss a project that would focus on improving the knowledge and pedagogical skills of primary school teachers in Jamaica with regard to teaching English in a Creole-speaking environment. This project is the Professional Development of Primary School Teachers (PDPST). It arose out of a concern over the marginal improvement in the results of the Grade IV Literacy Test, which is administered to children at the end of their fourth year in public primary schools, despite continued injections of resources by the Ministry of Education, Youth and Information. This concern was heightened by the mediocre English language passes at the secondary level in the Caribbean Examinations Council (CXC) exams, which students take at the end of four years of high school education. English is the language of instruction and assessment at all levels of the educational system, but for a majority of children who enter that educational system, it is not the home language and does not have a significant presence in their communities. Instead, Jamaican Creole (JC) performs those functions. Despite this linguistic reality, many elementary school pedagogies treat children as English speakers.

We felt, as a team, that we could support teachers by training them to become language-aware. This involved enhancing their knowledge about the roles of Jamaican English (JE) and Jamaican Creole (JC) in the society, and their understanding of the differences between the two languages, as well as introducing them to pedagogies that would allow them to make use of that knowledge. We felt that this would translate into better Language Arts (LA) teaching, which we contend, would in turn translate into better student performance in the various English language tests, indeed, into better performance across all subjects, given that their delivery is in English. This led to a series of workshops between October and December 2015, as a pilot at the University of the West Indies (UWI) campus, with forty Grades 3 and 4 teachers from eight schools in Kingston. This pilot later informed our model delivery of a series of workshops in February and March 2019. This second set of PDPST workshops was delivered to Grades 1 through 4 teachers from five schools across Jamaica, by graduates we had trained.

This chapter is informed by the second series of PDPST workshops, and is based on the teachers' language biographies and final workshop evaluations. We were interested in examining the language histories of the participants in the study. Also of interest was an examination of the attitudes towards the two languages which teachers brought with them, and how the workshops may have impacted these attitudes. Given the linguistic landscape in Jamaica, we thought it important to help the teachers to examine their own attitudes towards language, even before delving into the structures of each language. As such, our two guiding questions were:

> How did the teachers in the PDPST workshops describe themselves in terms of their language identities at the start of the workshops?
> In what ways did the teachers change some of their perceptions about JC/ JE based on the workshops?

In answering these two questions, we use critical discourse analysis (CDA) as both a method and a theory. As a method, we use "identity," one of Gee's (2005) seven building tasks to analyse the data with his preset questions as a guide. As a theory, we use a blend of Gee's discourse theory, along with Bryan's (2010) language-as-arena metaphors, and related literature to help interpret the teachers' language biographies and evaluations.

Critical Discourse Analysis and Bryan's (2010) Language-as-Arena Metaphors

CDA has been used in various educational studies to examine issues of power and identity (Rogers, 2004; Lewis-Fokum and Colvin, 2017; Lewis-Fokum, 2019). Gee (2005) reminds us that "language has a magical property: when we speak or write, we design what we have to say to fit the situation in which we are communicating. But at the same time, how we speak or write creates that very situation" (p. 10).

Gee (2014a) distinguishes between "discourse" and "Discourse." While *discourse* refers to "language in use," or "stretches of oral or written language" (p. 183) which can be analysed, *Discourse*, with a capital "D," includes more than text and can be defined as "ways of recognizing and getting recognized as certain sorts of who's doing certain sorts of what's" (p. 184). It is through language, whether written or spoken, along with other behaviours, that we get recognized as enacting particular socially constructed identities. As Gee (2014b) further explains, "[w]e use language to get recognized as taking on a certain identity or role, that is, to build an identity here and now" (p. 33). Within this chapter, we will be using the written discourses of the teachers' language biographies and final evaluations to examine and explain how they construct and re-construct their identities as competent teachers.

However, it was important for us to add a Caribbean lens to Gee's (2005) CDA by integrating local literature since this best reflects the language dynamics and language situation. Bryan's (2010) language metaphors were a good fit, as through language, identities are constructed. As she points out, "[e]veryone is interested in language and feels they have some contribution to offer on the matter. The topic assumes an even more charged relevance when it inevitably becomes wrapped up in issues about who we are and where we place ourselves (or are placed) in society" (p. ix). This idea echoes Gee's description of discourse as having the capacity to build or construct our identities.

Bryan's overarching metaphor is that language is an arena which can be viewed from three different angles. First, the arena can be viewed as the physical, social, or cultural spaces which form the context in which language is used, and which determine the choices made by language users (2010, p. x). The implication is that the classroom is not a neutral space: it, too, constitutes an arena in which power relationships, attitudes, and ideologies are brought to the production and interpretation of speech events. Second, the arena is about performance—that is, language is about roleplaying: "In one sense, teachers in classrooms, involved in the "act of teaching," are always engaged in performance and display, with props, scenery, and a supporting cast of characters" (p. x)—acts which require deliberate language choices. Third, language can be viewed as a contest. For the Anglophone Caribbean, there has been a socio-historical contest between the English languages of the colonizer, and the languages of the colonized, primarily the West and West-Central African languages of the enslaved (and later the Asian languages of indentured labourers). Out of this contest emerged English-lexifier creole languages which were created by the enslaved. This last metaphor is viewing language from beyond the realm of individual identity to national identity:

> Language is used to define who we are; to sustain our culture and develop the bonds of cultural identity. To take on a new language means to adopt that language's definition of self. The arena becomes even more open for contestation when that language is English. Because of its imperial past, English more than any other language invokes notions of ideological domination and repression (p. xii).

To summarize, therefore, we situate the three language-as-arena metaphors within the framework of CDA, in which Discourse is about an individual's ways of getting recognized, whether by speaking, writing, or acting in a particular context. Specifically, as it relates to language as performance, we see the issue of language identity construction emerging clearly. Both teachers and students take on specific identities when they speak JC or JE within the arena of the classroom. We contend in this chapter that though different, both of these languages are ours, both "define who we are."[2] Nevertheless, true to Bryan's language-as-arena, there has always been a struggle between these two languages from a socio-historical perspective, and from an identity construction perspective.

Language in Jamaica

Since DeCamp (1961), the term *Creole continuum* has been used to characterize the language situation in Jamaica. The continuum may be defined as a theoretical construct which "locates all variation, including socially conditioned variation on a unidimensional scale that extends from the most English-like [known as the *acrolect*] to the most Creole-like [the *basilect*]" (Kouwenberg and Singler 2011, p. 293). The area between acrolect and basilect, which is said to be the locus of variation, is known as the *mesolect*. It has been conceived as an "area of interaction" since "its existence has been, and continues to be, dependent on the cross influences from the two extremes" (Craig, 1971, p. 372). The creole continuum is referred to by DeCamp (1971, p. 350) as a "continuous spectrum of speech varieties" which overlap and are so finely articulated that they cannot even be divided into a finite number of discrete codes (Patrick, 2002). The extremes themselves may be said to be idealizations since it may not be that there are groups of speakers whose speech consists exclusively of features belonging to either pole. Nonetheless, it has traditionally been assumed that communities in rural areas would be more likely to have speakers of more basilectal forms (see Patrick, 1999, p. 49 for example), and that more acrolectal features would likely be found in urban areas which are less isolated in geographic and socioeconomic terms (Rickford, 1987, for example).

In this complex language situation, English is the official language, and the vocabulary base for JC—which we say therefore is English-lexified. The consequences are far-reaching. Though linguistically, JC is a language in its own right, with a sound system, lexicon, word formations, and grammatical structures distinct from JE, the similarities in vocabulary and pronunciation cause speakers to believe that the languages are similar in other respects as well. This results in a lack of awareness among speakers of the differences between the two languages, and often, in a belief that they are using JE when they are not, and in surprise that JC is not understood by non-Jamaican speakers of English.

A further consequence of the English-lexifier status of JC lies in the attitudes of its speakers towards it. Because of the social hierarchy and power relations between colonizers and colonized, slave owners and enslaved, JC—which emerged as the language of the enslaved—became associated with low prestige, as opposed to English, the language of power, of social advancement, and of social status (Christie, 2003). Louise Bennett, perhaps the most significant cultural icon of Jamaica, made it her life's mission to address this shame which speakers of JC associate with the language, by showing its value as a reflection of our culture, that it is a language in its own right, and that Jamaicans have reason to be proud that they are its speakers.

Today, as well as continuing to be the language of home and community, associated with positive values such as friendship, identity, and solidarity, JC is also making headway into domains which were traditionally reserved for JE only, and is becoming a symbol of national identity and pride (Christie, 2003; Carrington, 2001; Shields-Brodber, 2014). Nonetheless, it is still the prevailing view, even among native speakers of JC themselves, that JC is nothing but "bad English" or "broken English," and those in authority at home and at school are known to chastise the younger generations when they speak it.

Beliefs about JE as "language," and JC as "broken," as well as attitudes towards JE speakers as educated and prestigious, as opposed to JC speakers as poor and stigmatized, are carried into schools by children whose competence and production are predominantly JC, but include English and English-like elements. Kennedy's (2017, p. 53) code weaving is used to refer to these patterns, evidenced in the speech of the pre-primary school children she studied. Following Craig's (1980) terminology, she distinguishes between "superficial weaves, involving phonological and lexical features, and structural weaves, which combine syntactic features of the languages" (p. 53). Like woven cloth, the languages, though from separate strands, create a pattern from the intertwining of the languages by its speakers, which makes it difficult for them to differentiate the two codes.

The PDPST Approach and Other Language Arts Projects

We now seek to contextualize the PDPST workshops in terms of other Language Arts education projects that have set out to achieve the goal of improving students' competence in the English language.

Similar to the Language Materials Workshop (LMW) of the 1970s and 80s, we tried to infuse our approach with local literature, which would contain both languages—JC and JE (Bryan, 2014, p. 8). An example is our use of a traditional story "Anansi and Snake," which we modified to include both languages in order to facilitate a discussion of how the two languages are used in different contexts, and in relation to different audiences.

The Literature-Based Language Arts Project (LBLAP) in the early 2000s focused largely on input of the target language—English—by immersing Grades 1 and 2 students in a rich variety of texts that were predominantly written in English, and using various literacy strategies for promoting reading and writing skills in English (Lewis-Smikle 2006). In contrast, our project focused more on the importance of language awareness for both teachers and students, and emphasized the need for explicit teaching of English grammar and for extensive oral practice in the language. We advocate for input of the target language, but realize that with the tremendous amount of code weaving occurring in our language situation, and the limitations of the English language input that teachers are able to provide, full English immersion is not possible. Rather, the PDPST project aims at both rich English language input and awareness of the differences between the two codes. As such, within our project, we advocated for teachers to use a variety of texts to provide input of the target language, while recognizing that the input received from teachers would typically be characterized by a range of features from both languages. Other authors (Shields-Brodber, 2014) have also noted that there are insufficient models of English for Jamaican children, due at least in part to the expanding reach of Creole into many formal spaces. Therefore, the PDPST project adopts the view that in addition to providing input of the English language, teachers must also become linguistically aware of the status of both JE and JC as "language," and cognizant of the features of each language and the differences between them (Bryan, 2014; Kennedy, 2017;

Pollard, 2003). With this type of knowledge base, teachers can then help their students to become better at "noticing" the features of the languages spoken in the classroom, and in turn, the students should also have a growing ability to identify these features as either JE or JC.

The Jamaican Language Unit at the University of the West Indies also conducted the Bilingual Education Project (BEP), a pilot project delivered to children in Grades 1—4, in three primary schools during 2004—2008. The project involved the bilingual delivery in JE and JC of the full primary school curriculum. Carpenter and Devonish (2010) discuss the outcomes for one of the participating schools on a Grade 3 Language Arts test, showing that the project attained its goal to "do no harm . . . to pupils' competence in English," but failed to "produce an increase in Language Arts skill levels in English," or "in absolute literacy levels" (p. 173), although participating pupils produced moderately better results in a free-writing task in English than non-participating pupils (p. 180).

The PDPST project differs from the BEP in a significant way. Unlike the BEP, our project does not use JC as a primary medium of instruction alongside English. Rather, our project focused on building teachers' language awareness as the basis for enhancing Language Arts pedagogies and improving English-language learning outcomes.

PDPST: A Brief Overview

The PDPST workshops consisted of seven sessions, twice per week, with each session lasting approximately two and a half hours. These sessions were held after school hours, during the months of February and March 2019, and were conducted by graduates of the University of the West Indies, with a significant background in Linguistics at the undergraduate level, and in some instances, also at the graduate level. Most of these graduates were also trained teachers, and several were employed as teachers at the secondary level. A trainer-of-trainers model was used as we, the authors, trained these graduates to conduct the workshops through a training course which was informed by our first pilot of 2015.

The PDPST workshops presented linguistic content linked to specific pedagogical strategies appropriate to the primary school curriculum for Grades 1—4. The aim was for the teachers to implement the pedagogical strategies in their classrooms after each session and report their experience in the next session. Unfortunately, this was not always possible, given the competing demands of the curriculum and the scheduling of various school events. The linguistic content covered during the workshops and the linked pedagogical strategies are included in Appendix A.

For the purpose of this chapter, we analysed data based on the teachers' language biographies and their final workshop evaluations, as we were interested in how the teachers described their language journeys, and what impact the workshops had, if any, on their language identities. Although five schools participated in the study, we only had access to the language biographies and final workshop evaluations from four schools at the time of this writing. Of the four schools, two were in rural Jamaica, one was in what could be described as a peri-urban area, and the fourth was located in downtown Kingston. Thirty-six teachers submitted their language biographies to the workshop trainers, and twenty-eight teachers completed the evaluation questions at the end of the delivery of the training workshops.

Teachers' Language Biographies as a Resource

Bryan (2010) explains that one of the roles of the English language teacher in a Creole-speaking society is to use her or his own language journey as a resource, since many "Caribbean teachers have experienced the same linguistic struggles that their students encounter intuitively, at the very least, [and] know how language can be used to mediate power in the wider society" (p. 154f). However, though seemingly obvious, this would require a radical shift in thinking on two levels. The first shift is that teachers have to acknowledge that many among them are not native speakers of English—an acknowledgment which challenges their identity and legitimacy as teachers in a context where English is the official language and the language of instruction. Underlying this is the acknowledgment that two languages co-exist, and that the first language of the majority of our nation's speakers, including primary school teachers, is JC, which is related to but different from English. The second shift is that teachers would need to acknowledge their own struggles with language, which in turn requires greater language awareness on their part and reflection on their own language identities. Both of these shifts are critical if teachers are to continue to increase their knowledge and hone their pedagogical craft of English Language Arts teaching. Below is a long but useful quote from Bryan (2010), where a teacher recounts part of her own language journey and her struggle to improve her grasp of English:

> There are times when I really don't make the switch with the tenses . . . if I write, I might have so much problem as with the spoken language. I am not that comfortable with this. Maybe because of my home environment that I am from, it's not a practised thing . . . I speak Creole at home, but not the basilect. Mrs. C. realized it and she pointed it out to me; she called me one day and said to me, ". . . you have the ability to be a honours student, but there is one thing that may pull you away from it, and that is your language," and she just pointed it out by talking to me and encouraged me, like when I made the mistake she would change it around and put it the better way, the right way of saying it, and that was basically it for me; and knowing she believed that I had the potential to do it really encouraged me (pp. 160—161).

Like many of the teachers in the PDPST workshop, this teacher shares the experience of having grown up in an environment in which the language of home is exclusively, if not predominantly, JC, while the language of education is English, and underlines the challenges of having to learn the second language within this particular linguistic context without consistent appropriate instruction.

Instruments and Data Analysis

Gee (2005) constructed a set of questions designed to examine how language is used to build significance, activities, identities, relationships, politics, connections and sign systems, and knowledge (pp. 98—101). In what follows, we apply the questions set out by Gee in analysing the discourse of the teachers' language biographies and evaluations, and then use CDA in seeking reasonable explanations of the teachers' discourses.

In order to measure the impact of the PDPST training programme on teachers' language awareness, we began by asking teachers to write their language biographies in order to tease out their social and emotional ties to the two languages, and to facilitate positive attitudinal change through the workshops. It is the analysis of these biographies and the final workshop evaluations that are the focus of this chapter.

The introduction to the language biography activity which we conducted was as follows: "A language biography reflects on your history of language learning, and how that history relates to your current patterns of language use. The following questions are intended to guide your writing." The four questions we asked are integrated below in the descriptions of what the teachers wrote. A full list of the evaluation questions is provided in Appendix B.

In order to analyse the data from the language biographies, and from the final workshop evaluations, we identified recurring/repeated words and themes. Thereafter, we used Gee's (2005) building task of identity using the following preset questions:

> What identities (roles, positions), with their concomitant personal, social, and cultural knowledge and beliefs (cognition), feelings (affect), and values, seem to be relevant to, taken for granted in, or under construction in the situation? How are these identities stabilized or transformed in the situation? In terms of identities, activities, and relationships, what Discourses are relevant (and irrelevant) in the situation? How are they made relevant (and irrelevant), and in what ways? (p. 111).

Answering these questions meant reading the data multiple times, noting the repeated expressions, and eventually creating concept maps showing the relationships among different keywords. Also, specific quotes from teachers' language biographies or final workshop evaluations, which illustrated a particular theme, were highlighted.

Description of Findings

In this section, we review what the language biographies, submitted by thirty-six teachers, revealed about the teachers' attitudes towards the languages, as well as how the course impacted the teachers, as indicated by them in their final evaluations, submitted by twenty-eight teachers.

The Teachers' Language Biographies

As explained in the preceding section, teachers were given four questions which they were told were intended to guide their writing. We note that the majority of teachers addressed the questions individually. What follows is a summary of their responses.

Language Biography Question 1: *What kind of speaker do you consider yourself to be? A speaker of both Jamaican Creole and Jamaican English? Or a speaker of only one of these?*
Twenty-eight of the thirty-six teachers, or 77.8 percent, said that they were speakers of both languages. Two teachers gave unclear responses, three self-identified as JE speakers, and another three as JC monolinguals. The language biographies thus reflect the growing trend towards a greater acceptance of JC, and is in line with the claim that many Jamaicans accept the notion of a bilingual language identity (Devonish and Carpenter, 2007).

The teachers' responses also reflect the observation of Kennedy (2017) that children are exposed to much interweaving of the two languages, as many of the teachers recounted that they were exposed to both languages from an early age. Most of the teachers were exposed to JC and JE at home, in church, and within the community, and it was really only in the setting of school and work that there was more exposure to English.

Language Biography Question 2: *If you are speaker of both languages, do you have a dominant and a weaker language, or do you consider that you are equally proficient in both?*
Fifteen (41.7 percent) of the teachers viewed themselves as equally proficient in both languages, and 11 (30.5 percent) as proficient speakers of JC. Only seven teachers (19.4 percent) saw themselves as more proficient speakers of JE. There were three (8.3 percent) responses which included a non-response, and two unclear responses.

As seen in the quotes below, the teachers' responses to the issue of proficiency were quite nuanced as they tried to reconstruct their language identities in the language biography written task. This raises the issue of what it means to be proficient in a language, and in particular, the extent to which one must be proficient in a language in order to teach it.

The issue of proficiency was highlighted by one teacher, in particular, who wrote that while she is *more competent in Jamaican Creole, [she] can navigate [the] English language with a fair level of competence.* Only a minority identified JE as their dominant language. Another teacher made it clear that *I do not consider myself a JE speaker*. Such a confession of a primary school teacher is a big ideological shift in that the teacher feels safe enough to declare her JC language identity without being judged negatively.

These two quotes, however, contrast with another teacher who stated that she is *proficient in both verbally*. However, she has *difficulty spelling JC words*. This teacher feels confident speaking both languages, but has indicated that the writing of JC is challenging. And while writing JC might be difficult, one teacher noted that *JC [is her] dominant, most comfortable [language]*. The most poignant quote comes from yet another teacher who said that she is *proficient in both. I speak JC fluently, but is proficient at writing JE, or so I think*. Her language identity construction here reflects, on the one hand, confidence, and on the other hand, doubt. She is confident about speaking JC, believes she is proficient at writing JE, though is not sure. Interestingly, her doubt about her proficient writing is reflected in the grammatical error she makes with the verb to be—*I speak JC fluently, but is* (versus am) proficient at writing JE*. An error such as this illustrates what Kennedy (2017) refers to as "structural weaving" (p. 2), since this error is not a matter of spelling or pronunciation ("superficial weaving"), but has to do with the requirements of the morphosyntax.

Language Biography Question 3: *What language inputs were you exposed to?*
Since many of the teachers identified themselves as speakers of both languages, it is not surprising that in terms of input, many, though not most of them (14 of 36 teachers, or 38.9 percent), said they were exposed to *both languages* or a *mixture* of the two languages throughout their lives. For some teachers, the exposure to both languages was throughout their lived experience in which JC and JE were heard at home, school, and in the community. Other teachers were more specific about where exposure to the languages occurred, and the spaces which had more JC or JE. For example, one teacher described her input as follows:

*In my home, JC was used by my parents and primary caregivers, but I was exposed to JE on radio and news (TV). In school, teachers used **both** languages, while students spoke creole. Community members spoke creole, while at church, there was a **mixture of both**. In my training and work environment and development as a teacher, the use of the JE is more dominant* [our emphasis].

Other teachers gave specific sources of input of English, and these included the following:

- Poetry at the basic school level
- A grade one teacher who *translated*
- The Jamaica Library Service book mobile
- Parents or guardians who insisted that they *taak gud* or *speak properly*
- The minister's wife or persons from overseas
- Older siblings in high schools
- Lecturers who spoke in Standard Jamaican English (SJE)
- Readings of the [news]paper, books, journals, educational videos in university years
- The language of the text at school

In summary, the media, specific types of speakers, and textbooks were sources of English input for these teachers in their younger years.

In contrast to the others, one teacher who self-identified as a *speaker of one language, the Jamaican English,* shared that JE was heard throughout her lived experience at home, on television and radio, and at school by teachers and fellow students. While she did not identify the type of school that she attended, another teacher spoke about being exposed to more English when she went to a privately run elementary school, as opposed to a government school. Finally, another teacher shared that although she was exposed to JC throughout her life, as a mother she has *limited* her use of JC at home, as she does not like to hear children speaking Creole. In other words, in addition to code-switching, she was monitoring her own language use in relation to the acquisition of JE for her own child.

Language Biography Question 4: *What effect did these inputs have on your learning of Jamaican Creole and Jamaican English?*
Only twenty of the teachers responded to the question of the impact of the language input on their learning of JC and JE. Teachers expressed familiar sentiments about the impact of JC on their language learning.

One teacher noted that JC placed a *limit* on her ability to learn English as competently as she would have wanted at an early age. Another shared sentiment that we had heard in the very first pilot in 2015, was that teachers used JC in their classrooms mainly for *fun, scolding*, and some amount of explaining (*I may say something in Creole for them to understand*), as opposed to English, which was the dominant language used for instruction. And yet another teacher, mentioned that JC was *natural*, with the implication that JE was not as easily learned. Indeed, for many of the teachers, they shared that their own English language skills improved with greater levels of education:

> The exposure to JC did limit the extent of me learning SJE efficiently at an early age. However, with the training and learning process throughout primary, high school, and college, this has allowed me to be proficient in SJE.

Not surprisingly, teachers reported challenges to learning English. It was seen as *very difficult* with rules that were confusing. One grade two teacher reported that this was especially so since the English language has so many exceptions. Nevertheless, other teachers wrote that they were *comfortable* with both languages, and that exposure to both languages was *vital, positive,* and *more effective*. For some teachers, the impact of their language journey allowed them to have a *good grasp of both languages* so they were able to use the languages within *appropriate* contexts. Finally, for a few of the teachers, they admitted that they were still learning about the two languages. Here are quotes from two of these:

> This [language input] impacted my language because I practiced the Creole more than [SJE], and for English language, you must practice daily to improve and [learn].

> The effects of been* exposed to both languages at different times in my development has peeked* my interest in learning more about both languages so that one day I will be fluent and proficient in both languages.

Teachers' Evaluation of the Workshops

Twenty-eight teachers submitted final evaluations of the PDPST workshops. Much like the language biography, the evaluation instrument comprised a number of questions intended to serve as a guide. The full instrument may be found in Appendix B. In what follows, we summarize their responses to questions relating only to how the course developed their awareness of language issues in Jamaica, how it helped them to be able to explain the language differences between JC and JE, and the extent to which the course helped them to know how to present these language differences to students. The relevant questions are as follows:

> Application and specific skill development.
> a. In what ways did the course help to develop your awareness of language issues in Jamaica?
> b. How did the course help you to be able to explain the language differences between JC and JE?
> c. To what extent did the course help you to know how to present these language differences to students?

All but one teacher reported that the PDPST workshops were transformative for them. This particular teacher said that *the course did not help, as* [she] *was aware of the challenges*. We note that the other teachers who submitted final evaluations frequently used the comparative form *more* to indicate the ways in which the course transformed their thinking about the languages in Jamaica. The most frequent response was that the workshops made them *more aware* about the language differences between JC and JE. Similarly, two teachers commented that they were now *more cognizant* of the rules of the languages. In terms of their feelings, a few teachers mentioned feeling *more comfortable* about the two languages and *more tolerant*. Indeed, some teachers felt that both languages should be *accepted* and *value[d]*. Some teachers also wrote that the course *helped* them to *better explain* the differences and gave them *different activities* which the students *enjoyed*. Several teachers also went on to share how the workshops had impacted their students, with one teacher sharing that her students, as a result of her implementing some of the strategies from the workshops, were now speaking and writing *without fear*. Below are four quotes which reflect the descriptions identified:

> This course helps me to understand that **JC is not to be pushed aside** but to use it to **foster the English language**. I am now **more comfortable** to help the students to understand that there is a difference between JE and JC.

> *The language differences between JC and JE is that it promotes awareness to the transition from JC to JE. This course allows a **better explanation** of the language differences between JE and JE*, by allowing the students to speak the JC and translate into the JE for themselves **without fear**.*

> *Participating in this course has helped me to be **more cognisant** of the Jamaican Creole (JC) and the Jamaican English (JE), as well as the rules that govern both languages . . . .. I am now **more aware** of the different pronunciations, and I have realized that some words that are pronounced in JC mean the same in JE . . . .. As a result of the experience, I am now empowered to direct children into switching codes from JC to JE.*

> *The PDPST course has helped me to be **more aware** of the language issues both in society and in my classroom. It helped me to be **more tolerant** when children don't say the correct JE pronunciation, and this provides me with the opportunity to give them both ways (JC and JE).*

The most pervasive discourse within both the teachers' language biographies and their final evaluations was that of bilingualism. As mentioned earlier, many of the teachers considered themselves to be proficient in both languages, and stated that their own language inputs when growing up had included both JC and JE throughout home, community, and education. The value of bilingualism was reaffirmed for the teachers through the workshops, as evidenced by their comments in the final evaluation. From the teachers' comments, the course added to their knowledge of both languages, gave them useful teaching strategies for teaching English, and helped them to determine when JC ought to be used in the classroom. Teachers wrote that they were now *more aware* of the *language differences,* and could better *distinguish* between the two in terms of pronunciation, spelling, and meaning. Interestingly, no teacher mentioned being able to identify the differences in terms of grammatical structures, signalling a general lack of confidence in regards to morphosyntax. Below is an example of a teaching episode that one participant described in her final evaluation which relates to differences in pronunciation:

> *Contrasting was particularly useful in teaching tricky vocabulary. During one session, the students could not figure out the word "model" . . . .. The word "magl" was written on the board, and the more phonetically capable ones instantly pronounced the word and demonstrated the meaning. I was then able to present the target word and discuss the tricky syllable. In short, **Jamaican Creole was used as a tool of instruction for an English word.***

This is a good example of one of the goals of the workshops—that is, the use of contrastive analysis during teachable moments to allow students to notice the differences between JC and JE. As such, during the workshops, we had taught the teachers the JLU-Cassidy[3] orthography of JC and had recommended that they compare those forms with English words which the students found difficult to pronounce.

Finally, perhaps one of the most poignant quotes is from a teacher who wrote the following in her final evaluation:

> *At the beginning of this course, we began by looking at the language in Jamaica.* **As an educator, I spent most of my time focusing on perfecting the L2 and not giving the L1 its place.**

Here, we see evidence of transformation from one way of thinking to another type of discourse about language in the arena of the classroom. We suggest that it is a movement away from focusing solely on English and ignoring the mother tongue of the majority of the children (JC), to a focus on valuing the mother tongue and using it as a resource to speak and write in English more competently. Or, as another teacher stated:

> *This course helps me to understand that* **JC is not to be pushed aside,** *but to use it to foster the English language.*

Discussion

Three themes have emerged from the teachers' submissions: the pervasive discourse of bilingualism, the treatment of JC in the classroom, and the question of teacher proficiency in English.

Theme 1: The Pervasive Discourse of Bilingualism

Linguists such as Carrington (2001) and Christie (2003) have described how, over the years, JC has become more accepted in the public domain, in part due to the arts, such as through the beloved poetry of Louise Bennett-Coverley. Certainly, her poetry has been recited in many school performances, thereby allowing teachers and children to speak the mother tongue without fear of embarrassment in the school space. Education may indirectly have contributed to this increased acceptance as well, as many speakers with a largely Creole-speaking background have brought their language with them as they have moved up the socio-economic ladder (Shields-Brodber, 2014). The PDPST workshops aimed to reinforce this discourse of bilingualism, as we take as our basic premise the value of embracing both languages. On the one hand, it is important for teachers and students to value their mother tongue as a language which bears their national and cultural identity (Bryan, 2010). On the other hand, English is the official language of Jamaica, and an international language. As such, those who use it well are better able to negotiate multiple social spaces. Learning JE in addition to JC gives one the power of choice (Warner-Lewis 2015). As Pollard (1998) has mentioned, the ideal Jamaican student is one who is "bilingual" (p. 11). Teachers' language biographies seemed largely to confirm this ideal, as they were comfortable affirming their identity as speakers of both languages. Through the workshop series, they also became more aware of the classroom as a bilingual space, in which both languages can have a place.

Theme 2: The Treatment of JC in the Classroom

Although the majority of the teachers identified as speakers of both languages and to a large extent embraced JC, one challenge they had was how best to treat JC within the classroom space. While classroom observations showed us that teachers used JC for disciplinary measures, such as scolding, as well as for fun, whether telling jokes or stories, it seems as if they seldom used it as a teaching tool. Despite instances in which teachers used JC to explain difficult concepts, the concept of JC as a teaching tool seemed fairly new, judging from their evaluations. What the PDPST workshops offered were two ways of treating JC within the arena of the classroom. First, it was an important part of our workshop series to examine the language situation and the attitudes that we have towards JE and JC. Given the complex history behind the language situation, it is important for teachers to unpack any negative feelings towards either language. Second, in addition to valuing JC, our approach was to recognize the mother tongue as a resource in the teaching and learning of English (Kennedy, 2017). Rather than chastising students for speaking their native language, or treating it as ungrammatical English, we encouraged teachers to foster in themselves and in their pupils an awareness of the forms they are using and how those of JC differ from those of JE. This method allows pupils to realize that their own language, JC, has forms which, though different from JE, are valid. By having teachers study the two codes in terms of phonology, syntax, semantics, and the lexicon, and then equipping them with strategies to pass this knowledge on to their students, they would be able to systematically take advantage of teachable moments in the English Language Arts period, and to see how to integrate JC into their classroom teaching, and treat it as a resource rather than a hindrance for English language learning. Teachers' evaluations showed that this insight had emerged during the workshop series.

Theme 3: The Question of Teacher Proficiency in English

An important question that Murray and Christinson (2011) ask, is whether or not a non-native speaker of English can teach English. Their response is yes. Worldwide, there are many teachers who are non-native speakers of English who teach English, and do so effectively. What is important is that the teachers be trained in the necessary content knowledge and pedagogical skills in order to teach the language effectively. A part of that training we contend, especially in our Creole-speaking environment, and given our language history, is an acknowledgment that many of our teachers are really themselves second-language speakers of English. This would require a huge shift in the overall discourse about English language teachers in Jamaica. It involves a movement away from the once-held assumption that Jamaicans are all monolingual speakers of English, with some speaking a broken, simplified version of the language—the traditional view of JC.

The language biographies revealed that while the teachers seemed comfortable with their identity as speakers of both languages, they were not as confident about their level of proficiency with both languages, nor with their proficiency in JE. Teachers therefore acknowledged the need to become more aware of the languages they speak within the classroom space. This awareness can only come through treating a knowledge of language as the subject matter of the primary Language Arts teacher (Murray and Christinson, 2011, p. 69), and integrating that knowledge into teacher training.

This discussion of proficiency in the language of instruction also raises the issue of what teachers at the primary level ought to know. Certainly, it is impossible to know everything about a language, and learning a language, especially a second or third language, is often a lifelong endeavour. What is clear from the PDPST workshops is that while teachers found it easier to grasp the surface differences between the languages (spelling, vocabulary, and pronunciation), teachers needed more time to fully grasp some of the structural differences (morphosyntax). This is reflected in the teachers' evaluations, which typically included comments pertaining to what they felt they had learned about pronunciation, spelling, and meaning. Notably absent were similar comments regarding morphosyntactic notions, despite the emphasis these had received in the workshops.

Critical Discourse Analysis and Identity Work

Language is inextricably linked to identity. This is why within the PDPST workshops it has been important to us to begin the workshop series with a session on language and society. This session has multiple goals, including providing the workshop participants with some basic sociolinguistic tools for understanding the linguistic landscape of Jamaica, but it also has been critical to us that teachers unpack their own attitudes towards JC and JE, given the historical tensions between them. Where does identity construction and re-construction fit in all of this? First, teachers did this unpacking about their own language attitudes through the writing of the language biographies, and then reflecting on those attitudes in parts of the evaluation. Second, if we agree with Gee (2014, p. 2) that language "allows us to take on different socially significant identities," then one can argue that through language, teachers can appropriate identities of proficient or competent monolingual English speakers, or of proficient or competent bilingual speakers of JE. Recall the teacher in the long quote above from Bryan (2010) who shared how she struggled with shifting tenses which impacted her sense of competence in English. Recall, too, the teacher within the workshop space who identified herself as proficient in both languages yet doubted her own competence in writing JE (*proficient in both. I speak JC fluently but is proficient at writing JE, or so I think*). In contrast, another teacher claimed that *I can navigate [JE] with a fair level of competence*. Not all, but many teachers struggle with this identity of being competent with the language of instruction—English.

We can also look at this identity construction and reconstruction from the lens of Bryan's (2010) language-as-arena metaphors. Within the physical and sociocultural space of a workshop, there is the expectation that learning will take place. Having a workshop right after school was challenging for the teachers, as some expressed. However, the energy with which the facilitators conducted the sessions, and the growing meaningfulness of the content made the PDPST workshops worthwhile for the teachers in the long run. Within the workshop space, we aimed at moving beyond the rhetoric of the contest between the two languages, to one of conciliation. We did this by teaching the participants the JLU-Cassidy orthography for writing Creole, thereby expanding the value of JC as a written language. And finally, the major aim of the PDPST workshops was to equip teachers with linguistic and pedagogical content in order to perform as highly proficient users of the English language within the space of the classroom. Based on the final workshop evaluations, we achieved this goal to some extent, but mainly at the surface linguistic levels of the languages, as opposed to the structural differences between the two languages. In other words, based on the teachers' reports, they can perform as more knowledgeable educators about the linguistic differences between the two codes in relation to spelling, pronunciation, and vocabulary.

Conclusion/Implications:

Based on a thematic examination of the teachers' final workshop evaluations, all but one teacher felt that the PDPST workshops had helped to develop awareness of language issues in Jamaica. The teachers' awareness about the language situation was greater at the end of the sessions, and they felt more comfortable with the inclusion of JC in the classroom space as a tool for instruction in learning JE. One of the lessons that we have learned coming out of the model delivery of the PDPST workshops is the importance of language identity as a key component of any language workshop within Creole-speaking environments in order to challenge negative attitudes towards the home language and its use in the classroom. As such, language biography activities are useful in building awareness of these attitudes. Another lesson is that while the teachers grasped some of the surface differences between JC and JE covered in the workshops, more work needs to be done to help teachers to better understand the deeper grammatical linguistic differences between the two languages.

Appendix A

Unit	Content	Activity
Unit 1: Language in Society and Critical Language Awareness	Linguistic: • The linguistic approach to the study of language • Language in society and in the classroom • Variation in language • The impact of social and cultural context in language use Pedagogical: • Raising awareness of the functions performed by JC in society • The use of elements of RAFT (Role-Audience-Function-Topic) to develop language awareness	• Identifying a regional (or other) element in one's own speech and that of others • Elaborating elements of the Hymes' S-P-E-A-K-I-N-G model, and applying it to communicative situations • Class simulation of the story 'Anansi and Snake' modelling the DRTA (Directed Reading Thinking Activity) pedagogical approach • A simulated collaborative activity in the form of a short role-play based on the 'Anansi and Snake' story using RAFT
Unit 2: Morphosyntax of JC and JE, Part 1	Linguistic: • Morphemes and their functions in language • Pluralization in JC and JE • Vocabulary expansion in JC and in JE. Pedagogical: • Using Craig's Augmented Language Experience Approach (ALEA) to teach JE plural formation • Developing activities which focus on morphological analysis	• Text analysis for the discovery of challenging elements for JC native speakers • Determining when dem is needed in JC to give a plural reading • Suggesting the forms and meanings of parts of words • Moving from talk to writing by the teacher, to reading, editing, re-reading and writing by the students • Interactive reading of the poem "What makes a friend?"; selecting rich texts suitable for such an exercise

Unit 3: Language acquisition	Linguistic: • Characteristics of first and second language acquisition • The nature of learner language in second language acquisition • Factors contributing to the incomplete acquisition of a second language • The importance of language awareness in second language acquisition	• Identifying acquisitional stages in negation and the plural • Discussion of the roles of motivation and learner personality in second language acquisition
	Pedagogical: • Usefulness of error analysis in examining students' work, to discover the stage they may have reached in their acquisition of English • The features of enthusiastic reading; the value of Interactive Read Alouds	• Using error analysis to identify students' strengths, to distinguish between mistakes and errors, and to identify a grammatical error to be targeted for re-teaching • Practice in reading sentences using different voices, pacing etc., and discussion of their effects on interpretation • The use of affective and connection questions
Unit 4: Phonological Awareness	Linguistic: • The role of spelling in achieving literacy • Spelling vs pronunciation • The cognate advantage in phonology • Phonotactic analysis to identify systematic differences in JC and JE consonant clusters	• Identifying words which are pronounced identically in JC and JE and those with systematic differences in the two languages • Identifying initial 'onset' and final 'rime' clusters in JE and in JC
	Pedagogical: • Teaching phonological awareness and spelling using Contrastive Analysis, within the context of Shared Reading • The use of phonics and analogy to teach rimes which differ in JC and JE	• Class simulation using a poem to demonstrate how poetry can help students with difficulties in pronunciation • A group activity involving the poem "What makes a friend?" which illustrates JE rimes which are different in JC

Unit 5: Morpho-syntax of JC and JE, Part 2	Linguistic: • Concord in JE in the simple present tense, and the contrast between the JE and JC treatment of the present tense • Aspects of the formation of interrogatives which are similar vs different in JC and JE Pedagogical: • Using the 4 stages of a grammar mini-lesson within ALEA to teach concord • Using the mini-lesson within ALEA to teach the JE rule of subject-auxiliary inversion	• Creation of simple present tense sentences using verbs provided and subjects given by a colleague • Identifying differences in the word order of questions in JE and JC • Application of ALEA to Wendy's Wonderful Week (Literacy 1-2-3 material) • Including the "I do – We do – You do" sequence • Moving from free talk to controlled talk
Unit 6: The lexicon	Linguistic: • The complexity of language learning • Content teaching as an opportunity for language teaching • Advantages and dangers of the Bilingual Lexicon Pedagogical: • Using an adapted Directed Reading Activity • How to support students in their acquisition of JE words	• Identifying patterns in the uses of words in JC datasets • Analyzing how differently the JE cognate behaves • A group planning activity using texts provided for this purpose with the goal to identify how language teaching can be integrated into content teaching • Mini lessons, with reinforcement through writing
Unit 7: Final perspectives	Linguistic: • Linguistic elements of a text as covered in the course Pedagogical: • Mining a text for teachable elements at the level of phonology, lexicon, morphology, and syntax	• Identification of challenging and teachable elements in texts • Planning and preparing a text for teaching, including pre-reading, during-reading, and post-reading activities

Appendix B. Instrument Questions

Language Biography

A language biography reflects on your history of language learning, and how that history relates to your current patterns of language use. The following questions are intended to guide your writing.

1. What kind of speaker do you consider yourself to be? A speaker of both Jamaican Creole and Jamaican English, or a speaker of only one of these?

2. If you are speaker of both languages, do you have a dominant and a weaker language or do you consider that you are equally proficient in both?

3. What language inputs were you exposed to?*

4. What effect did these inputs have on your learning of Jamaican Creole and Jamaican English?

Final Evaluation

Please use the following as a guide when reflecting on the course, and be as honest and complete as possible in your responses.

1. Presentation of content (e.g. organization, clarity, use of materials, logical sequence of topics)

2. Sharing your experiences of teaching using a 'PDPST' strategy (e.g. usefulness of discussion, feedback provided)

3. Encouragement of participation and discussion by trainer

4. Content of the course:

    a. To what extent were the concepts presented in a teacher-friendly way?

    b. To what extent were the concepts presented in a student-friendly way?

    c. Which aspects of the course were/were not at an appropriate grade level?

    d. So far, what content area(s) have you found most relevant to your classroom experience?

    e. What content area(s) do you still find unclear?

5. Application and specific skill development.

    a. In what ways did the course help to develop your awareness of language issues in Jamaica?

    b. How did the course help you to be able to explain the language differences between JC and JE?

    c. To what extent did the course help you to know how to present these language differences to students?

    d. What teaching strategy/strategies did you find most useful so far? What was useful about it? How did your students respond?

    e. Which strategies might you now try out in your own teaching? Why?

    f. What teaching strategy/strategies did not work? And why not?

    g. Which strategies are you still hesitant to try? How come?

6. Identify what you consider to be the strengths of the course.

7. Identify area(s) where you think the course could be improved.

8. What additional supporting materials, assignments, or practice worksheets do you think you would have benefited from?

9. What area(s) would you benefit from knowing more about?

10. Would a follow-up course be useful, and why?

11. What overall rating would you give the course: excellent, good, average, poor, very poor?

12. Are there any other comments you would like to make about any aspects of the workshops?

Endnotes

1 This paper reports on a project for which ethical approval was given by the UWI Ethics Committee (application number ECP 236, 16/17). Participating teachers provided informed consent for the use of their data for the purpose of research emanating from this project.

2 This comment was shared by one of the teachers in our first pilot study in 2015, in which she mentioned that English was also part of our linguistic heritage.

3 JLU is the Jamaican Language Unit/Di Jamiekan Langwij Yuunit at the University of the West Indies (Mona, Jamaica). Frederic Cassidy was a leading advocate of a writing system for Jamaican Creole and, with Robert Brock Le Page, published *The Dictionary of Jamaican English* in 1967 (second edition, 1980, 2002).

References

Bryan, B. *Between Two Grammars: Research and Practice for Language Learning and Teaching in a Creole-Speaking Environment.* Kingston, Jamaica: Ian Randle Publishers, 2010.

Bryan, B. "'English as an Arena, Not a Subject': Language Learning and Teaching in Post-Independence Jamaica." *Lectures on Language Education: A Monograph.* Edited by Beverley Bryan. Kingston, Jamaica: School of Education, University of the West Indies, Mona, 2014, pp. 2—32.

Carpenter, K. and Devonish, H. "Swimming Against the Tide: Jamaican Creole in Education." *Creoles in Education. An appraisal of current programs and projects.* Edited by B. Migge, I. Léglise and A.

Bartens. Amsterdam and Philadelphia: John Benjamins, 2010, pp. 167—181.

Carrington, L. "The Status of Creole in the Caribbean." *Due Respect: Essays on English and English-Related Creoles in the Caribbean in Honour of Professor Robert Le Page.* Edited by Pauline Christie. Kingston, Jamaica: University of the West Indies Press, 2001, pp. 24—36.

Christie, P. *Language in Jamaica.* Kingston, Jamaica: Arawak Publications, 2003.

Craig, D.R. "Education and Creole English in the West Indies." *Pidginization and Creolization of Languages.* Edited by D. Hymes. Cambridge: Cambridge University Press, 1971, pp. 371—91.

Craig, D.R. "Language, Society and Education in the West Indies." *Caribbean Journal of Education,* vol. 7, no. 1, 1980, pp. 1—17.

De Camp, D. "Social and Geographical Factors in Jamaican Dialects." *Creole Language Studies* II. London: Macmillan, 1961, pp. 60—84.

De Camp, D. "Towards a Generative Analysis of a Post-Creole Speech Continuum." *Pidginization and Creolization of Languages.* Edited by D. Hymes. Cambridge: Cambridge University Press, 1971, pp. 349—70.

Devonish, H. and Carpenter, K. "Towards Full Bilingualism in Education: The Jamaican Bilingual Primary Education Project." *Social and Economic Studies,* vol. 56, nos. 1 and 2, 2007, pp. 277—303.

Gee, J.P. *An Introduction to Discourse Analysis: Theory and Method.* New York: Routledge Taylor & Francis Group, 2005.

Gee, J.P. *How to do Discourse Analysis: A Toolkit.* London and New York: Routledge, 2014a.

Gee, J.P. *An Introduction to Discourse Analysis: Theory and Method.* London and New York: Routledge Taylor & Francis Group, 2014b.

Kennedy, M.M. *What do Jamaican Children Speak? A Language Resource.* Kingston, Jamaica: University of the West Indies Press, 2017.

Kouwenberg, S. and Singler, J. "Pidgins and Creoles." *The Cambridge Handbook of Sociolinguistics.* Edited by Rajend Mesthrie. Cambridge: Cambridge University Press, 2011, pp. 283—300.

Lewis-Fokum, Y. and Colvin, C. "Tracing the Discourses of Accountability and Equity: The Case of the Grade Four Literacy Test in Jamaica." *Changing English*, vol. 24, no. 1, 2017, pp. 11—23.

Lewis-Fokum, Y. "Unpacking Educational Policy and Practice in Jamaica Through Critical Discourse Analysis: A Theoretical Framework and Methodology." *Decolonizing Qualitative Approaches for and by the Caribbean*. Edited by Saran Stewart. Charlotte, NC: Information Age Publishing, Inc., 2019, pp. 93—114.

Lewis-Smikle, J. "Literacy and Learning through Literature in the Junior Years: A Prototype Project." *Caribbean Journal of Education*, vol. 28, no. 1, pp. 85—110.

Murray, D.E. and Christison, M.A. *What English Language Teachers Need to Know*, vol. 1. New York and London: Routledge Taylor & Francis Group, 2011.

Ortega, L. *Understanding Second Language Acquisition*. London and New York: Routledge, 2013.

Patrick, P. *Urban Jamaican Creole. Variation in the Mesolect*. Amsterdam and Philadelphia: John Benjamins, 1999.

Patrick, P. "Modelling Synchronic Variation: The (Post-)Creole Continuum." University of Essex, 2002.

Pollard, V. "Code Switching and Code Mixing: Language in the Jamaican Classroom. *Caribbean Journal of Education*, Vol. 20, No. 1, 1998, pp. 9—20.

Pollard, V. *From Jamaican Creole to Standard English: A Handbook for Teachers*. Kingston, Jamaica: University of the West Indies Press, 2003.

Rickford, J. *Dimensions of a Creole Continuum*. Stanford: Stanford University Press, 1987.

Rogers, R. *An Introduction to Critical Discourse Analysis in Education*. Mahwah, New Jersey: Lawrence Erlbaum Associates Inc., 2004.

Shields-Brodber, K. "Coexisting Discourses and the Teaching of English in the Creole-speaking Environment of Jamaica." *Education Issues in Creole and Creole-Influenced Vernacular Contexts*.

Edited by I. Robertson and H. Simmons-McDonald. Kingston, Jamaica: University of the West Indies Press, 2014, pp. 207—224.

Warner-Lewis, M. "Patois is Not Enemy of English." *Jamaica Gleaner*, 2015, Retrieved from http://jamaica-gleaner.com/article/commentary/20151005/patois-not-enemy-english.

PATWA A YAAD, ENGLISH ABROAD:
LANGUAGE AND ECONOMIC DEVELOPMENT IN JAMAICA

Tka C. Pinnock

During my childhood years, I lived in a small rural community in the tourist town of Ocho Rios, St. Ann, Jamaica. My grandmother, affectionately known as Miss Mama, had a shop[1] that seemed to be the centre of community life. As a young child, that shop served as my daycare, then my after-school care, and my summer camp. The shop—*our* shop—was a quotidian space. It was part of my family's and our neighbours' everyday existence—whether they stopped in to purchase goods, share some new or *old* gossip, seek a word of advice, or request that my grandmother, who was one of the very few older adults in our community who had a formal education, correspond with some official person on their behalf. It was the place where I found new friends—children whose families had recently moved into the community. It was a meeting place of sorts. In this everyday space of the shop, as I suspect with many everyday spaces in villages across Jamaica, life is narrated in Patwa—colourful, bold, and delicious. And so it is unsurprising that as a "pickney raise inna shop,"[2] Patwa was my first, and up until secondary school, primary language.

By the time I entered a prominent all-girls high school in St. Andrew, Jamaica, I had sufficiently mastered the English language to pass the Common Entrance,[3] and as I learned, *surprisingly,* to sound "less country" to my new "town" classmates. Having attended an elite preparatory school, I was well-aware that there was something wrong—less than—in speaking Patwa, or at least not being able to speak Jamaican Standard English. Preparatory schools—even in rural areas—serve as a microcosm of class differences in Jamaica, and I understood early on that the language people used and how they spoke could betray or portray a class position. I, of course, could not articulate it in this manner as a child, but I sensed that "poor," "black" people spoke Patwa, and everybody else spoke "English." Not until I moved to *town*, however, did I realize that Patwa—or rather, a particular non-Kingston version of Patwa—was connoted with being rural, and hence, arguably backward. For the first time, I had peers who boldly asserted that they did not speak a "lick of Patwa," and did not intend to learn. This was most certainly not the case. I cannot recall any of my peers not understanding Patwa, and most indulged—even a little—in speaking the lingua franca. Some of this class-based (and ideological) bias against Patwa is rooted ". . . in our cultural memory of shame and inferiority vis-à-vis an imposed British standard" reflecting "the weight of a colonial past that lingers into the linguistic present" (Henry, 2012, p. 99).

I had never given much thought to the role language had played in my life while resident in Jamaica or in its diaspora, having migrated to Toronto, Canada in my teens. It was common for me to occupy a space of "both/and." I knew how and when to code-switch—even in the same sentence—between Canadian English, Jamaican Standard English, and Jamaican Creole. I continue to "dip and slide along the socio-linguistic continuum of Standard English and Patwa" (Henry, 2012, p. 100), sometimes unknowingly, and other times quite deliberately when attempting to share a sentiment which only Jamaican Patwa seems capable of fully capturing and expressing. My code-switching is not just a feature of my diasporic experience, but a practice I engaged in even while resident in Jamaica. As someone who moved between "country" and "town," I also moved between variations of Patwa. I recall a high school geography field trip in my senior year to the parish of St. Thomas, where while doing a sketch of the landscape, I refereed to a roadway as a "pass"—much to the entertainment of my geography teacher—who pointed out that I must be from country because "only country people" would use that terminology. This movement is not only a rural/urban phenomenon but runs along the uptown/downtown divide in Kingston,[4] which is well-known across the island. In conversation with fellow Jamaican authors Kei Miller and Marlon James, Nicole Dennis-Benn discusses her experience of living in Vineyard Town, Kingston, while attending a high school in upper St. Andrew. Dennis-Benn shares that she wore "a mask of social respectability" at school to fit in with her peers—most of whom were from Jamaica's upper- and middle-class families. This "mask of respectability" included speaking "proper English" (Dennis-Benn, 2019).

Though I was aware of the ongoing debates about the proper place of Jamaican Patwa in the island-nation's sociocultural and political landscape, my deeper curiosity in the matter, which has led to this commentary, was sparked by a conversation among diasporic Jamaicans at a celebration of Louise Bennett-Coverley, affectionately known as Miss Lou. In September 2019, as Coordinator of the Jean Augustine Chair in Education, Community and Diaspora at York University, I had the privilege of co-planning an evening in honour of the centenary of her birthday. The evening featured a viewing of a recording of one of her live performances at a Toronto high school in the late 1980s, followed by presentations on her life and legacy. A fruitful and impassioned dialogue then ensued, as is common when Jamaicans gather. While there was no doubt about the warmth of feelings for Miss Lou, the discussion quickly shifted to Patwa, and its place in the island's cultural identity and its possible integration into the educational system.

I was not surprised at the tenor of the conversation. More than a few attendees disagreed with the suggestion that Patwa should become an official language or a language of instruction in schools. The conversation reflected familiar attitudes prevalent in Jamaica. As Patrick Gallimore asserted in one letter to the editor in the *Jamaica Gleaner*:

> Teaching a class of students in Patois would be doing those students, particularly at the primary and secondary levels of the Jamaican education system, a disservice. Why? Because it would cripple or severely weaken those students' ability to learn, grasp, communicate in, and eventually, master the English language (Gallimore, 2019).

Yet what I *did* find shocking was one audience member's position that the Jamaican government should abandon any such suggestion because Jamaicans needed to speak English so that when they migrated, they would be able to fit into their host country and find employment.

This comment piqued my interest as a student of Caribbean political economy and development: why would Jamaica—a sovereign state—determine its language policies by the potential integration needs of Jamaican immigrants in their host countries? While Jamaica has long been a labour-exporting country (Nurse, 2004), and consequently, has needed to be attentive to the needs and interests of its diaspora, I was curious about the expectation that the seemingly unrelated socioeconomic needs of Jamaicans outside of Jamaica should dictate its domestic sociocultural policies. In attempting to make sense of these connecting tissues between Jamaican language policy, migration, and migrant socioeconomic success, I turn to political economy to consider what happens when we begin to view language—Jamaican Creole and Jamaican Standard English—as an exploitable economic resource.

Without an extensive excavation of the scholarly and policy literature, one can assert that post-Independence Jamaica has suffered from high debt and low economic growth (Lewis, 2017; Lewis and Kirton, 2015). As Jovan Scott Lewis sharply puts it, the Jamaican "economy can be characterized as one of comprehensive and inescapable precariousness, or as a state of *sufferation*" (Lewis, 2014, p. 12). Revealing its particular Jamaican character, Lewis asserts, "sufferation is a descriptive public discourse used in Jamaican society to denote a condition of being existentially and economically stuck . . . . [It] is a state, a condition, and a position in which one economically struggles." It describes "an arrested self-determination and self-realization couched in structural inequality" that not only defines the lives of everyday Jamaicans, but also the Jamaican state with its stagnant growth, foreign dependence, and high debt (Lewis, 2014, p. 13).

Under these national economic circumstances, tourism and remittances—where remittances have been embedded within the "policy" of migration—have become consistent policy responses by the Jamaican state. Presently, tourism is Jamaica's "bread and butter"— contributing approximately 50 percent of Jamaica's foreign exchange inflow, and generating more than 350,000 jobs annually (Silvera, 2020). Indeed, upon its election in 2016, the Jamaica-Labour-Party-led government established a five-pillar growth strategy for the Ministry of Tourism—"5 x 5 x 5"—which targets securing five million visitors in five years and earning USD $5 billion. Remittances to the island are also an important source of foreign exchange. According to the Bank of Jamaica, deficits in the country's Balance of Payments current account have been consistently reduced by remittance inflows (Ramocan, 2011, p. 1). Remittances are a crucial source of financial support not only for many individual Jamaican families, but also for the state itself. Using the public education system as a case study, Giselle Thompson argues that in the face of structural adjustment and neoliberal austerity, the Jamaican state has become reliant on diasporic philanthropy to meet its public policy commitments: it is a weak state relying on its strong diaspora (Thompson, 2021).

In this political-economic context, language can become "a resource that . . . can be exchanged for other symbolic or material resources" (del Percio, Flubacher and Duchêne, 2016, p. 55). It can take on an increasingly central role in the transnational circulations of capital, commodities, and labour, and can become a key tool in capitalist reproduction by the state. I wish to suggest that in the case of contemporary Jamaica, language—both English and Patwa—has served as an economic resource. Though the state may not have a formal policy commitment in this regard, it has managed to deploy and convert some of its linguistic capital to meet its economic development needs. This conversion, however, is not neutral, traversing long-standing contestations about the proper place of English and Patwa in Jamaican society (Farquharson, 2015), and (re)producing new, yet familiar, forms of stratification amongst speakers—everyday Jamaicans—as producers of language.

A quintessential element of "Brand Jamaica" (Johnson and Gentles-Peart, 2019)—its image, identity, and reputation—is Jamaican Creole. Global fascination with, and interest in, Patwa have grown through the internationalization of Jamaican reggae and dancehall, Rastafarianism, and the expanding diaspora in such global cultural centres as London, New York, and Toronto. In the fiercely competitive global marketplace of tourism, symbolic, often linguistic, resources add value to standardized products (Heller, 2010, p. 104). Despite its undervaluation by elites at home, Patwa is part of constructing "authenticity" for the global tourist consumer familiar with marketing images of Jamaica as a friendly, laid-back island, where everyone and everything is *"irie."*[5] Take for example, Lewis's analysis of Volkswagen USA's 2013 Super Bowl advertisement, "Get Happy."

> It featured a white American office worker in a nondescript company of manifestly disgruntled and pessimistic employees, and opened with the classic nine-to-five worker moan: "I hate Mondays." In the advertisement, the lead actor, speaking in Jamaican patois, encourages everyone to be more optimistic with a heavy dosing of "Jamaicanized" phrases, such as "Turn that frown upside down." When the positive affirmations fail, he eventually succeeds by giving a few colleagues a ride in his Volkswagen Beetle, and they begin speaking in patois as a result (Lewis, 2017, p. 67).

Though the advertisement drew criticisms from the Jamaican media for being a racist caricature, it nonetheless epitomizes a prevailing image of Jamaica in the global tourism market—an image intricately tied to Patwa as a language. The Jamaican state is also implicated in the (re)production of said image. In a recent video produced by the Jamaica Tourist Board (JTB) UK office, two JTB staff give a tutorial on Patwa. The staff preface their lesson with a commentary on the "profound effect" of Patwa on Jamaican culture (Jamaica Tourist Board UK, 2020). Undoubtedly, as a language, Patwa is exploited as a tourist commodity by the state.

Tourists expect a Jamaican experience whose authenticity is measured not by the lived realities of island life, but by the globally circulated images of an island paradise with restorative landscapes, warm people, and beautiful Patwa. This expectation of an "authentic Jamaican experience," which includes hearing/using Jamaican Creole, does not easily square with tourists' expectations of excellent guest service, which require service providers in the tourism industry to communicate in English, the language of the globalized business world. I propose that these dual expectations engender a bifurcated notion of everyday Jamaican-ness along the borders of "tourist" spaces. Jamaicans within these spaces are assumed to operate in English, while those outside operate in the exoticized Jamaican Creole/Patwa.

The pre-eminence of Patwa in tourism, however, is not indicative of a more general regard for the importance of the language. For many Jamaicans, the creative and entertainment industries are the only "acceptable" domains circumscribed for [Patois] (Farquharson, 2015, p. 169). To quote Paul Shoucair in his letter to the editor that appeared in the *Jamaica Gleaner*: "Patois' only strength is as an oral storytelling language and has almost no value in the arena of technology or commerce" (Shoucair, 2019). The elites (and aspiring elites) of Jamaican society have invested in the idea of Jamaica as an "English-speaking" country and perceive Patwa as a globally irrelevant language that serves to disadvantage Jamaicans and Jamaica in engaging with the outside world. As newspaper columnist Glenn Tucker—who self-describes as a sociologist and educator—wrote:

> Electronic technology has contracted the world into a global village. The "Jamaican"-speaking population is only .041 percent of the world's population. Who are we going to convince to learn Patois in order to do business with us? Our relevance in the world depends on our ability to supply a need and negotiate a reasonable price (Tucker, 2012).

The structuring role of macro political-economic conditions in shaping the sentiments that Patwa is an obstacle to socio-economic advancement both in Jamaica and internationally (Farquharson, 2015) should not be underestimated. Still, we must underscore that these sentiments are also the scar tissues from British colonialism and the young nation's fight against its own feelings of inferiority.

The hegemonic ideology in Jamaica holds English to be the language of the elite and of the upward socially mobile. Patwa remains connoted with poverty, backwardness, and the un(der) educated (Farquharson, 2015). The constant hostility towards Patwa is as much about class and race as it is about protecting/ensuring Jamaica's capacity to participate in the global economy. Historically, race and colour were closely related, such that a colour-coded hierarchy has commonly substituted for a racial one in Jamaican society, with "whites" at the top, "browns" in the middle, and "blacks" at the bottom. Contemporary social stratification still broadly reflects this colonial racial and colour classification, with "brownness" now at the top of the racial/colour hierarchy (Thame, 2017). So while a majority of the population identify as African-descended, "blackness" does not map onto a White/Other ordering, and is further complicated by class and skin colour. Farquharson contends that:

The beginning of hostility towards the language [Patois] roughly coincides with the implementation of universal adult suffrage in Jamaica, i.e., when adult Jamaicans of all races, social classes, and linguistic backgrounds got to participate in the political decision-making process. This period also coincides with Louise Bennett's consistent use of Jamaican in print and in the audiovisual media, which blossomed into activism for the acceptance and preservation of the language (Farquharson, 2015, p. 162).

While the hostility towards Patwa may be even pre-date 1944, it is clear that language is and has been deeply implicated in the social relations of race, colour, and class, and the insecurities of the aspiring elite.[6] Yet we cannot ignore how the links between English as the language of global business and Jamaica's place in the global political economy shape the country's policy decisions on language.

Contemporary globalization has created new markets for skilled and feminized labour, which developing states like Jamaica produce and export. Its status as an English-speaking country allows it to attract businesses such as North American call centres, as well as continue to produce and export labour to meet the labour needs of the Global North. Studies show that about 80 percent of university graduates in Jamaica migrate (Ramocan, 2011, p. 71). Though not without its challenges (Lewis and Kirton, 2015), such a high rate of international migration acts as a pressure valve for a stagnant domestic labour market and fuels remittances as a source of financial support for both individual Jamaicans *and* the Jamaican state. There are expectations by the Jamaican government that many Jamaican migrants will become "remittance senders," and will choose to remain in their respective host countries even in times of economic crisis (Ramocan, 2011, p. 71). Despite public platitudes to making "Jamaica the place of choice to live, work, raise families, and do business" (Planning Institute of Jamaica, Vision 2030), the country's sluggish economic situation continues to propel the migration of highly educated/skilled Jamaicans.

It is plausible that given the state's reliance on remittances, along with its formal strategy of training professionals for export (Lewis and Kirton, 2015, p. 187), those in power will continue to uphold English as the official language and the language of instruction. In the production of labour for export, language becomes an important marker of the communication capacity and productive potentiality of future immigrants. It then becomes of prime importance that citizens are suitably prepared to migrate and become successful in their host countries. Under these conditions, there are greater returns on investment in English than Patwa, except in the areas of tourism and cultural export.

By placing the ongoing debate on language in Jamaica in a wider context of global political economy and development, it becomes clear that language is a resource deployed as a tool for development. This may not be a formal strategy of the state, but the broad commodification of Jamaican Creole/Patwa to increase the competitiveness of the tourism product, along with the continued investment in the idea of Jamaica as an English-speaking country in global business, suggests that there is at least a recognition by the state of its linguistic capital. A worthwhile project for the Jamaican state is to determine the effective conversion of this capital to meet its development needs. Such a project necessarily entails placing Patwa on equal footing with Jamaican Standard English in the sociocultural space, and authentically addressing the affective complexes attached to language in Jamaican society. A recognition of the intimate ties between language and development may yet offer a path towards an official bilingualism. But even if not, I contend that the state's recognition of language as an economic resource may engender space for us to acknowledge the social exploitation at play in our engagement with Patwa more directly. In both the global cultural arena and the global marketplace, the Jamaican brand cannot be divorced from its Patwa. Yet the language and the ordinary Jamaicans, who in their speaking, regenerate and reinvent it, are discriminated against on home soil. A reframing (of the question) of language in political economic terms may allow us to revalue Patwa outside of the cultural domain, and to fruitfully engage with the place of our two languages in Jamaica's sociocultural *and* economic development. Perhaps then we can move beyond the fractured notion of *Patwa a yaad, and English abroad.*

Endnotes

1   This refers to a Jamaican corner shop, which is similar to bodegas and convenience stores in North America. Much smaller in size than a supermarket, they typically sell household items, food stocks, and sometimes, liquor.

2   "Pickney raise inna shop,"—a child raised in a/the shop. It is typical for children whose primary caregivers operate corner shops or small stores in Jamaica to spend their after-school time and weekends in the shops or stores—whether or not they were assisting with tasks.

3   Introduced to Jamaica in 1957, the Common Entrance Examination (CEE) was a national exit examination that students at the primary level were required to take to gain placement in a secondary school. The CEE had three parts: English, Mathematics, and Mental Ability. As Buttrick (1995) found: "The test of mathematics is easier for most students than is the English test, which is 'class-biased,' in that many children from poor families do not find books at home, nor is standard English spoken there" (p. 358). I would argue that not speaking standard English at home also applies to many families who would be considered middle class. This is certainly true for my family.

4   Uptown/downtown references a rough calculus and division of the middle/upper classes (uptown) from the working classes (downtown) in Kingston, Jamaica.

5   "Irie"—good, pleasing, nice; initially associated with the speech patterns of Rastafarians, the term has been widely adopted within Patwa and is featured in the tourism industry as short-hand for the good feelings associated with the island.

6   Returning to the conversation between Jamaican authors Kei Miller, Marlon James, and Nicole Dennis-Benn, Miller notes that language and the use of Patwa are social issues for Jamaica's middle class, not the upper classes. The place of Patwa may trigger insecurities for those with "Brown" middle-class aspirations, more so than those already securely middle and upper class. Miller goes on to note that there is a moneyed middle-class with historical ties to wealth, and an intellectual middle class that emerged post-independence. These multiple identity formations complicate our discussions of the proper place of Patwa. See https://www.youtube.com/watch?v=IUC2SqxKJhg.

References

Buttrick, J. "About the Common Entrance Examination." *Social and Economic Studies*, vol. 44, no. 2 and 3, 1995, pp. 358—364.

Del Percio, A., Flubacher, M. and Duchêne, A. "Language and Political Economy." *The Oxford Handbook of Language and Society*. Edited by

O. García, N. Flores and M. Spotti. New York: Oxford University Press, 2016, pp. 55—75.

Dennis-Benn, N., Miller, K. and James, M. "Jamaican Letters: Past, Present, Future." *Key West Literary Seminar,* September 2019, https://www.youtube.com/watch?v=IUC2SqxKJhg.

Farquharson, J.T. "The Black Man's Burden?—Language and Political Economy in a Diglossic State and Beyond." *Zeitschrift für Anglistik und Amerikanistik,* vol. 63, no. 2, 2015, pp. 157—177.

Heller, M. "The Commodification of Language." *Annual Review of Anthropology,* vol. 39, no. 1, 2010, pp. 101—14.

Henry, A. "Patwa: Its Power, Politics and Possibilities." *Jamaica in the Canadian Experience: A Multiculturalizing Presence.* Edited by Carl E. James and Andrea Davis. Halifax: Fernwood Publishing, 2012, pp. 98—105.

Jamaica Tourist Board UK, "The Jamaican Dialect Patois Has a Profound Effect on Today's Vibrant Popular Culture, and it Has a Cool Factor." Facebook, July 30, 2020, https://www.facebook.com/watch/?v=918129965359901.

Johnson, H. and Gentles-Peart, K. (eds). *Brand Jamaica: Reimagining a National Image and Identity.* Lincoln: University of Nebraska Press, 2019.

Gallimore, P. "Leave Jamaican Patois Alone." *Jamaica Gleaner,* November 15, 2019, https://jamaica-gleaner.com/article/letters/20191115/leave-jamaican-patois-alone.

Lewis, J.S. "Rights, Indigeneity, and the Market of Rastafari." *International Journal of Cultural Property,* vol. 24, 2017, pp. 57—77.

Lewis, J.S. "Sufferer's Market: Sufferation and Economic Ethics in Jamaica." PhD thesis, London School of Economics and Political Science, 2014.

Lewis, P. and Kirton, C. "Migration and Remittances in Development: A Study of Jamaica." *Migration and Development: Perspectives from Small States.* Edited by W. H. Khonje. London: Commonwealth Secretariat, 2015, pp. 186—243.

Nurse, K. *Diaspora, Migration and Development in the Caribbean.* Ottawa: Canadian Foundation for the Americas, 2014, pp. 1—12.

Ramocan, E. G. "Remittances to Jamaica: Findings from a National Survey of Remittance Recipients." Remittance Survey 2010, Kingston: Bank of Jamaica, 2011.

Shoucair, P. "Patois' Only Strength is Oral Storytelling." *Jamaica Gleaner*, December 21, 2019, https://jamaica-gleaner.com/article/letters/20191221/patois-only-strength-oral-storytelling.

Silvera, J. "Tourism Reopening a Matter of Economic Life or Death—Bartlett." *Jamaica Gleaner*, June 5, 2020, https://jamaica-gleaner.com/article/lead-stories/20200605/tourism-reopening-matter-economic-life-or-death-bartlett.

Thame, M. "Racial Hierarchy and the Elevation of Brownness in Creole Nationalism." *Small Axe*, vol. 54, 2017, pp. 111—123.

Thompson, G. "Weak State, Strong Diaspora: A Case Study on Education in Jamaica." *The Handbook on Caribbean Education*. Edited by E. J. Blair and K. A. Williams. Charlotte, NC: Information Age Publishing, 2021, pp. 297—312.

Tucker, G. "Stop This 'Teach Patois' Nonsense!" *Jamaica Gleaner*, August 29, 2012, https://jamaica-gleaner.com/gleaner/20120829/cleisure/cleisure2.html.

Planning Institute of Jamaica. "Welcome to Vision 2030 Jamaica," http://www.vision2030.gov.jm/.

PATWA: POWER, POLITICS, AND POSSIBLITIES[1]

Annette Henry

> Persons belonging to national or ethnic, religious, and linguistic minorities (hereinafter referred to as persons belonging to minorities) have the right to enjoy their own culture, to profess and practise their own religion, and to use their own language, in private and in public, freely and without interference or any form of discrimination.
>
> —*United Nations Declaration on the Rights of Persons Belonging to National or Ethnic, Religious and Linguistic Minorities*

In Praise of Jamaican Language

I had the pleasure of my mother living with me for the last six years of her life. Now that she has passed on, my one constant link to Jamaican language and culture has also departed from my life. Our elders are living archives; they link us to an intergenerational cultural memory. As I would come home and slip into my most comfortable clothes, so was the feeling of hearing my mother's Jamaican speech—the affect, inflections, the pet names for every family member, the gestures, such as kissing her teeth, the plural markers (di bwoy-dem), and the particular tones of voice, rhythms germane only to Jamaicans, and dare I say, Jamaican mothers. I'll miss the reduplication—"kete-kete," or "long, long time"—the unique vocalizations—"Eh-eh!"—the discussion of dreams in the morning, and the stories of duppies and rolling calves. Even her laugh! A Jamaican laugh rises up from the depths of the lower belly, full, joyous, and unapologetic. Ah, the metaphors, the everyday creativity, and the poetry of the language! The use of sayings, proverbs, and other Jamaicanisms are significant cultural ways of theorizing. The joy of hearing a Jamaican talk is like biting into a sweet mango, juices running down your chin and onto your hands.

Language and Identity

About six months after her retirement, my mother confessed, "I'm so glad I don't have to speak Standard English anymore!" This utterance was a surprise. Always eloquent, always articulate, she never gave the impression that the Standard English varieties of Britain or Canada, places where we lived, were an imposition. She had never given the impression that she longed to relax into a more personalized form of speech—albeit, it was the language of home, her family, her feelings, her heart.

In raising her children, my mother emphasized the reality that Black people are judged the moment we open our mouths. My parents knew, without reading the research, that in the UK and Canada, Black/ Jamaican students are often stereotyped as deficient because of their language, and sometimes erroneously placed in remedial classes or embarrassed by teachers in front of peers. The languages we speak are implicated in society's view of us, and our views of ourselves. Once, I heard some Latina friends debating whether one could be a "real" Latina if she didn't speak Spanish. I wondered, *Can one call herself a Jamaican if she doesn't speak "patois?"*[2]

Across social classes, many children of Jamaican descent are raised to disregard or dismiss Jamaican language, known as Creole to linguistics, and patois to its speakers. Attitudes regarding the use of Jamaican Creole vary according to region, social status, age, and gender (The Jamaican Language Unit, 2005). Indeed, our foreparents, who received a particular kind of British colonialist education, were taught that patois was an inferior and illegitimate vernacular. In Caribbean countries, contemporary efforts to establish Creoles as national languages and languages of instruction have been welcomed by some, scorned by others, and even met with great suspicion and accusations of "keeping our children back." In Jamaica, opponents argue that Jamaican Patois should remain the language of the home and other informal settings. It is widely accepted, in practice and in research (Bialystock, 2001; Nero and Stevens, 2018), that speaking one's home language does not inhibit literacy development in the wider society. However, the ideological biases against Caribbean Creoles are deeply entrenched in the dominant society and in our cultural memory of shame and inferiority vis-a-vis an imposed British colonial standard. My parents had some Jamaican-Canadian friends in Ontario in the 1960s. The husband introduced himself and his wife with an affected "British" accent: "My wife is Jamaican, and I am British West Indian," he explained. I was only nine years old, yet I remember being struck by the discrepancy between this man's thinking and his actual language practice. A Native American colleague once confessed that he never writes on the board while teaching because he sometimes makes spelling mistakes while speaking and writing simultaneously. He feared that his students would think, "That Indian can't even spell!" These examples reflect the weight of a colonialist past that lingers into the linguistic present. Language discrimination—linguicism—and the pressures to attain an uncomfortable standard of language use affect our sense of identity, sense of competence, and affect our perceptions of success in the wider world.

The Meanings of Patwa

Jamaican Creole—or Patois, or Patwa—can represent a secret language, a language of power, of self-determination, of pride, of resistance, of comfort, of inclusion, of solidarity, of struggle, and of voice. We may joyously dip and slide along the sociolinguistic continuum of Standard English and Patois, sometimes with intention, for rhetorical or stylistic purposes, and at other times, imperceptibly. When I was a schoolteacher, I would witness students codeswitching between English and Patois with great delight when they didn't want the (white Canadian) teachers to understand, when they wanted to show solidarity, and when they wanted to defy the social norms of Eurocentric Canadian schooling that stresses a particular "standard." Canadian youth who are not Jamaican often perceive the language as "cool." Popular culture, music, and the media have helped to enhance this "coolness." Language frames our desires, subjectivities, and social and cultural worlds.

Language, by nature, is ever evolving. Jamaican Creole in Jamaica and beyond reflects a colonialist past where languages, cultures, and histories have struggled, melded, and are constantly created anew in a postcolonial present. Contemporary Jamaican Standard English (JSE) is influenced by other World Englishes (especially American). In this globalized and post-colonial world, influenced by the Internet, social media, and transnationalism, the language of Jamaica and Jamaicans represents processes of hybridity, cross-fertilization, and syncretism. Jamaicans in Canada and in Jamaica speak a language of multiple locations and borders.

Poets Theorizing Language

Poet and essayist Marlene Nourbese Philip has written copiously about "the anguish that is English in Colonial societies" (Philip, 1989, p. 11). She writes:

> ... and english is
> my mother tongue
> is
> my father tongue
> is a foreign lan lan lang
> language
> l/anguish
> anguish...
> (Philip, 1989, p. 56)

Philip feels that she has no choice but to use English as the base from which she works, but it is a father tongue for her—an international, written language, rather than a mother tongue—a localized and personalized one (Philip, 1989). Father tongues, rather than mother tongues (Creoles), remind us, in some sense, of a pervasive "master discourse" (Davies, 1995), a language which categorizes and positions us in a discourse "that reflects the realities of those who must *speak through more than one language/culture at once*" (Chancy 1997, p. 11). Consider Grace Nichols, one of many Caribbean poets who captures this multiplicity:

> I have crossed an ocean
> I have lost my tongue

From the root of the old one
A new one has sprung (Nichols 1984, p. 63).

These poets express how we embrace the world with an insider/outsider linguistic consciousness. Loving Jamaican language and culture involves a recognition of the colonialist past as well as the challenges of living in an ever-changing global society. This "new tongue" that "sprung" has necessarily been embroiled in dissent and controversy.

The idea of a Patois Bible has long exemplified this controversy from the moment it was proposed by Faith Linton in the 1950s, when she was an English and Literature teacher. To coincide with the fiftieth anniversary of Jamaican Independence, the *Jamaican New Testament*, (JNT) was released in 2012 in Jamaica and Britain, where there is a large Jamaican population. Articles published in Jamaican and international newspapers in anticipation of the Bible translation project reflected some of the national resistance to the project. Consider the following cartoon from the *Jamaica Gleaner*, in which Bruce Golding, then prime minister, expresses his sentiments:

(*Jamaica Gleaner*, July 1, 2008)

The Jamaican Creole translation project describes its sole aim as one of providing Jamaicans the Bible "in their heart language."[3] Online commentaries of ordinary citizens worldwide reveal a range of reactions to this project. Some believe that it makes a mockery of God and spirituality. One person referred to it as a "Joke Bible" (Ade-

Gold, 2008). Another wrote on *Jamaicans.com* that when people will hear the parson read from the patois Bible, "Nuff people ago dead wid LAUGH" (Dennis, 1998). Some Christians, however, have claimed that it creates a relationship with a more intimate God. The *Daily Mail* cites a Jamaican pastor who says, "People feel liberated. They say they are able to visualize the Bible better" (*Daily Mail* Reporter, 2010). The Rev. Courtney Stewart, general secretary of the Bible Society of the West Indies argues, "The Scriptures have the greatest impact when you hear it in your mother tongue. So this translation to Creole is affirming the Jamaican speaker's language, and it is very, very powerful" (*Daily Mail* Reporter, 2010). To the question, "Does *God* speak Patois?" Oscar Green (2021) responds, "Absolutely! Any Jamaican Christian will tell you that they communicate with Him daily," and as for God's preferred language: "*a patwa iim luv chat*" (73).

Despite the fundamental right to use one's own language in private and public (*Declaration on the Rights of Persons Belonging to National or Ethnic, Religious and Linguistic Minorities*), the King James Version of the Bible has been intricately interwoven into everyday Jamaican culture and music. It is an ingrained part of Jamaican life for the unschooled and erudite alike. Indeed, as some argue adamantly in favour of its literary value, Lindsay Johns, who describes himself as a "staunch atheist," writes to the *Daily Mail*:

> [N]othing can compare with the rich, mellifluous, and hypnotically beautiful cadences of the magisterial King James Version and the cultural and literary touchstone it has now become. The phrases, allusions, and imagery are . . . an acknowledged masterpiece of literature in its own right (Johns, 2011).

Hubert Devonish, Professor Emeritus of the Jamaica Language Unit at the University of West Indies, Mona Campus, explained, "We've now produced a major body of literature in the language, whatever people may think about it one way or the other. And that is part of the process of convincing people that this thing is a serious language with a standard writing system," (David McFadden, 2012).

What Does it Mean to be Literate in the 21st Century?

Post-Independence musicians, writers, and other artists have been instrumental in redefining and concretizing Jamaican national and diasporic identities through literary and social texts. Some Jamaican educators and linguists have been grappling with the complexities of envisioning Jamaica as a bilingual country (English and Jamaican Creole) and Jamaican Creole as a veritable language amid resistance; they have been working out practical matters such as standardizing orthography and finding suitable curricula and pedagogy for biliteracies in Jamaican schools (see Moren and Moren 2007; Devonish 2010; Linton, 2015; Nero and Stevens, 2018). These efforts are cloaked in debates about how best to prepare children with the necessary twenty-first century literacies. Opponents question the appropriateness of Jamaican Creole in the curriculum as a tool in preparing global citizens. Some even point to the contradiction that the very people who advocate formalizing Creole in schools received a traditional Eurocentric education and send their own children to elite preparatory and secondary schools. These issues of Jamaican language as the medium of instruction are not unrelated to Canadian debates of culturally and linguistically relevant curricula and pedagogy for Jamaican-Canadian students, and how to validate and build upon the home language practices that students with Jamaican backgrounds bring to the classroom. Canadian classrooms in urban areas would be more linguistically diverse than the classrooms of their Jamaican counterparts. However, teachers' understandings and validations of mother tongues, and the ways in which children may speak and write can act as springboards for dynamic critical literacy practices in Canadian classrooms, and in the case of Jamaican Patois, instill a sense of pride for one's language that centuries of colonial thinking have eroded.

Students in Jamaica and abroad can benefit from formally learning Creole and learning about Creole. They will appreciate its history and hybridity (Cooper, 2011; Kowenberg, et al., 2011). This learning is part of what Vèvè Clarke named "Diaspora Literacy" (1990), which involves people of African heritages understanding their languages and cultures from informed, indigenous perspectives. Understanding and validating one's linguistic heritage contributes to sustaining an intergenerational cultural memory and involves understanding correspondences with West African languages and the social and political history of languages in contact. Indeed, Caribbean languages are cloaked in histories of exile and slavery and reveal a people's creative strategies for linguistic and cultural survival.

Since 2008, the UN General Assembly has recognized the necessity to preserve and protect all languages of all peoples. In her message for International Mother Language Day, 2012, Irina Bokova, then director-general of UNESCO, emphasized, "The language of our thoughts and our emotions is our most valuable asset. Multilingualism is our ally in ensuring quality education for all, in promoting inclusion and in combating discrimination" (Bokova, 2012). As the Declaration of Rights above underscores, people have the right to conduct their daily lives in their mother tongue. The validation of Creoles in the curriculum does not impede English literacy. One does not exclude the other. In bilingual educational contexts, children's literacies increase in both languages. Importantly, we need to recognize and appreciate the spectrum of language practices in various social and cultural contexts in Jamaica, the Caribbean and in the diaspora (Youssef 2004). A Creole-inclusive language curriculum can contribute to understanding the rich cultural and political histories of the Caribbean and of Caribbean Canadians. Educators need to ensure equitable access to a quality *"both/and"* education for students of African heritage (Henry, 1998; Bryan, 2010)—an education that allows students *both* to understand their lives, histories, and languages, and dream about their futures from their own informed, indigenous perspectives. *And* an education that affords students equitable access to twenty-first century knowledges with the required critical literacies to participate as confident, competent international citizens in a globalized, transnational world.

Endnotes

1 This is an updated version of an essay which first appeared in *Jamaicans in the Canadian Experience: A Multiculturalizing Presence*. Carl E. James and Andrea Davis, eds. Halifax: Fernwood Press, 2012, pp. 98—105.

2 Linguists would call Jamaican language a "Creole," whereas the everyday Jamaican would refer to it in a range of ways: Patois, Patwa, Jamaican, and unfortunately, "bad" or "broken" English. Creoles are languages

with origins in one or two other languages, as Grace Nichols expresses in her poem in this essay. For the purposes of this chapter, I use Jamaican Creole, Patois, and Patwa rather interchangeably. Creoles have their own rule-governed grammars and sound systems. Much of the vocabulary of JC is English-based, a reality that has helped to promote the notion that it is a corrupt, inferior form of English. The lines of demarcation between dialects, creoles, languages are often geopolitical. For example, a dialect of a particular language might have less similarity than two distinct languages.

3   Historically, the Bible has always been translated into people's vernaculars, and this Creole project is no exception. A team returned to the original Greek and compared with English translations and translated the ideas in culturally appropriate ways. (See http://jamiekanbaibl.org/lib/runPeople.php, and CBC Sunday Edition, http://www.cbc.ca/thesundayedition/shows/2010/12/19/december-19-2010/.)

References

Ade-Gold, C. "Patois Bible, A weh yuh a seh!" *Jamaica Gleaner*, June 23, 2008, Retrieved April 1, 2012, http://jamaica-gleaner.com/gleaner/20080623/news/news9.html.

Bialystok, E. *Bilingualism in Development: Language, Literacy and Cognition*. Cambridge: Cambridge University Press, 2001.

Bokova, I. "International Mother Language Day: Mother Tongue Instruction and Inclusive Education," 2012, http://www.un.org/en/events/motherlanguageday/.

Bryan, B. *Between Two Grammars: Research and Practice for Language Learning and Teaching in a Creole-Speaking Environment*. Kingston: Ian Randle Publishers, 2010.

Chancy, M.J.A. *Framing Silence: Revolutionary Novels by Haitian Women*. New Brunswick NJ: Rutgers University Press, 1997.

Clark, V. "Developing Diaspora Literacy and Marasa Consciousness." *Comparative American Identities*. Edited by H. Spillers. New York: Routledge, 1991, pp. 40—60.

Cooper, C. "Governor General Gives Throne Speech in Patois." *Jamaica Gleaner*, November 6, 2011, http://jamaica-gleaner.com/gleaner/20111106/cleisure/cleisure3.html.

"Di ienjel go tu Mieri . . .:Jamaican Church Creates Patois Gospel of Luke After Congregation Fails to Grasp King James Bible." *Daily Mail*, December 21, 2010, Retrieved March 15, 2012, http://www.dailymail.co.uk/news/article-1340185/Jamaican-church-creates-patois-Bible-congregations-struggle-understand-standard-English-version.html#ixzz1qX5yFu5n.

Davies, C.B. "Hearing Black Women's Voices: Transgressing Imposed Boundaries." *Moving Beyond Boundaries, vol.1: International Dimensions of Black Women's Writing*. Edited by C. Boyce Davies and M. Ogundipe-Leslie. New York: New York University Press, 1995, pp. 3—15.

Dennis, L. "Di Bible in Patois." Jamaicans.com, August 20, 1998, Retrieved April1, 2002, http://www.jamaicans.com/culture/jatimes/bible.shtml.

Devonish, H. "Professor Hubert Devonish, Advocate for Jamaican Patois as a Language." Jamaicans.com, January 1, 2010, Retrieved March 15, 2012, http://www.jamaicans.com/speakja/patoisarticle/JamaicanPatoisLanguage-2.shtml.

Green, O. "God and Patois in Jamaica." *Caribbean Journal of Theology*. vol. 20, 2021, pp. 67—74.

Henry, A. *Taking Back Control: Black Women Teachers' Activism and the Education of African Canadian Children*. New York: State University of New York Press, 1998.

The Jamaican Language Unit. *A Proposal for: Bilingual Education Project*. Department of Language Linguistics and Philosophy, The University of the West Indies, Mona, Jamaica. Unpublished Manuscript, 2004.

The Jamaican Language Unit. "The Language Attitude Survey of Jamaica." Department of Language, Linguistics and Philosophy: University of the West Indies, Mona, Jamaica, 2005, Retrieved April 1, 2012, http://www.mona.uwi.edu/dllp/jlu/projects/

Report%20for%20Language%20Attitude%20Survey%20of%20Jamaica.pdf.

Johns, L. "Lord Have Mercy! Jesus, Unno Ready Fe Dis?" *Daily Mail*, December 19, 2011, Retrieved March 15, 2012, http://johnsblog.dailymail.co.uk/2011/12/lord-have-mercy-jesus-unno-ready-fe-dis.html.

Kouwenberg, S., Anderson-Brown, W., Barrett, T., Dean, S., Lisser, T., Douglas, H., and Scott, J. "Linguistics in the Caribbean: Empowerment Through Creole Language Awareness." *Journal of Pidgin & Creole Languages*, vol. 26, no. 2, 2011.

Linton, F. "UNESCO Guidelines and Jamaican Patois." *Jamaica Gleaner*, April 15, 2011, Retrieved July 7, 2012, https://jamaica-gleaner.com/gleaner/20110415/cleisure/cleisure3.html.

McFadden, D. "Jamaica Gets First Patois Bible." *Caribbean Life*, December 11, 2012, Retrieved July 6, 2012, https://www.caribbeanlifenews.com/jamaica-gets-first-patois-bible/.

Morren, R. and Morren, D. "Are the Goals and Objectives of Jamaica's Bilingual Education Project Being Met?" *Summer Institute of Linguistics International Electronic Working Papers 2007—2009*.

Nero, S. and Stevens, L. "Analyzing Students' Writing in a Jamaican Creole-Speaking Context: An Ecological and Systemic Functional Approach." *Linguistics and Education*, vol. 43, 2018, pp. 13—24.

Nichols, G. *The Fat Black Woman's Poems*. London: Virago, 1984.

Philip, M.N. *She Tries her Tongue: Her Silence Softly Breaks*. Charlottetown: Ragweed Press, 1989.

Philip, M.N. "Managing the Unmanageable." *Caribbean Women Writers: Essays From the First International Conference*. Edited by S. R. Cudjoe. Wellesley MA: Calaloux Publications, 1990.

Project for Jamaican Creole. "About the Project," 2012, http://jamiekanbaibl.org/lib/runHome.php.

Youssef, V. "Is English We Speakin: Trinbagonian in the 21st Century." *English Today*, vol. 20, no. 4, 2004.

"WAA GWAAN?"[1]:
THE CONSTRUCTION OF BLACK LANGUAGE AND IDENTITY IN TORONTO

Carl E. James

Jamaican slang was big growing up. I grew up in an area with a lot of Jamaicans, and we even had a Jamaican neighbour. However, I would not say that they represented the largest nationality in my area. Despite this, Jamaican Patwa was used frequently by many, particularly by racialized people. To be honest, there are some words now that I use frequently that I forget have Jamaican origins. I still continue to use "Man dem"[2] with non-Jamaican friends who I grew up with, but also with non-Jamaican friends who grew up in different hoods. I actually don't even think of "Man dem" as a Jamaican thing anymore (Jama, of Ethiopian descent).

Similarly, reflecting on their language experiences growing up in their racially diverse Northwest Toronto community, "Afro-Latinx and Afro-Caribbean" brothers, Jon and Rian, whose home language was Spanish, also acknowledged that the Jamaican language had "a big influence" on them. And as Jon stated: "From elementary to high school, many of my friends were Jamaican." But even though it was common, or more likely, for young people to have Jamaicans friends—given that Jamaicans comprise a majority of the Black Canadian or "Afrodiasporic" (Campbell, 2012a) population (Statistics Canada 2007)[3]—as Rian asserted: "There was this affinity for the Jamaican language by virtue of being Black."

In this chapter, I reflect on Black youth's "affinity for the Jamaican language," and its role in helping to define them as Black people residing in Canada. As such, the Jamaican language does not merely serve as a primary reference or influence for the language of Black Canadian youth because most of them are of Jamaican descent. Rather, it is a product of their active construction of an identity that speaks to their "difference" as Canadians or Torontonians—in which colour, race, gender,[4] and in some cases, dress—mark them as foreign or outsiders, and not African American[5] (Campbell, 2012a; James, 2012a, K. James, 2001; Walcott and Abdillahi, 2019). In discussing the use of "Black Toronto" language and its relationship to the Jamaican language,[6] I reference comments related to me in Spring 2021 by Jama, Jon, Rian, and Addie, who were in their late twenties-early thirties. They discussed with me how, as Rian puts it, "Jamaican language and culture have been synonymous with the identity of many Black Canadians." Through conversations, written texts, and follow-up clarifications—essentially, telling me "waa gwaan"—they provided insights that are used here to tell of the construction, articulation, and use of Black Toronto language, and its relationship to Jamaica and Blackness.

Toronto's Black language:

In their article, "Black English in Toronto: A New Dialect?" Baxter and Peters (2013) write that "ongoing research on ethnic variation in Toronto English has found that younger generations of Italian- and Chinese-Canadians generally assimilate" to dominant speech pattern of Toronto, suggesting that "their English does not differ significantly from that of speakers of British/Irish heritage" (p. 1). But in the case of Black individuals, their "preliminary study" indicates that:

> Second-generation Black Torontonians have not assimilated to the larger English-speaking speech community in the way that second generation speakers of other ethnicities . . . have been found to do. The persistence of difference appears to be linked, at least in part, to language transfer from Jamaican Creole, or perhaps dialect transfer from Jamaican English . . .. The evidence suggests that Black speakers in Toronto may be speaking a new and different variety of English. We have found that this variety is spoken by Black residents of different neighbourhoods, including Black enclaves like Jane and Finch, as well as non-enclave suburban neighbourhoods (Baxter and Peters, 2013, p. 11).

The researchers further observed that their study participants, particularly those from Jane and Finch,[7] considered themselves to be "not only more visible, but actively marginalized, oppressed, and isolated by mainstream society." This contributed to the "very insular, tight-knit community" with "very loyal and supportive" members (p. 11). Therefore, it should be of no surprise, as the researchers submit, that "such an entrenched separation from the larger community would also have a linguistic effect" (Baxter and Peters, 2013, p. 11).

The Jamaican language—or "Jamaican Creole, or patois, or patwa," as Annette Henry writes (in this collection) "can represent a secret language, a language of power, of self-determination, of pride, of resistance, of comfort, of inclusion, of solidarity, of struggle, and of voice." Campbell (2012b) adds that it is also a language of empowerment, protest, protection, and endearment—and in the case of young Black men, it serves in their assertion of masculinity, and to "combat the micro-aggressions of daily racism and devaluation" (p. 123). Developed in colonial Jamaica, where enslaved Africans, in the words of Raven Wilkinson, "hybridized the languages of oppression— English, French, Spanish, and Dutch—and their own West African languages," the language that was created (cited in Wijekoon, 2020; see also Cooper, 2016) has gained much prominence locally and transnationally. With its rich lexicon, wordplay and sound, the language as it is spoken outside of Jamaica is not merely the result of migrant Jamaicans who have maintained their mother tongue in diasporic spaces such as Toronto and London (England),[8] but through the music such as reggae, ska, dancehall, and other genres of music (Campbell, 2012a; K. James, 2001: Martis, 2016), as well as the poetry and prose of icons like Louise Bennett-Coverley (see Bennett, 1966; Cooper, 1993; Morris, 2014).

In his essay, "The Gwannings," which opens with "Eh, wha a gwan my yout," [What's going on] Mark Campbell (2012b) tells us that "the day my mother corrected me[9] for asking my friend 'What's gwanning?'[10] was the first time I paid attention to the very creative ways in which the Patois/Patwa word 'gwan' has been transmitted into the Toronto context," where, while "being treated like a standard English word," gwan, as he points out, "somehow acquired an 'ing' ending" (p. 124). Similarly, writing some ten years earlier about asserting his Canadian identity as a Black person of Caribbean background, high school student Kai James (2001) pens: "Black Canadian youth have created a cultural blend that is unique and truly Canadian." For instance, the Jamaican greeting, "Wha' gwaan?" and the Canadian version, "What's going on?" became "What's gwanning?" (p. 19).

Furthermore, as Campbell signals, language, like culture, is always evolving—taking on meanings, symbols, accents, and essence in relation to the social and political contexts of its users and creators. As a symbol of Blackness for individuals who identity as Black, and those with whom they socialized in the culture of Blackness, the Black language of Toronto—representing community, resistance, and mobilization (Campbell, 2012a; K. James, 2001; Martis, 2016)—will be the means of communication. So as Campbell (2012b) writes, one should not be surprised to hear Tamil, Filipino, and Vietnamese youth using Black Toronto language.[11] And it might be argued that a level of recognition was shown when Premier Doug Ford said, in Patwa: "Ten a yuh yard"[12]—one of twenty-two languages he used on January 21, 2021—in admonishing Ontarians to "Stay at home" to avoid getting or spreading COVID-19 (see Davidson, January 21, 2021).

Further, in her *Globe and Mail* article, "Di Sound in di City," columnist Dakshana Bascaramurty (2017) writes: "After decades of West Indian immigration to the GTA, patois-peppered English has begun to feel like a distinctively Toronto thing."[13] And she goes on to say:

> Caribbean culture has become so influential in the city that bits of the patois language and the accent that goes with it have filtered down to much of the rest of the population, including Drake, creating what both linguists and visitors to the city notice as a very distinctly suburban Toronto sound. South Asians in Mississauga respond to questions with ahlie [you lie] as an affirmation or to state skepticism. Croatians in Malvern will say, from time, in reference to something that happened long ago. Somalis in Rexdale will greet each other with a Wah gwan? rather than asking, What's up.

Linguists like Derek Denis, University of Toronto, have argued that "when immigrants from a variety of backgrounds come together in one place, such as London, New York, Paris, or Toronto," what frequently emerges are "dialects of the local language that include words from multiple ethnic groups"—which he refers to as "multi-ethnolects," and such dialects are usually spoken in working-class neighbourhoods

(Anderson, 2019). Denis recalls that in 2015, when telling students that researchers began hearing the word "*man*" being used in the place of "I" in immigrant neighbourhoods of London, England, a young woman spoke up, saying: "But we have something just like that here." The student later shared with Denis messages she had received from friends—such as, "*Mans* has work in the morning. How about you?" The professor went on to theorize that "*mans/man* evolved" in both London and Toronto "independently, but from the same Caribbean language" (Anderson, 2019). The fact is, as Wijekoon (2020) writes, "The experiences of Toronto's Black communities are reflected in the Black communities of London, England, where the Jamaican diaspora, along with many of London's vibrant immigrant communities, has created "Multicultural London English," a dialect that is strikingly similar to what is found in Toronto" (see also, Bascaramurty, 2017).[14] In London, England, *Jafaikan* or *Jafaican*, described as "a blend of *Jamaican* and *African*," and "a new multicultural dialect," is not a word, as Quinion (2006) writes, "you'll find in any dictionary, but it can be heard on the streets of London . . . that is appearing among young Londoners, whether their parents are of Bengali, West Indian, Arab, Brazilian, or English stock."[15]

That generations of Black students of Caribbean and African descent—and their peers[16]—are, as Dakshana Bascaramurty (2017) points out, "lacing their speech with patois," makes it "no longer a Jamaican language, but a black language." And as with all other languages, there is a Toronto version in which individuals engage in a form of speech alternation or "code-switching" (Myers-Scotton, 2017). In other words, Black language and Canadian English are spoken in certain contexts and amongst certain people and groups. This switching from one language to another often functions in the production of new versions of both languages (Campbell, 2012b; K. James, 2001).[17] For instance, in the case of Black Toronto language, there is "a faint, but audible accent that is accompanied by high levels of what linguists call t/d-deletion—dropping the final T or D in a word, as in 'I can' wai' to go there,' or 'She pass' her exam yesterday'" (Bascaramurty, 2017). In what follows, I explore what my four raconteurs—Jama, Jon, Rian, and Addie—had to say about their use of Toronto's hybrid of the Jamaican language, or "Toronto Black Language," while growing up. They reflect on the role of the language in their construction of identities, and how music helped to facilitate or advance the language. And the section ends with unabbreviated reflective accounts from Rian and Addie.

Language, Identity, Music: Growing Up with "Toronto Black Language"

As mentioned earlier, participants in my discussions of "Jamaican language" indicated that the language figured prominently in their lives and friendships while growing up in their respective racially diverse communities. And it is often in these kinds of communities that individuals engage in conversations in which their speech is interspersed with "patois" (Bascaramurty, 2017) as they code switch (Myers-Scotton, 2017) and develop assorted "dialects" (Anderson, 2019). Here is how Jon remembers life growing up with his friend and speaking the language:

> Jamaican culture has undoubtably become part of Toronto's mainstream culture. As an Afro-Latino growing up Toronto, a city with a strong Black population of Jamaican descent, many of my friends were Jamaican. Naturally, by hanging out with my friends and their families, I became familiar and was influenced by the beauty and richness that is Jamaican culture and language. While visiting my friends' homes, I became familiar with Jamaican food, music, and language. At a young age, although I am an Afro-Latino from the Dominican Republic, a part of my socialization during my formative years was shaped by these friendships. Reggae, dancehall music, and home-cooked Jamaican meals like oxtail, curry goat, jerk chicken, and rice and peas were not foreign to me.

Jon went on to say that growing up around his Jamaican friends made it possible for him to become familiar with some common words and phrases—such as "Wah gwaan," "Ting," "Ah lie," "Man dem," and "Yute" [youth]—which became part of their daily communication. And he affirmed that "it is not only the use of these words that has shaped Toronto's mainstream culture, but quite foundationally, the Jamaican accent used to pronounce these words. In fact, sometimes a Jamaican accent is used outside of these words in an attempt to sound Jamaican." Here, Jon is alluding to the fact that words and sound sometimes overlap, and sometimes not.

Concurring with his brother, Rian also mentioned the "immense and widespread contributions" that Jamaica and Jamaican people have been having on "the larger Canadian society and the world." He notes that an important part of this contribution is "the Jamaican language, Patois, which is used broadly across the GTA by people of all races and cultures." As such, it is not uncommon to hear "Asians or South Asians from Brampton using terms like 'ah lie' to affirm a statement or question its validity; Russians from Scarborough saying 'lang time' in reference to something that happened a while ago; or Somalis from Rexdale saying 'wha gwan mandem' [what's going on, friends] while greeting each other and referring to a group of predominantly men." Referring to how the language figured in his interactions with his non-Black friends, Jama recalled that he has a Filipino friend with whom he grew up, and today when they talk with each other, their conversations "would just be in slang and we would obviously be using many Jamaican patios expressions." However, generally, according to Jama, "an exchange today" with longtime friends—like one "who works in the government or another friend who works in finance," and are not of Jamaican descent, would go something like:

> **Friend:** What's manz saying?
> **Me:** I'm free later to link [meet] up, but I need to handle this ting first.
> **Friend:** Ah right den, dun kno [I know].
> **Me:** Alright, easy fam.[18]

Similarly, constructing what a conversation about the pandemic might be with his friend, Jon said that it might go like this:

> **Me:** Yo, wha ah gwan with the mandem?
> **Friend:** Jus chillin, fam.
> **Me:** Notin' to do during lockdown, ah lie?
> **Friend:** Yah fam, de ting is crazy out here right now.

Discernable in these participants' assertations is the relationship of language to identity. For as Rian affirmed, engaging with the Jamaican language and related accent "has largely become part of the identity of Black Canadians." Correlated to this point, is the fact, as Jama attests, that:

Not everyone could get away with using Patwa. Sometimes you would have non-Jamaicans policing other non-Jamaicans on their use of Patwa. For example, a Somali youth might "page" (potentially another form of Patwa meaning to warn) a white kid for using "our" slang. The white youth will be looked as a wannabe, or wigger (white nigger). Honestly, sometimes these white youth will try to defend their use of certain slang because they "identify" with it. I am not sure what they identify with exactly, but our similar class position must have created some illusion in their head of the similarities of our experiences.

As Jama indicates, for Black youth in Toronto, similar class position—such as being of working-class background—does not entitle white youth to use their Black language. For while there is a race-class intersection, as is the case in the production of all languages, for many Black youth it primarily a raced language (since some who are using it are no longer in the lowest classes).

Essentially, then, as Rian maintains, "in a remarkable fashion, Jamaican language and culture have been synonymous with the identity of many Black Canadians"—for, as he explained, "shared cultural stories of resistance" contributed to his feeling like a Jamaican. So people who "were not Jamaican but still Black (like me) would adopt the language as our own. In some ways, you could uphold your Blackness[19] by speaking Patois as a way to show others that you were not *white*" (see also Collins, 2017). Therefore, it is not because people of Jamaican descent represent the largest Black *ethnic* group in Canada (see Statistics Canada 2007, 2019) why their presence—through language, culture, music, etc.—is evident or felt in Canada, particularly Toronto, but because of the politics of identity related to their "shared stories" with other Black groups. In addition, there are also efforts by Black Canadians to differentiate themselves from African Americans. As Rian put it: "the Black Canadian identity has been created in contrast to Black American identity for global recognition . . . . This is also a "ting" (another Jamaican word meaning "something") where Black Canadians seek to indicate that we are not mirror-images of Black Americans."

Further, arguing that white supremacy and the culture of whiteness has much to do with the ways in which Black people (see Collins, 2017), Jamaican language, and Black culture and identities are obfuscated and despised, Rian went into a persuasive analysis that is worth quoting at length:

Jamaican culture, similar to other Black cultures, are [sic] partially constrained by white imagination and white logic, which are seen through manifestations of stereotypes or assumptions that say, for example, anyone who is Black in Canada is automatically Jamaican. This has happened to me, an Afro-Latinx and Afro-Caribbean whose parents are from the Dominican Republic. I've been mistaken for being Jamaican countless times without even reciting a word of Patois. To a certain degree, this identity stereotype may be related to the fact that many Black people in Canada, whether African or Caribbean, have both been influenced by or have adapted the Jamaican language and culture. So it goes far beyond just speaking Patwa or eating rice and peas and oxtail. The racial stereotype has more to do with the popular narrative of whiteness—that Black Canadians are a homogenous group—and ignores the uniquely complex forms of Black culture, indigeneity, and art. The pathology of stereotype often exists when there is a refusal of Black Canadians to enact white cultural norms in spaces traditionally sanctioned by whiteness.

Presentability politics play a role in labelling Black people "unprofessional" or "ghetto" for acting in ways that are inconsistent with traditional white norms of language, dress, and culture. On the contrary, when a white person "borrows" the Jamaican language and says, "that's my bredrin, yo," referring to anyone who is a friend or colleague, they are seen as acting in a friendly fashion. This troubling dynamic exposes the truth that anti-Black racism permeates the very fabric of Canadian culture and society. Black men in particular are often seen through a white gaze as violent, predatorial, promiscuous or as "gyalist" (a Jamaican slang describing a man who lures many women to him).[20] Conversely, white men who obsessively seduce and deceive women are devoid of such stereotypes against the white racial group. It is implied that white people are given a "pass" to say and do whatever they please with little to no cultural or systemic retribution. And white celebrities and artists who sample aspects of Black culture (like language, accent, food, dance, or dress), mainstream media applaud them for their trendiness and economic prowess in a world built on capitalism, greed, and white supremacist logics. This very illuminating contradiction allows white artists like Justin Bieber to sample Jamaican art and not be seen as culture vultures.

In addition to conversations—especially among friends—music is another medium by which the Patwa language was cultivated among young people, as well as gained prominence and world recognition. In fact, as Jon said it, "The influence of Patois on me was undoubtedly cultivated by having Jamaican friends and listening to Hip Hop, Reggae, and Dancehall music." Campbell (2012a) sees Hip Hop in Canada as based on a culture of intertextuality and hybridity which makes for a plausible and "temporary version of Black Canada consisting of overlapping African diasporas" (p. 45). Also, Martis (2016) writes that Hip Hop icon Drake helped to produce "Toronto-speak"—also known as "Drake-cabulary."[21] Specifically, in reporting on Drake's contributions to the language, Bascaramurty (2017) writes:

> In early 2015, just before he dropped his mixtape *If You're Reading This It's Too Late,* Drake released a short film, Jungle, in which he spoke with a faint Jamaican accent, mixing in a bit of patois, the distinctive vernacular of the country—a flavour that emerged on many tracks and came out even stronger in 2016's Views. Many listeners, particularly in the United States, were perplexed: Why was the rapper with an African-American father and Jewish-Canadian mother suddenly speaking in a way that suggested he was from the islands? Most living here, though, recognized the sound. It's just a GTA ting.

Likewise, Rian commented that with, "Cock up yuh bumpa, siddung pon it!" [Prop up your buttocks, sit down on "it"],[22] Drake "infamously" communicated his familiarity with Patwa. And not withstanding the fact that people questioned "how someone of his background could speak the language enough to perform it on a global stage through Hip Hop," the fact remains that culture and language are boundless and transnational. Besides, Rian also credited "eminent Canadian Hip Hop pioneer Kardinal Offishall," of Jamaican descent—also considered to be "Ambassador of Hip Hop" in Canada—for his role in promoting the music. Indeed, it was Kardinal Offishall who "walks listeners through Toronto slang in his 2001 hit, "BaKardi Slang" (Wijekoon, 2020).

This reflection on the Black language of Toronto would be incomplete without mention of swear, or curse (cuss), words which, as in all other languages, are used to convey displeasure, anger, surprise, cynicism, excitement, or simply solicit a laugh. In her blog post, Shanna Collins (2017), who describes herself as "a Black woman raised in the United States," writes that the "particularly menacing undertone of *'bumbaclot'* as a pointed cuss [word] deeply resonated with me as an African descendant without a direct connection to my own indigenous African language." On this subject, Jon recalls using such words as "bumbaclaat and bloodclot" [bumboclaat and bloodclaat], which are words often used in everyday conversations among high school friends. And Jama would add:

Even though it was not as common, white kids would make use of some terms like Wha'gwaan, [Waa gwaan], or some curse words. One famous curse word was bumboclaat, which I have used many times but still don't know what exactly it means. But we all knew it was a curse word. Even the white teachers knew. I remember this Tamil youth yelling out "bumbaclot" in class, thinking that the teacher would not know what it is. This upper-class, middle-aged white woman sternly warned him not to repeat the word. She said this with a weird sense of pride because she knew what the word meant. We were all shocked as well, and the class burst out laughing. I say this just to show the reach of Jamaican Patwa. I'm not sure how many white teachers know swear words in Oromo, Tamil, or Tagalong, but I would put money on it that many of them will know the common swear words in Patwa.

By way of ending this section, the following unexpurgated reflective comments by Rian and Addie should serve to illuminate how much these young men have engaged with the language that they regard as shaping and delineating their Blackness.

Rian: "That sounded so cool."

I first became acquainted with the Jamaican language (Patwa) in elementary school. Growing up in Rexdale, there were a lot of Jamaican children and families living in my community that would speak it around me. My closest friends, Dwayne and Paul, were both Jamaicans. Whether this had to do with proximity, or that I just gravitated more towards them because they were Black, Canadian, and Caribbean, I don't know. But I knew then that this was an identity that I could relate to being Dominican-Canadian. My fascination with the Jamaican language started as soon as I heard Paul say: "Did you talk to dat ting yo?"—referring to the beautiful girl in my Grade 5 class. I remember thinking, *That sounded so cool*. It also resonated with me because "ting" sounded so much like the English word "thing," but said with an accent and in shorter form. The way he said it was also very similar to how Dominicans cut their words or sentences and speak Spanish with their own accent, employing their own colloquialisms which are often not understood by other Spanish-speaking countries in Central or South America. To Dominicans, this is a way of being "cool" and of having their own Spanish-Caribbean identities.

Most of the girls I liked were Jamaican, too. Their confidence and strong identity always intrigued me. In Grade 9, I met my high school sweetheart, who was from Clarendon, Jamaica. I felt like I had to learn the Jamaican language in order to talk to her. I started watching *Shottas* (a popular movie that was out at the time)[23] and listening to Reggae and Dancehall music (it was what she listened to). It became clear to me at an early age that to fit in and to have style, you had to "chat" Patwa. During high school, when Drake and Tory Lanes (two popular Canadian Hip Hop artists) hit the scene and started mixing their music with Patwa words, the words were solidified as a popular slang. It became more popular to mix Hip Hop terms with Jamaican Patwa. At one point, I remember it became not normal to not know Patwa because it was all over. It was beneficial to know the language as well so that you could navigate your way around the community and local food places like Caribbean Cuisine or Willy's Jerk (to get that rice and peas and fried chicken). It was also beneficial to know Patwa so that no one from the community could make fun of you, without you knowing.

I loved speaking the language[24] so much, it functioned sort of like a form of acceptance. It was a way of letting others know that I was one of the "cool" kids. If you didn't speak any Patwa, you were disconnected from the culture, and thus labelled lame or boring. I started to speak the language not just around my Jamaican friends, but literally all the time. I would use words like "Low mi nuh" to tell others to leave me alone, or "Yuh dun know" to let them know that I spoke a different language, and that I had my own culture that I was part of, outside of the white European culture (which rarely accepted me). Patwa quickly became a third language for me after English and Spanish. Even now, I listen to music, and if the song is good, I say, "Big chune" [Big tune] to acknowledge how good it sounds. I think, now that I'm older, however, I use the language more intentionally as a way of challenging the norm in places I work, and in social institutions that are traditionally white. I use it to code switch whether I want to be funny, cool, or even disguise what I'm saying so that only those who are meant to understand it, can identify it. This is my way of being myself, which I think gives permission to the young people I work with to do the same.

Addie: "Patios roots me in my people, and my people's experiences."

As an Afro-Jamaican Torontonian, Patios is intrinsically enmeshed with my identity. It's attachment to the words that I produce through the sounds of my voice or the slight inclination my accent breathes life into what it means to be Black in Toronto. It is nestled deep between my collarbones. It's an expression that finds its meaning in the closeness of my childhood, and the struggles of my people. To me, Patios is a celebration of my ancestors. It's largely African influence, with remnants of the Indigenous Taino people, and the English and Spanish. All of which is housed in my body and expressed through my Jamaican expressions.

Like many Toronto youth, language is a part of my identity. It is a marker for my struggles and marginalization that we all experience as Black youth, and our constant reimagining and creating of space in a country that shuts us out of its definition of citizen. For me, Patios roots me in my people, and my people's experiences. It connects me to the struggles of my parents and the struggles of Black youth nationwide, as they are constantly trying to find space and create opportunities for futurity.

In a place where unbelonging is often a felt experience, holding onto my Jamaican language is one of the ways I hold onto my Jamaican-ness.

Conclusion: "Jamaican language and culture go far beyond speaking Patwa or eating rice and peas and oxtail."

As Jon, Rian, Jama, and Addie have indicated, Patwa is a language that has been serving them in the construction of their sense of community, to exercise agency, resist their marginalization and homogenization, and mobilize against what Shanna Collins (2017) calls "linguistic colonialism," which operates to disparage their language. But the fact is, while I invited these young men to talk with me about the place of Patwa in their lives while growing up, and there is concurrence that the language with its salutations, slangs, "cuss" words, related accent, and code-switching emanate from Jamaica, they also made it clear that in the diasporic spaces of Canada, there are variations to the language (Campbell 2012a), in that the language is being modified by its Canadian speakers—many of them of non-Jamaican descent, Canadian born, of African origin, and English second-language speakers. The point is, this engagement with the place of Patwa in the lives of Black youth in Toronto was not to, as Campbell (2012a) warns against, "Jamaicanize blackness, as often happens in Toronto Afrodiasporic communities" (p. 51). Rather, our attempt here is to do as Campbell suggests—show the articulations, utterances, sentiments, subjectivities, and specificities of Afrodiasporic youth and people of various generations with the "language" and variations of Blackness.

Acknowledgements

I am indebted to Karim Jamal, Percival Robinson, and brothers Jonathan Rua and Ryan Rua for their contributions to this essay. Their comments, texts, explanations, and insights contributed significantly to what I have been able to produce in this chapter. Thanks to all four of you for willingly engaging with me in the many conversations and follow-up clarifications I sought.

Endnotes

1. "Waa gwaan?"—What's going on? Also note that "waa" is sometimes spelt "wha" or "wah." Readers will observe an inconsistency in word spelling, which might be attributed to the individuals' lack of familiarity with the standardized spelling, and hence they construct spelling as they go.

2. The term or slang is often used to mean "group of men friends;" or used to address a male individual.

3. According to Statistics Canada (2007), in 2006, Black people represented just under 7 percent of the total Greater Toronto Area (GTA) population, and 16 percent of the total for "visible minority" population. And a significant vast majority of Black Torontonians were of Caribbean descent—that is about three hundred thousand people of which more than half were of Jamaican descent representing the largest Black group in Canada. By 2016, the Black population of Canada numbered about 309,485 of which 30 percent were of Jamaican descent—most of whom were first and second generation in Canada (Statistics Canada, 2019).

4. Insofar as gender intersects with race and colour, these identity characteristics operate together in the construction and/or reading of an individual's presumed difference—in terms of, for example, their behaviour, speech pattern, tone, and interactions. Context notwithstanding, the reading of an individual's "difference" in relation to these identity characteristics also serves as a marker of their "otherness" and assignment of outsider status. Something like "with that kind of behaviour, or based on the way they talk, they can't be Canadian."

5. It tends to be the case that Black people in Toronto are not immediately or often constructed as African American since the Black people who an individual is most likely to meet would have been of Caribbean

descent—especially Jamaican. This reflects the immigration patterns that contributed to Jamaicans making up the significant proportion of the Black Canadian population (Statistics Canada, 2019; Walker, 2012). Hence, the language or accent of many Black Torontonians would likely be influenced the pervasive presence of Jamaicans.

6   It is true that there is much debate as to whether there is a "Jamaican Language." In fact, *Jamaica Travel Guide, Frommer's* (n.d.) states that "The official language of Jamaica is English, and the unofficial language is a patois. Linguists and a handful of Jamaican novelists have recently transformed this oral language into written form, although for most Jamaicans, it remains solely spoken—and richly nuanced. Experts say more than 90 percent of the vocabulary is derived from English, with the remaining words largely borrowed from African languages. There are also words taken from Spanish, Arawak, French, Chinese, Portuguese, and East Indian languages." Writing in *Babble Magazine*, Steph Koyfman (July 12, 2019) proffers: "Though English is technically the official language, Jamaica is home to a unique linguistic legacy unlike any other in the world." And in an interview with Xavier Murphy on Jamaica.com, sociolinguist, Professor Hubert Devonish of the University of the West Indies, described as "one of the strongest advocates fighting for Jamaican Patois as a Language," and a leader in advancing and promoting a writing and spelling system for Jamaican language, asserted that "in the same way that the language of Spain is Spanish; of Turkey, Turkish; Norway, Norwegian," so is the language of Jamaica, Jamaican. "Patois is the term originally used for regional dialects of French in France and has been extended to described French-lexicon Creoles of the Caribbean, like St. Lucian. In fact, the spelling "Patwa" has been used to describe St. Lucian French Creole. The most accurate label is, therefore, Jamaican." See also Devonish (July 28, 2008) "End Jamaican language apartheid."

7   Jane and Finch (which is marked by the intersection of Jane Street and Finch Avenue) is a marginalized, low-income inner-suburban neighbourhood in the northwest area of Toronto with a racially mixed population of South Asian, Asian, Black, and European (largely long time Italian residents). And while South Asians make up a significant percentage of racialized population, the area is thought of as a "Black area" (Baxter and Peters, 2013; Friesen, 2018; James, 2012b).

8   Martis (2016) contends that "patois is more than just an island *ting*: it's a language holding Jamaicans around the world together."

9   Nadia Hohn, a teacher and author of the picture book, *A Likkle Miss*

Lou: How Jamaican Poet Louise Bennett Coverley Found Her Voice, also said that "growing up in a Jamaican family in Toronto's Rexdale neighbourhood," she, too "was discouraged by her parents from speaking in Jamaican Patois" (Porter, 2019).

10 Campbell inferred that this mother corrected him for his use of Patwa. But it is also possible that the Toronto version, "What's Gwanning?—of the Jamaican Patwa sounded particularly odd to his mother—who might have expected "Waa gwaan?," that she intervened by correcting Campbell.

11 Despite the affinity to and use of the language by others, there are still claims of appropriation of the language (Anderson ,2019), and in some cases, especially for dark-skinned people, using the language further marginalizes them, or subjects them to a white gaze of fascination and imitation (Bascaramurty, 2017; Yancy, 2008, 2013). The fact is, colour plays a role and makes a difference in the use of the Jamaican language. For dark-skinned people, the language might contribute to them being read as "exotic" among some, "backward," "uneducated," or from rural Jamaica among others. For lighter-skinned people or white Jamaicans, their use of the language might be seen as a representation of them being "ordinary people" and having the ability to relate to common folks.

12 Premier Ford meant to say: "Tan a yu yaad," (Stand/Stay at your yard/home) but said "Ten a yuh yard"—which Jamaicans and speakers of Jamaican around the world found to be hilarious.

13 Bascaramurty (2017) also makes the point that "the original speakers are undecided whether it's a tribute or a travesty." And Campbell (2012b) writes that the use of the language presents "an interesting conundrum" for even as the expressive culture of Black youth becomes popularized, "innovative Black youth are still disproportionately devalued, criminalized, and systemically marginalized" and therefore held back from "contributing to the betterment of Canadian society" (p. 120).

14 Pamoda Wijekoon quotes Raven Wilkinson as saying: "There's actually a lot of debate about people from London thinking that people from Toronto are stealing their slang . . .. Like I said, it's problematic to think that [the dialect is] just from those places, because it's not."

15 Quinion (2006) says that *Jafaican* was created by "black Londoners whose parents migrated "to the UK in the 1940s and 1950s from the West Indies, the majority from Jamaica."

16 Referencing the UK context, Bascaramurty (2017) mentions that "by

the 1990s, white, British-born youth were speaking confidently in a mix of English and patois."

17 But Jacqueline Peters, a linguist who studies the pattern of code switching, believed that not "many of them would be able to speak what we call 'standard' English," so she would not "call it code switching" (in Bascaramurty, 2017).

18 "Fam"—family, abbreviated, is meant to indicate a close relationship.

19 According to Campbell (2012a), "Blackness in Canada sits at the intersection of the hegemonic construction of the nation and the reality of a doubly diasporized people" (p. 49).

20 More specifically, it is Jamaican slang for a man who has several relationships—serious and otherwise—with multiple women (nof gyal), which makes him a "gyalis[t]".

21 It is noted in several blog posts and on social media that Drake bears some responsibility for the increasing incidences of "public patois faux pas" among suburban white boys who are drawn to his music. Also, he has been criticized for being a "culture vulture" for his performance of "embodied Caribbeanization"—a form of "intra-racial appropriation" represented in his adaptation of Jamaican phraseology and sound (Persadie, 2019).

22 This could be read as a sexual line directed at a woman by her male partner suggesting, depending on context, how she might engage with him while they engage in a variety of activities, including riding a motorbike, dancing, or sexual intercourse.

23 *Shottas* is a film about two young gunmen who grew up together on the streets of Kingston, Jamaica moved to Miami, Florida, where they continued with their street hustling and criminal activities. After they were deported to Jamaica about twenty years later, they continued with their illicit activities. Shottas is derived from the Jamaican verb "to shot" [to shoot], so that shooters become "shottas" [also referred to as "gunmen"].

24 It should be noted that Rian posited that "Jamaican language follows unique linguistic and cultural codes and traditions that makes it difficult for non-Jamaican people to understand, adapt, or copy. This is true whether one is speaking words like 'respect' or 'bless,' which could mean anything from a greeting to a farewell, or even a thank you—depending on the context and how it's said. Jamaican language comprises of English words with an African syntax that are uniquely and complexly

constructed with an accent that is authentic to only Jamaicans. In this way, Jamaican words can have several meanings, and thus can be misinterpreted by lots of people outside of the culture. Take the word, 'bad' for example, which in Jamaican culture could mean anything from 'good,' to actually meaning 'bad,' depending on the cultural context."

References

Anderson, S. "Do You Know Toronto Slang? Youth Are Drawing From Several Languages Spoken by the City's Immigrants to Create a Novel Form of English." *University of Toronto Magazine*, October 2, 2019, https://magazine.utoronto.ca/research-ideas/culture-society/do-you-know-toronto-slang/.

D. Bascaramurty, "Di Soun in di City." *The Globe and Mail*, August 4, 2017, https://www.theglobeandmail.com/news/toronto/popularization-of-patois-stirs-up-complex-feelings-for-torontos-westindiancommunity/article35884529/.

Baxter, L. and Peters, J. "Black English in Toronto: A New Dialect?" *Proceedings from Methods XIV*, pp. 2013, pp. 1—14. https://www.academia.edu/2966441/Black_English_in_Toronto_A_New_Dialect.

Bennett, L. *Jamaica Labrish*. Kingston: Sangster's Book Store, 1966.

Campbell, M. V. "'Other/ed' kinds of Blackness: An Afrodiasporic versioning of Black Canada." *Southern Journal of Canadian Studies*, vol. 5, nos. 1 and 2), 2012a, pp. 46—65. https://www.academia.edu/5240771/_Other_ed_kinds_of_Blackness_An_Afrodiasporic_Versioning_of_Black_Canada.

Campbell, M.V. "The Gwannings." *Jamaica in the Canadian Experience: A Multiculturalizing Presence*. Edited by C.E. James and A. Davis. Halifax: Fernwood Publishing, 2012b, pp. 120—128.

Cassidy, F.G. and Le Page, R.B. *Dictionary of Jamaican English*, Kingston: University of the West Indies Press, 2002.

Collins, S. "If You Don't Accept Caribbean Patois as Valid, You're Probably Anti-Black." *Medium*. October 4, 2017, https://medium.

com/@janelane_62637/if-you-dont-accept-caribbean-patois-as-a-valid-you-re-probably-anti-black-8e2a23b42338.

Cooper, C. "Disguise up de English Language: Louise Bennett's Anansi Poetics." The Michael Baptista Lecture, York University, Toronto, Ontario, Canada, November 3, 2016.

Cooper, C. "Culture an Tradition an Birthright: Proverb as Metaphor in the Poetry of Louise Bennett." *Noises in the Blood: Orality, Gender, and the "Vulgar" Body of Jamaican Popular Culture.* Durham: Duke University Press, 1993, pp. 37—46.

Davidson, S. "Doug Ford Releases Video Urging People to Stay Home in 22 Languages." *CTV News*, January 21, 2021, https://toronto.ctvnews.ca/doug-ford-releases-video-urging-people-to-stay-home-in-22-languages-1.5276384.

Devonish, H. "End Jamaican Language Apartheid." *Jamaica Gleaner*, October 28, 2018, Retrieved July 2021, https://jamaica-gleaner.com/article/commentary/20181028/hubert-devonish-end-jamaican-language-apartheid.

Devonish, H. *Languages and Liberation: Creole Language Politics in the Caribbean.* Kingston: Arawak Publications, 2007.

James, C.E. "Students 'at risk': Stereotyping and the Schooling of Black Boys." *Urban Education.* vol. 47, no.2, 2012a, pp. 464—494.

James, C.E. *Life at the Intersection: Community, Class and Schooling.* Halifax: Fernwood Publishing, 2012b.

James, K. "What's Your Background?" *Talking About Identity: Encounters in Race, Ethnicity and Language.* Edited by C.E. James amd A. Shadd. Toronto: Between the Lines, 2001, pp. 17—19.

Koyfman, S. "What Language is Spoken in Jamaica?" *Babble Magazine*, July 12, 2019, https://www.babbel.com/en/magazine/what-language-do-jamaicans-speak.

Martis, E. "How the Language of Jamaica Became Mainstream." *Fader*, September 1, 2016, https://www.thefader.com/2016/09/01/how-jamaican-patois-became-mainstream.

Morris, M. *Miss Lou: Louise Bennett and Jamaican Culture.* Kingston: Ian Randle Publishers, Ltd., 2014

Murphy, X. "Professor Hubert Devonish, Advocate for Jamaican Patois as a Language." Jamaica.com, 2008, Retrieved July 2021, https://jamaicans.com/jamaicanpatoislanguage-2/.

Myers-Scotton, C. "Code-Switching." *The Handbook of Sociolinguistics*. Edited by F. Coulmas. Oxford: Blackwell Publishing, 2017, pp. 217—237.

Persadie, R. "Sounding the '6ix': Drake, Cultural Appropriation, and Embodied Caribbeanization." *MUSICultures*, vol. 46 no. 1, 2019, pp. 52—80.

Porter, R. "Miss Lou's Sweet Jamaican Patois Speaks to a Whole New Generation." *Toronto Star*, August 16, 2019, https://www.thestar.com/entertainment/books/2019/08/16/miss-lous-sweet-jamaican-patois-speaks-to-a-whole-new-generation.html.

Quinion, M. "Jafaikan." *World Wide Words: Investigating the English Language Across the Globe*, April 29, 2006, https://www.worldwidewords.org/topicalwords/tw-jaf1.htm#:~:text=Jafaikan%20or%20Jafaican%20is%20a,Indies%2C%20the%20majority%20from%20Jamaica.

Statistics Canada. "Diversity of the Black Opulation in Canada: An Overview." *Ethnicity, Language and Immigration Thematic Series*, February 27, 2019, https://www150.statcan.gc.ca/n1/en/pub/89-657-x/89-657-x2019002-eng.pdf?st=JZDfC8VW.

Statistics Canada. "2006 Community Profiles, Toronto, Ontario (Code535)." *Statistics Canada Catalogue, no. 92-591-XWE*, Ottawa, 2007, https://www12.statcan.gc.ca/census-recensement/2006/dp-pd/prof/92-591/details/page.cfm?Lang=E&Geo1=CMA&Code1=535&Geo2=PR&Code2=35&Data=Count&SearchText=Toronto&SearchType=Begins&SearchPR=01&B1=All&Custom=.

Statistics Canada. "Diversity of the Black Population in Canada: An Overview." *Ethnicity, Language, and Immigration Thematic Series*, February 27, 2019, https://www150.statcan.gc.ca/n1/pub/89-657-x/89-657-x2019002-eng.htm

Yancy, G. "'Walking While Black in the 'White Gaze.'" *The New York Times*, September 1, 2013, https://opinionator.blogs.nytimes.com/2013/09/01/walking-while-black-in-the-white-gaze/.

Yancy, G. *Black Bodies, White Gazes: The Continuing Significance of Race*. London: Rowman & Littlefield Publishing, 2008.

Author Biographies

Lillian Allen, who hails from Spanish Town, Jamaica, is an acclaimed foremother of Canadian Poetry and a leading international exponent of Dub Poetry. She is a two-time Juno award winner for *Revolutionary Tea Party* and *Conditions Critical*. Her latest book, *Make the World New* is edited by Ronald Cummings (Wilfrid Laurier University Press, 2021).

Pamela Appelt was born in Jamaica, migrated to Canada in 1966, worked as a researcher in medical biochemistry at McGill University and became the first female Afro-Canadian to serve as a judge of the Court of Canadian Citizenship. Appelt is co-executor of the Estate of the Hon. Louise Bennett-Coverley and played an instrumental role in bringing the Louise Bennett-Coverley Archives to the McMaster University Library.

Pamella Archer is a Senior Teacher and Head of the Social Studies Department at Central High School in Clarendon, Jamaica. She received her teacher training at Mico University College and has taught Social Sciences at the secondary level for over 20 years. She holds a Bachelor of Science degree in International Relations and a Master of Arts degree in Teacher Education and Teacher Development from the University of the West Indies, Mona.

Everton Cummings is an Adjunct Lecturer with the School of Education at the University of the West Indies, Mona and a consultant with the Joint Board of Teacher Education in Jamaica. He completed his doctoral studies in Curriculum, Teaching and Learning with a focus on Teacher Education at the Ontario Institute for Studies in Education (OISE), University of Toronto. Cummings has served in the fields of secondary and tertiary education, in Jamaica and Canada, for more than 31 years.

Andrea A. Davis is an Associate Professor in Black Cultures of the Americas in the Department of Humanities at York University in Toronto, and co-editor of the *Journal of Canadian Studies*. She is the author of *Horizon, Sea, Sound: Caribbean and African Women's Cultural Critiques of Nation* (Northwestern University Press, 2022).

Honor Ford-Smith is an Associate Professor in Environmental Arts and Justice in the Faculty of Environmental and Urban Change and Associate Director of the Centre for Latin America and the Caribbean (CERLAC) at York University. She works at the crossroads of performance, politics and justice and her many publications are rooted in a tradition of radical Caribbean anticolonial, transnational feminist thought and performance theory.

Clive Forrester, who earned his PhD in linguistics from the University of the West Indies, Mona, teaches linguistics, academic writing, and the language and literature of the Caribbean in the Department of English Language and Literature at the University of Waterloo. Forrester previously taught at York University where he introduced popular courses on Jamaican language.

Amah Harris, M.Ed., is an award-winning cultural and social activist and a pioneer in the field of Black Theatre in Canada, whose work promotes positive imaging of Caribbean and African Peoples and the harmonious co-existence of Peoples. Harris's impactful international productions and experiential workshops have been recognized with her inclusion in *100 Accomplished Black Canadian Women* (2018).

Annette Henry is a Professor in the Department of Language and Literacy Education and cross appointed to the Institute for Gender, Race, Sexuality and Social Justice at the University of British Columbia. Her scholarship examines race, class, language, gender and culture in socio-cultural contexts of teaching and learning in the lives of Black students, Black oral histories, and Black women teachers' practice in Canada, the U.S. and the Caribbean.

Carl E. James holds the Jean Augustine Chair in Education, Community & Diaspora at York University, Toronto. He has written on the educational, social and cultural lives of Black and Caribbean youth – noting the ways in which inequitable societal and institutional structures mediate their experiences, opportunities and achievements. With Andrea Davis, James co-edited *Jamaica in the Canadian Experience: A Multiculturalizing Presence* (Fernwood, 2012).

Michele A. Johnson is a Professor in the Department of History at York University, Toronto, where she previously served as Director of the Harriet Tubman Institute for Research on Africa and Its Diasporas. She is co-editor of *Historie sociale/Social History* and author, co-author and co-editor of publications focusing on the social and cultural histories of Jamaica and Canada.

Michèle Kennedy is a Senior Lecturer (retired) in the Department of Language, Linguistics and Philosophy at the University of the West Indies, Mona. Her research includes a study of the speech of three-year old children, focusing especially on the acquisition of lexical and morphosyntactic structures.

Silvia Kouwenberg is a Professor of Linguistics and Dean of the Faculty of Humanities and Education at the University of the West Indies, Mona. Her research and publications focus on Creole Studies, particularly on the formal properties of creole languages and their historical emergence in Berbice (Papiamentu) and Jamaica (Jamaican Creole).

Yewande Lewis-Fokum is a Lecturer at the School of Education at the University of the West Indies, Mona. Her areas of research include English language and literacy. Her work has been published in peer reviewed journals such as *Changing English*.

Tka C. Pinnock is a doctoral candidate in the Department of Politics at York University, Toronto. Her research interests lie at the intersection of feminist political economy, political ecology, and globalization where she explores the everyday politics of life work in the Caribbean.

Olive Senior is the Poet Laureate of Jamaica 2021-2024, and the award-winning author of 20 books of fiction, nonfiction, poetry and children's literature. Her most recent are *Pandemic Poems: First Wave* and *Hurricane Watch: New and Collected Poems*. In 2021, four of her books were listed among the Bocas-sponsored "100 Caribbean Books that Made Me." In 2022 her first book, *Summer Lightning*, was among the 70 books from the Commonwealth chosen for the BBC and the Reading Agency's Big Jubilee Read to coincide with the Queen's Platinum Jubilee.

Jennifer Walcott is a retired teacher of English in Toronto, who started writing as a child in Jamaica. Her verses are published in *Calling Cards: New Poetry from Caribbean/Canadian Women* (2005), *Your Daily Poem.com*, *Calabash, The Antigonish Review*, as well as in two chapbooks, *Poems from Ocean Wilderness* edited by Patrick Lane.

Klive Walker is a UK-born Jamaican-Canadian author, music historian, cultural critic and exhibition curator. His specialization is reggae but he also writes about rock, hip hop, dancehall, jazz, cinema and photography. His publications include *Dubwise: Reasoning from the Reggae Underground* (2005) and essays in *The Global Reggae Reader* (2012) and *Ears, Eyes, Voice: Black Canadian Photojournalists 1970s-1990s* (2019). He is co-curator of the *Rhythms and Resistance: Caribbean Music in Toronto* exhibition at the Friars Music Museum in Toronto (2022).

Index

A

Abrahams, Roger 98
Academy of Canadian Cinema and Television 24
acrolect 153
Adisa, Opal Palmer 2–3
African Caribbean 38
African heritage 8, 94, 200
Afrodiasporic 205, 217
Aitken, Madame di Mena 42
Akers, Glenn 99
Allen, Lillian v, 2, 4, 6, 17, 19, 58–59, 111, 227
Alleyne, Mervyn 94, 99
Anancy/Anansi 44, 48
Anderson, Benedict 37
Anthony, Trey 58
anticolonial 4-5, 17, 37-38, 40, 42, 48, 228
Appelt, Pamela v, 4, 23, 59, 227
Aunty Roachy/Aunty Roachie 20, 31–32, 44, 48
authenticity 103, 186

B

backative 33–35
Bailey, Amy 42
Bailey, Beryl 99
Bailey, Carol 2
ballad 5, 83
bandana 4, 31, 40, 45
baraka-clarke, amuna 2
Barclay, Alexander 103, 108
Bascaramurty, Dakshana 208–210, 214
basilect 153, 158
Baxter, Ivy 44
Beckwith, Martha 101
Belafonte, Harry 57
Bennett, Cornelius 68
Bialystok, Ellen 125
bilingual v, 83, 156, 160, 167, 169, 174, 199–200
Bilingual Education Project (BEP) 156
bilingualism 140, 165–167, 189
biliteracies 199

Black
  American 212
  Canadian 9, 205-206, 208, 211-213, 228, 230
  identity 9
  Language vi, 9, 205–206, 208–210, 212, 214
  people 17, 94, 121, 182, 194, 205, 212-213
  Toronto 9, 206, 208–209
Blackness 5, 21, 37, 187, 206, 208, 215, 217
body knowledge 124
Bogues, Tony 39
Bokova, Irina 200
Bolland, Nigel 94
Brand Jamaica 8, 185
Brand, Dionne 58
Brathwaite, Kamau 69–70, 94, 98
Breeze, Jean Binta 17
Bronfman, Alejandra 2
broughtuptcy 32, 33
Brown, Aggrey 122
Burgie, Irving 57
Burke, Mavis 24

C

call and response/call-and-response 39, 41
Canadian English 182, 209

Caribbean Examinations Council (CXC) 149
Caribbean Pioneer Women of Canada 24
Carrington, Lawrence 99, 166
Cassidy Writing System 87-90
Cassidy, F.G./Cassidy, Frederic 6, 86–90, 100, 170
centenary 1, 58, 183
Césaire, Aimé 38–40, 44
Christie, Pauline 99, 154, 166
Chronixx 142
Clarke, Austin 58
Clarke, Edith 42
Clarke, Vèvè 199
Clifford, James 64
code switching 162, 182, 195, 209-210, 216-217, 221
code weaving 154-155
Collier, Gordon 99
Collins, Shanna 214, 217
colonial v, 3, 5, 17, 37–38, 40–42, 45–46, 48, 74, 93, 95, 98, 109, 133, 182, 187, 195–196, 199, 207
colonialism 26, 71, 74, 94, 98, 187, 217
Commonwealth Immigrants Act 71
constructivist pedagogy 134-135
convergence 6, 94
Cooper, Afua 58
Cooper, Carolyn 3, 40, 138

Index

Cooper, Rev. Thomas 108
Coverley, Eric 64, 68
Coverley, Fabian 4, 25
creolisation 94, 97
Critical Discourse Analysis (CDA) 150-152, 158, 169
Cudjoe, Selwyn 70
culture vulture 213
Cummins, Jim 125
curse 43, 101, 214–215

D

D'Costa, Jean 95, 99, 139
dancehall 57, 185, 207, 210, 213, 215, 230
Davis, Natalie Zemon 95, 108
Denis, Derek 208–209
Dennis-Benn, Nicole 183
Devonish, Hubert 99, 156, 198
dialect 1–2, 25, 34, 57, 68, 86, 97–98, 107, 121, 132, 141, 206, 209
dialogic phenomenology 124
diaspora 5, 8, 56, 58–59, 64–66, 70, 80, 121, 182–185, 199–200
diasporic 5, 57, 59, 67, 70, 182–183, 185, 199, 207, 217
Dinkie Mini 44
discourse vi, 5, 7, 33, 37, 45-46, 67, 70, 107, 125, 129, 149-152, 158-159, 165-169, 184, 196
Drake 208, 214, 216

E

embodied 38-39, 41, 43–44, 48
embodiment 40
Ethington, Ben 2

F

Farquharson, May 42
father tongue 196
film 45, 58, 69, 121, 214
Fleischmann, Ulrich 99
Fleras, Augie 66
Folkway Records 57
Ford, Doug 208
Ford-Smith, Honor v, 4–5, 37, 40, 42, 58–59, 64, 228
full-body/full-bodied 40, 45

G

Gallimore, Patrick 183
Garvey, Marcus 42, 57
gender/gendered 1-2, 5, 26, 37, 41, 48, 80, 96, 105-106, 194, 206, 228
Genie Award 58
Gingell, Susan 2
Gloudon, Barbara 68
Golding, Bruce 197
Goodison, Lorna 58
government 1, 4, 25-26, 39, 42, 77, 138, 143, 162, 184-185, 188, 211
Grant, D.R.B. 23

Green, Oscar 198

H

Harbour Front Centre 4, 25
Harding, John 108
Hart-Cellar Immigration Reform Act 77
hero 4, 19, 34–35, 122
higgler 44
hip hop 213–214, 216, 230
Hohn, Nadia 3
huckster 44

I

icon 1–2, 34, 58–59, 66–67, 154, 207, 214
identity v-vi, 9, 18, 41, 45, 48, 66–67, 85, 107, 131-133, 139, 150-154, 157, 159-161, 167-171, 183, 185, 194-195, 205-206, 208, 210-213, 215-217
indigenous 8,86, 93, 130, 135, 199, 200, 214, 216
International Festival of Authors (IFOA) 58-59
irie 134, 186
irony 39, 45, 71, 75
ironic 43, 45, 70, 142

J

Jackson, J.R. 109
Jackson, Mrs. 109–110

Jafaican 209
Jamaica Federation of Women (JFW) 42
Jamaica Information Service (JIS) 1–3, 5
Jamaica Welfare 42
Jamaican
  Creole (JC) 2, 6, 7 65, 70, 86-87, 94-95, 99-100, 104-106, 108, 111, 132-145, 150, 152-158, 160-176, 182, 184-186, 189, 194-197, 199, 201, 206-207, 229
  English (JE) 86-87, 132-145, 150, 152-156, 160-175, 206
  Language Unit (JLU) 6, 87-90, 166, 170
  New Testament (JNT) 197
James, CLR 39-40.
James, Marlon 183
Jamiekan langwij i, iii, v, 2, 4, 6, 9, 88, 93-95, 99-100, 103, 107, 111
Jamiekan Langwij Yuunit 6, 88
Jean Augustine Chair in Education, Community and Diaspora 121, 183, 229
JLU-Cassidy 166, 170
John, Alma 57
Johns, Lindsay 198
Johnson, Linton Kwesi 17
Johnson, Thelma 24
Jolly, Denham 25
Juno Award 59, 227

Index

K

Kardinal Offishall 214
Kasinitz, Philip 77
kas-kas 33
King James Bible 138, 198
King, Ann Amelia 109
Klyde Broox 2
Knibb, Mary Morris 42
Kouwenberg, Silvia vi, 7, 99, 149, 229
Kru 96
Kwa 96

L

L'Ouverture, Toussaint 39
Lalla, Barbara 95, 99
Lamming, George 40
Language Arts (LA) 150, 155-156, 158, 168-169
Language Materials Workshop (LMW) 155
language-as-arena 151–152, 170
laughter v, 4, 23, 32, 34, 37, 39, 43, 48–49, 65, 73–74, 79, 136–137
Le Page, R.B. 6
learning process 123–124, 126, 141–142, 144, 163
Lewis, Jovan Scott 184, 186
Lewis, Matthew (Monk) 103-104
linguicism 195

linguistic 6, 45, 70, 72, 75, 77, 97, 99, 143, 150, 156-158, 169-174, 182, 185, 188-189, 193, 195, 197-200, 207, 217
linguistics 156, 194, 228–229
Linton, Faith 197
Literature-Based Language Arts Project (LBLAP) 155
Long, Edward 96-100, 104-107
Louise Bennett Close 4, 25
Louise Bennett Room 4
Louise Bennett Coverley Fonds 4

M

Mandiela, Ahdri Zhina 58
Mandingo 96
mannersable 34
Marley, Bob 17, 37, 63, 122
Marson, Una 41, 56
McKay, Claude 57
mesolect 153
migration v, 5, 56, 64, 66, 70-72, 74, 76-79, 140, 184, 188
Miller, Kei 183
Miss Kitty 137
Miss Lou v, 1-6, 15, 17-19, 21, 23-26, 31-34, 37, 40-41, 47, 58, 63-70, 79-80, 83, 85, 87, 89, 111, 121-122, 134, 139-140, 183
Mordecai, Pamela 2, 58
Morris, Mervyn 2, 43, 68-70, 99

mother tongue vi, 6, 121–122, 125, 166–167, 196, 198-200, 207

mouta massi 47

Multicultural London English 209

multi-ethnolects 208

multilingualism 200

Mutabaruka 137

N

National Hero 4, 19, 34-35, 122

Négritude 38

Neigh, Janet 2

Nettleford, Rex 43, 69-70

Nichols, Grace 196-197

Noormohammadi, Rezvan 125

Nugent, Maria 105–107

Nwankwo, Ifeoma Kiddoe 2–3

O

orthography v, 85, 166, 170, 199

P

Palaver International Literary Festival 25

Palmer, A.L. 109

Patois Bible 197–198

Patois 1,3, 57, 121-122, 126, 183, 186-188, 194-195, 197-199, 207-214

Patwa vi, 2-3, 6-8, 89, 94-95, 97, 99, 104-106, 108, 111, 129-130, 132-145, 181-183, 185-189, 193, 195, 198, 205, 207-208, 212-217

peasant 40, 44

pedagogical 145, 149, 156–158, 168, 170, 172–174

pedagogy 123, 134–135, 145, 199

Philip, Marlene Nourbese 196

Phillips, Lolita 23

Pollard, Velma 99, 167

post-colonial/postcolonial 17, 45, 48, 79, 196

Project for Advancement of Childhood Education 24

proscenium 38–39

Protoje 142

proverb 33, 44, 100-102

Pukkumina/Pocomania 41, 44

R

race 37, 39-40, 48, 56, 76, 80, 93, 129, 131, 187-188, 206, 211-212, 228

radio 44, 56-57, 68-69, 145, 162

Ramazani, Jahan 2, 67

Rampini, Charles 101

Rastafarianism 185

reggae 57, 142, 185, 207, 210, 213, 215, 230

remittances 184–185, 188

revolutionary 39, 122, 227

Richardson, Bonham 71

Roberts, Danny 144

Robertson, Ian 99

Robeson, Paul 39

Robinson, Kerene 68

Rodis, Katherin Verhagen 2

Royal Academy of Dramatic Art (RADA) 43, 56, 68

S

Scarborough 55, 63, 211

Scott, James 45

Senior, Olive v, 4, 31, 58-59, 230

Shoucair, Paul 187

signifying 39, 42, 45

Silvera, Makeda 58

Simmons-McDonald, Hazel 99

Solomon, Frances-Ann 58

Spencer, Aisha T. 2

St. George, Michael 58

Standard English (SE) 5, 7, 83, 122, 134, 143-144, 182, 184, 194-195, 207

Standard Jamaican English (SJE) 132-133, 136-138, 140-141, 143-145, 162-163, 182, 184, 189, 196

Stewart, Courtney 198

Stewart, John 100, 102, 107

sufferation 184

T

television 24, 34, 57-58, 68-69, 145, 162

Thompson, Giselle 185

Toronto v-vi, 3-5, 9, 23-25, 55-59, 63-66, 131, 134, 182-183, 185, 205-210, 212, 214, 216-217, 227-230

tourism 8, 49, 184-186, 189

transnational 8, 18, 67, 71, 80, 185, 196, 207, 214, 228

Tucker, Glenn 144, 187

U

United Nations 193

Universal Negro Improvement Association (UNIA) 41-42

University of the West Indies (UWI) 6, 87, 122, 130-131, 134, 150, 156, 198, 227-229

V

Vasquez, Shalene M. 2

Village Vaguard 57

W

Whitfield, Catherine 109–110

Whylie, Dwight 23

Wilkinson, Raven 207

Williams, Randolph "Ranny" 41

Windrush 56

working class 5, 37, 40-42, 44, 47-48, 66, 69, 71, 75, 208, 212

Wynter, Sylvia 38

Y

York University 3-4, 25-26, 58-59, 64, 121, 183, 228-229

young, d'bi/ d'bi.young anitafrika 2, 58